URBAN BUSINESS PROFILES

URBAN BUSINESS PROFILES

An Examination of the Opportunities
Offered by 18 of the Most Common
Types of Small Businesses, and
a Guide to Their Establishment
and Successful Management

SMALL BUSINESS RESEARCH LIBRARY SERIES
VOLUME ONE

Gale Research Company • Book Tower • Detroit, Michigan 48226

BIBLIOGRAPHIC NOTE

This volume represents a compilation of eighteen studies and a plan for preparing a business profile originally issued as a series of nineteen individual booklets in 1972. The booklets were prepared and jointly published by the Economic Development Administration and the Office of Minority Business Enterprise, both agencies of the United States Department of Commerce. The original catalog numbers were EDA-72-5980 through 5998.

An Omnigraphics Book

Library of Congress Cataloging in Publication Data

Main entry under title:

Urban business profiles.

(Small business research library series ; v. 1)
(An Omnigraphics book)
Reprint of 19 individual booklets prepared and jointly published in 1972 by the Economic Development Administration and the Office of Minority Business Enterprise, U.S. Dept. of Commerce.
Includes bibliographies.
1. Minority business-enterprises--United States--Case studies. 2. New business enterprises--United States--Case studies. 3. Small business--United States--Case studies. I. United States. Economic Development Administration. II. United States. Office of Minority Business Enterprise. III. Series.
IV. Series: An Omnigraphics book.
HD2346.U5U7 658'.022 79-14909
ISBN 0-8103-1027-9

Introduction

Through the combined efforts of the United States government and sectors of the private economy, the American dream of owning one's own business became a reality for women, blacks, Hispanics, and other minority group members in the late 1960's.

In an effort to provide further guidance for these new entrepreneurs, the United States Department of Commerce, through two of its agencies, the Economic Development Administration and the Office of Minority Business Enterprise, commissioned a series of profiles of the eighteen types of businesses most commonly started by minorities in urban population centers.

These business studies have several shared characteristics: A description of the industry or service is provided, along with information on the nature of the product and the potential customer. Also covered by the studies are such factors as an analysis of business feasibility, projections of attainable returns on investment, and special consideration of factors which may prove favorable to those considering establishing new urban related minority ventures. Guidance in establishing a business, especially as regards obtaining financing, is provided. Finally, each study closes with a useful bibliography and list of trade organizations.

As a further aid, the government agencies developed a guide to assist the new entrepreneur in preparing his own business profile. The guide was issued as the nineteenth component of the series.

This useful series has since gone out of print, and is no longer available through official government channels. Therefore, copies of the individual booklets comprising the *Urban Business Profiles* are virtually impossible to obtain. The present republication of the complete series of eighteen studies, and the plan for preparing a business profile, enables the user to consult the entire series in a sturdy, hardbound reference volume.

Urban Business Profiles is the initial volume in the Gale Small Business Research Library.

April, 1979
Detroit, Michigan

Table of Contents

BEAUTY SHOPS

Section Contents

URBAN BUSINESS PROFILE

Beauty Shops

(SIC 7231)

I. RECOMMENDATION

The beauty care industry is among the fastest growing service industries in the United States but is also characterized by one of the highest industry failures. The reason for this is that beauty shops, or "salons," are usually very small in size and cater to a limited and demanding clientele. A few dissatisfied customers can have wide-ranging ill effects on the business.

Consequently, while beauty shops are good investments under the proper conditions, the entrepreneur must approach the venture with caution. Unless the manager can attract qualified and personable stylist employees, chances of success are limited. If a good staff is lined up and proper marketing analysis and planning precedes the venture, however, chances of success and a good return on investment are relatively high.

The shop should be planned and located only after the client population is defined and carefully analyzed with respect to current consumer patterns. While a successful existing firm has an initial competitive edge, there will always be women willing to try new establishments. If these trial customers are satisfied, the word will spread quickly, and a market of regular clients should soon develop.

Initial venture capital will run between $10,000 and $20,000 for medium-sized establishments (3 to 6 operators). Stylists can be found through industry sources, beauty schools, employment agencies, or classified advertisements.

The beauty care industry is one of the few in which a well-defined minority market segment can be identified. Minority-owned beauty salons tend to have an advantage in serving members of their own community, and the rapidly increasing beauty consciousness in the minority population provides a strong basis of support for the operations of a well-planned and operated salon catering to this group's needs.

II. DESCRIPTION OF THE BUSINESS

A. Identification

A beauty shop is any establishment primarily engaged in offering services to women involving hair, facial, hand, and nail treatment. While primarily providing services, some retail activities are included. In most shops wig sales, for example, are a new revenue generator.

Beauty shops are classified for statistical purposes as Standard Industrial Classification (SIC) 723 (and as SIC 7231 on the four-digit level). Included in SIC 723 are establishments that offer both beauty services for females and, secondarily, barber services for males. This profile, however, is restricted to the female-oriented services, which constitute the bulk of activities within this general classification.

B. Dimensions

There has been a steady growth in the beauty care industry in the United States during the past decade. The following statistics from the *Census of Manufactures* illustrate this growth:

Year	Number of establishments	Total receipts	Number of employees	Total payroll
1958	110,395	$1,028,077,000	140,336	$342,053,000
1963	151,720	$1,617,959,000	203,738	$572,910,000
1967	179,209	$2,354,398,000	255,037	$943,298,000

During this period, 1958–1967, growth was common to all parts of the United States. Only two States, Delaware and Montana, have experienced a decrease in the number of beauty establishments—and in both cases, total beauty shop revenues continued to rise despite the decrease in establishments.

More recent data suggest that the growth trend has continued beyond 1967. A Bank of America report on beauty salons indicated that in 1969 there was a 9.5 percent increase in sales over 1968 and an 8.2 percent increase in employees over this same year period as compared to annual rates of roughly 11 percent in sales and 6 percent in employment for both the 1958–1963 and 1963–1967 periods, as illustrated in the table above.

Using these rates as a basis, the beauty shop industry (as defined by SIC 723) in the United States was in 1971 a $3½ billion per year business, employing over 300,000 individuals in some 200,000 establishments. Over half of these establishments are small proprietorships with no paid employees. Of those with employees, the majority are single proprietorships with two or three employees on the payroll.

C. Characteristics

1. Nature of the Product

Women frequent beauty shops for the purpose of becoming better groomed and consequently more attractive. Also the beauty shop often serves as a social meeting place where weekly or monthly information is exchanged with other regular customers or with the staff.

The services offered include a wide spectrum of hair, facial, hand, and nail treatment. Among the more common services are hair and scalp conditioning, hair shampooing, dyeing or tinting, cutting, setting, and styling; facials and makeup, nail filing and polishing; and hairpiece sales and care. Hairdressing and manicures have typically accounted for the largest portion of receipts over the years.

For the most part, beauty shop services are required by their clients on a regular basis. There is in addition a sizeable number of clients who frequent beauty shops only on special occasions (before a wedding, dance, or similar event), choosing to use home care at other times. However, most customers are regular beauty shop users who visit the shop weekly or every 2 weeks.

Prices for beauty shop services vary widely from establishment to establishment, and sometimes even from stylist to stylist within the same establishment. For example, the price of a haircut—which takes relatively little time and minimal supplies and equipment—can range from $2 to $8 or more. Price ranges are determined primarily by the skill and/or reputation of the stylist; customer-type (income level primarily), time to complete service, cost of supplies and equipment, and market considerations (such as price lists of competitors).

The higher priced services, such as permanent waving or hair coloring (ranging from $15 to $25 and up), are required on a less frequent basis by regular customers than are the lower priced services (shampoo sets, for example, at $5 to $7 and up) which are required weekly or every 2 weeks.

Many salons complement their service sales by selling beauty products as well. Some offer more specialized services such as electrolysis for removal of unwanted facial and/or body hair and makeup treatments. Others compete with department stores and specialty shops by offering a full line of wigs and accessories (wig stands, cleaners, special combs and brushes). However, no more than 15 percent of all beauty shops offer this wide assortment of services—most focus almost wholly on hair treatment and styling.

2. Nature of the Customer

Virtually all women desire some continuous form of hair grooming and/or treatment. They have three alternatives: (1) do it themselves, (2) have relatives or friends do it, and/or (3) seek professional services. The decision to take the latter route—to seek professional services either by going to beauty shops or, in rarer cases, by having beauticians come to them—is based upon such considerations as availability of time, income, desire for expert services, lack of household alternative (e.g., no appropriate product on the market), and extent of interest, trust, or patience in home treatment.

Accordingly, the best source of customers for beauty shops are, first, middle-aged and elderly housewives who have time and money, and are extremely sensitive about their changing hair and facial features, and, second, working women who have their own incomes, a need to look well groomed at all times, and who don't want the burden of home grooming added to their already full week of activities. In an attempt to concentrate on younger clientele, some beauty shops have gone "mod," employing wild posters, rock music, and occasionally combining beauty services with retail sales of women's clothes and accessories (the so-called "boutique treatment").

One major determinant of each salon's customer mix is its established policy regarding appointments. There are recognized advantages and corresponding disadvantages to maintaining a standing list of appointments. On the plus side, a fully booked schedule of regular customers means a steady income from these regular patrons, fewer telephone calls and appointment changes, less style changes and learning problems, less idle time, and a more congenial atmosphere. On the other hand, the full book generally consists primarily of low-profit services (sets, manicures, etc.) and may result in a less challenging and more routine operation with little or no chance to increase profits by serving new patrons. Accordingly, a common strategy is for new shops and/or new stylists to begin by permitting customers to book time, but, upon establishing a reputation and a sound customer following, to reverse the booking policy and schedule customers according to the time and workload desired by the shop or stylist. This results in a more interesting schedule of services, combining profitable and less profitable items and permitting open time blocks for new patrons.

The location of the beauty shop will depend upon the target population being served and also upon the strategy adopted regarding customer scheduling. Women often combine the beauty shop trip with other shopping chores, and consequently the location of the shop in proximity to shopping areas is considered highly desirable.

Consequently, beauty shops are found in most shopping centers. In such cases, the shop may have an "exclusivity clause" within its lease, restricting the presence of competing businesses such as wig and cosmetic shops. Further, a beauty shop in a shopping center that does not accept appointments may be able to negotiate a higher favorable lease on the basis that customers may fill their waiting time frequenting the surrounding shops. Other common locations, in additon to shopping centers, are hotels, apartment house complexes, and downtown office districts.

3. Staffing Needs and Skills

The beauty operator must possess skills in shampooing, cutting, setting, styling, straightening, permanent waving, bleaching, and tinting, and in giving manicures, pedicures, scalp and facial treatments, makeup analysis, and in eyebrow shaping. A knowledge of the cleaning and styling of wigs and falls is becoming more necessary as well.

Operators in beauty salons must be licensed by the Board of Cosmetology in each State. To be eligible for licensing a prospective operator must possess a diploma from an accredited beauty school. Licensing is contingent upon passing the State board examination, meeting age requirements (usually 16 years of age), provision of certification of good health and having completed the minimum years of required formal schooling (ranging from grades 8 to 12, depending on the State). Cosmetology laws in most States require that an operator have at least 1 year of experience before opening or managing a beauty salon. Completion of a State-approved cosmetology course (6 months to a year) is recognized as adequate preparation for the examination in most States; sometimes this can be substituted for a period of apprenticeship.

The majority of beauty shops are proprietorships with no paid employees. The shops with employees generally have no more than three or four beauty operators, although much larger shops do exist. Operators may secure different types of arrangements with the shop owner. In most cases, their salaries will be based upon a percentage of their total service sales. A minimum guaranteed weekly income may also be set. The usual commission paid to an operator is 50 percent to 60 percent of sales. Inexperienced stylists will generally accept a lower rate at first. A few owners permit operators to act as independent agents who rent a station in the shop for a fee and/or a commission. In such cases, the operators generally furnish their own supplies. Weekly earnings for beauty operators range from $80 to $100 for beginning operators to $300 and up for top stylists.

In larger shops, auxiliary staff may also be required. Such staff might include a shampoo girl, manicurist, electrologist, receptionist (who may also handle retail sales), and maintenance help. Some salons keep a minimum full-time staff and increase personnel on the busiest days—Thursdays, Fridays, and Saturdays. Specialists such as a manicurist and electrologist are paid either on the same percentage basis as stylists or on the basis of concession arrangements. A shampoo girl must be a licensed cosmetologist in most States, but she is likely to be either a stylist just starting out or an older operator who is not skilled in recent styling techniques. Receptionists receive a flat salary (around $100 per week) or may work for commissions from retail sales. Maintenance staff are paid by the hour at a minimum wage level.

The major advantage of a full-service auxiliary staff is that stylists can be freed to engage in the more lucrative services while the more basic and smaller revenue producing services are performed by less expensive staff. In only relatively few shops, however, is there sufficient volume to permit such economies of scale.

4. Competition and Marketing

The success of a beauty shop rests squarely on satisfying the perceived needs of the client. If a customer is satisfied with the service she receives, she will continue to frequent the establishment on a regular basis. Moreover, she will serve as the single most effective form of advertisement for the shop ("Where did you get your hair done? It looks terrific!. . ."). On the other hand, if she is *not* satisfied with the services received, she will be certain to mention this to friends and associates. The negative consequences can be significant.

It has been found (by the National Hairdressers and Cosmetologists Association as a consequence of the collective experience of its members) that women will accept poor workmanship much quicker than bad treatment in the shop. Thus, customer relations is of even greater importance than quality of services in securing and maintaining a contented and growing clientele.

Beauty shops typically compete on the basis of service, quality, price, and image. The customers of a given beauty shop tend to be of a more homogeneous nature than in most other service establishments. The reason for this is that most stylists tend to favor certain hair styles and other beauty aids. Consequently their client groups quickly define themselves as those women who prefer this range of styles. More often than not, the style range will be more common among certain groups of women than others (the young, the middle class, housewives, office workers, the wealthy, the country club set, etc.). Shop decor and the price list also reflect customer range.

While customer recommendations are the best form of advertisement, it is usually recommended by industry experts that between 1½ percent and 3 percent of total sales be utilized for advertising, with perhaps 5 percent being spent in the initial year of operation. Direct neighborhood mailing has generally proven to be more effective than television or radio spots. Contributing free hairdos for school, church, and fashion shows and for local theatrical productions—with an accompanying credit line in the program—is also a typically effective method of advertising. Product distributors and manufacturers will sometimes contribute advertisement funds or materials to the shop in behalf of their product lines. Beauty shops in shopping centers may be required to contribute to a tenant association which, in turn, will handle all advertisements for the entire complex. Offering free introductory services (such as haircuts) or reduced introductory prices to newcomers to the area through organizations like "Welcome Wagon" will also help attract new customers.

Chains, especially those in department stores, and franchise operations are growing in numbers and in the volume of business they do. Even though at present they constitute less than 10 percent of the country's beauty shops, they present the independents with their major competitive threat. These big business salons achieve high sales either by using the "assembly-line" system of budget salons or charging high prices in luxury salons noted for their chic. Franchised operations are often given preferential consideration in shopping center developments.

The small salon also has competition from home beauty products—although national advertising can help increase salon sales by introducing women to new beauty aids and making them more beauty conscious. More than a few women have come to the beauty salon after damaging their hair by misusing home products.

5. Ease of New Firm Entry

All States require that a beauty salon manager be a licensed cosmetologist and hairdresser. However, the requirements for securing such a license vary from State to State and are obtainable from the bureau of licenses in each State and city. Locational requirements in relation to health and zoning regulations, as well as specifications of equipment conditions, may make difficult securing a specific site.

In addition to the initial capital investment of between $1,500 and $10,000 depending on size and decor, a cash reserve will be necessary to meet preoperating expenses, including advertising, legal services, and advance rent. The cash reserve must be large enough to cover both business and personal expenses until the business is on a paying basis. The minimum time for achieving profitable operations is estimated to be about 3 to 4 months. July and August are considered the slowest months in which to open a new salon, unless the location is a resort area.

Since there is a high turnover rate in beauty shops, the prospective owner might consider buying an existing salon rather than starting from scratch. An existing shop should have the proper electrical wiring and plumbing and the necessary equipment. However, the buyer should be careful to investigate why the shop is being sold. Was it so successful that the owner wanted to enlarge or was he discouraged by the lack of business? He should also find out whether any of the employees will stay on; if they leave, many of the present customers may go, too.

Minority-owned and operated beauty shops are quite common in minority neighborhoods. The ability to develop such an establishment in an all-white or racially mixed area will depend upon prevailing racial attitudes rather than on economic or other institutional factors.

6. *Capital requirements and Financing*

The amount of initial capital investment (or startup costs) required to begin a new beauty salon is dependent upon the target market, the types of services to be performed, and the number of operators to be employed. At a minimum, a shop selling to a lower income group will require from $1,600 to $1,800; one servicing a middle income group may need from $2,000 to $3,000; and a luxury type shop from $5,000 to $10,000 and up. The largest single cost factor in the beginning will be the equipment, including shampoo sinks, styling chairs, curler stands, dryers, and mirrors. This equipment usually costs $1,000 per station and may be purchased on installment.

In addition, inventories for the retail sales of beauty products and/or wigs and accessories as required must be added to the total cost. A typical wig room with display cases and counter can run an additional $500 to $1,000.

Typical operating costs include the following.

a. Rent, utilities, telephone, insurance (6 percent to 10 percent of sales).

b. Salaries (50 percent to 60 percent of sales).

c. Initial advertising (5 percent of sales).

d. Improvements in space, including plumbing, electricity, painting, and sign costs (5 percent to 10 percent of sales).

e. Supplies for shop use (7 percent to 10 percent of sales).

f. Reserve fund (5 percent of sales).

Financing may be accomplished through the use of equity, commercial bank loans under Small Business Administration guarantees, and occasional minority business financing. An excellent guide to local sources of financial and technical aid is the *Directory of Private Programs Assisting Minority Business,* Office of Minority Business Enterprise, U.S. Department of Commerce, 1970.

Franchise operations are growing in importance in the industry and now account for almost 10 percent of all establishments. The franchise fee entitles the entrepreneur to several advantages (such as use of company's name, preferential treatment in seeking locations, training programs, access to suppliers, etc.), which in turn should aid the entrepreneur in securing financial backing.

7. Profitability and Risk

Beauty shops have been able to raise their prices on a regular basis throughout the past decade to more than compensate for increasing costs of operation. The average gross margin for the industry is between 20 percent and 35 percent of total sales. Franchise operations are, on the average, even more profitable.

A high turnover rate of establishments during the 1960's, coupled with the rapid growth of the industry as a whole, suggest that while beauty shop operations can be highly profitable for successful entrepreneurs, the risks are great. Success is linked directly to satisfying the consumer through both quality of service and courteous delivery of these services. A few dissatisfied customers can literally destroy the market for the establishment. Consequently, the failure rate is high. The risk can be minimized substantially by selecting qualified and experienced beauty operators and by taking all measures possible to insure that every customer is well treated.

8. Dependence on Economic Conditions

Historically, the beauty shop business has been relatively resistant to general economic trends. Recepits have declined noticeably during periods of general economic slowdown only in those shops primarily serving the lowest income groups. Further, retail sales of cosmetic products do not decline significantly during periods of general economic recession. This would suggest that beauty services and products are considered by women to be relatively indispensable.

III. ANALYSIS OF BUSINESS FEASIBILITY

A. Review of Key Factors

The following factors are essential to successful development of a profitable beauty shop:

1. Market

As a general rule of thumb, a total population of roughly 1,000 persons is required to support a shop. The actual client group of a given beauty shop will tend to be relatively homogeneous. Clients will usually reside in the same general locale and belong to the same general socioeconomic group. They are also likely to be further defined by life-style.

2. Location

Proximity to the client group is the overriding locational determinant. Within this framework, a preferable location is one with good accessibility and visibility (such as a major shopping street or shopping center), preferably on the ground floor. Plenty of parking near the shop is considered a must. Locations near other shopping facilities are desirable.

3. Site Requirements

The space required for a beauty shop will average 100 to 150 square feet per operator. This space requirement will allow for reception areas and storage. Wig rooms, coloring rooms, and retail sales areas (including boutiques) will require additional space.

Beauty care equipment places heavy demands on plumbing and electricity, and the building chosen must be able to accommodate these utility needs.

4. Complementary Services

In addition to the required beauty services, additional items are recommended to enhance the shop: free coffee, food vending machines, outside telephone service, charge accounts, recorded or taped music, and retail sales of beauty accessories.

5. Equipment

The basic equipment required to operate the business will average around $1,000 per styling station and include vanity and shampoo bowl, mirror, styling chair, curler stand, and dryer. Expendable supplies will range between 7 percent and 10 percent of total sales.

6. Management

The manager must first and foremost be concerned about keeping the customers satisfied. This requires a sound working knowledge of the business, an ability to work well with employees, an ability to maintain good customer relations and to handle angry or dissatisfied customers, and good management sense (regarding inventory control, retail sales operations, hiring of additional employees, etc.). Both men and women are found as managers of successful beauty salons.

7. Work Force

Beauty shops are very labor intensive, with salaries generally accounting for between 50 percent to 60 percent of total revenues. It is the stylists and beauty operators who attract most customers and cause them to frequent the establishment on a regular basis. There are few economies of scale for smaller operations. However, the larger beauty shops can permit staff specialization and service differentiation in order to free the best stylists from routine functions to concentrate on the higher priced services. The number of operators will depend upon market demand—there is no optimum size.

In addition to beauty operators, larger shops will maintain a receptionist and possibly a maintenance worker. Part-time staff may be employed during the peak period (Thursdays through Saturdays).

B. Special Factors for New Minority Ventures

There are no known industrial barriers acting to prevent minority ownership of beauty shops. Beauty shops are highly market-oriented, and there are both a growing demand for beauty services among minority consumers and a general acceptance of minority-owned and managed beauty shops. Consequently, any beauty shop—white or non-white owned—that provides high quality service should be able to locate a favorable market area to serve.

Because of the high turnover of shops, a possibly attractive way to begin a new venture is to buy a shop about to close. The conditions leading to the closure should, of course, be investigated in detail before making such a move. Beauty salon failure due to poor service will usually not seriously hinder a totally new operation locating in the same facility with a new name and new operators.

C. Projections of Attainable Returns on Investment

Representative projections of revenues and profits attainable are furnished for three common sizes and types of beauty shops: a single proprietorship with no employees, a proprietorship with three beauty operators, and a franchised operation with six operators.

1. One-person Operation

Revenues		
Beauty services	$15,000	
Retail sales	0	
Total revenues	$15,000	100%
Operating expenses		
Rent	$ 1,500	
Supplies	1,400	
Advertising	400	
Laundry rental service	200	
Utilities	500	
Maintenance and repairs	200	
Other (licenses and taxes, insurance, accounting fees, etc.)	1,000	
Total operating expenses	$ 5,200	35%
Gross operating profit	$ 9,800	65%
Other expenses (equipment, depreciation, and interest)	$ 750	
Net profit before taxes (before owner's compensation)	$ 9,050	60%

2. Proprietorship With Three Beauty Operations (including owner)

Revenues		
Beauty services	$40,000	
Retail sales	2,000	
Total revenues	$42,000	100%
Operating expenses		
Salaries and wages	$21,000	
Rent	3,600	
Supplies	3,700	
Advertising	1,800	
Laundry rental service	700	
Utilities	1,500	
Maintenance and repairs	500	
Other	800	
Total operating expenses	$33,600	80%
Gross operating profit	$ 8,400	20%
Other expenses	$ 2,400	
Net profit before taxes	$ 6,000	14.3%

3. Franchised Operation With Six Beauty Operators (including owner)

Revenues		
Beauty services	$80,000	
Retail sales	5,000	
Total revenues	$85,000	100%
Operating expenses		
Salaries and wages	$40,000	
Rent	7,200	
Supplies	8,100	
Franchise fees	6,000	
Advertising	2,400	
Laundry rental service	1,000	
Utilities	3,200	
Maintenance and repairs	1,000	
Other	2,600	
Total operating expenses	$71,500	84.1%
Gross operating profit	$13,500	15.9%
Other expenses	$ 3,000	
Net profit before taxes	$10,500	12.4%

IV. SUMMARY: ESTABLISHING THE BUSINESS

A. Approaching the Market

In determining where to set up a beauty shop, the overriding consideration is to be reasonably accessible to the target client group. In turn, the target group should be selected on the basis of perceived divergence between demand and available services. In this latter regard, a detailed analysis of (1) the services offered by competition and (2) the dominant client group of existing establishments in each alternative location should be undertaken.

Upon determining the target client group to be served and the general locale, a detailed analysis of alternative sites should be undertaken. Special consideration should be given to sites near shopping centers that offer adequate parking.

In the actual planning of the facility, the decor, complementary services, and the price list should be designed with the target client group specifically in mind. Stylists should be recruited on the basis of their interest in creating styles and providing beauty services for the target group. In the case of a franchised operation, the franchisee will help with both the shop layout and the hiring of personnel, as well as in setting up books and records.

There are several options open to a new firm wishing to introduce itself to the general public and particularly to its target population. Placing a large advertisement in a neighborhood shoppers' newspaper is generally a good investment. A mimeographed letter announcing the opening might also be sent profitably to selected addresses (neighborhood associations may exist and will have names and addresses for their areas). Radio and/or television spots are costly, but do reach sizeable numbers of persons. In the case of a shopping center location, the announcement of the opening probably will be handled through the center's tenant association. In the case of a franchised operation, the franchiser will arrange the grand opening and local advertising and may provide a guest star.

As a longer term marketing project, reduced rates may be offered to newcomers to the area through the local Welcome Wagon organization. Free styling for fashion shows and local theatrical productions may also be offered in return for a credit in the program. However, as stated several times already, the best form of advertising is through the satisfied customer.

B. Facility and Capital Requirements

As indicated above, roughly 100 to 150 square feet of floor space per operator is required for a typical beauty shop. This space requirement includes room for a reception area and for storage. Wig rooms, coloring rooms, and extensive retail sales areas will require additional space, depending on the scale of the operation. The building must be capable of accommodating the electricity and plumbing needs of the shop. The land must be appropriately zoned.

Equipment can be supplied by a single supplier. Installment terms are available. Usually a one-third downpayment (roughly $400 per operator) is required. Furniture, leasehold improvements, initial advertising, and supplies may run as high as $5,000 for a small four-operator venture. Larger operations (10 or more operators) will have proportionately higher startup costs.

A franchised operation will cost a little more to start than an independent operation. A franchise fee must be paid, plus future monthly payments of between 5 percent and 10 percent of monthly sales.

C. Financing

As indicated above, equipment can be purchased on installments, with a one-third downpayment typically required. Bank loans may be available to cover other capital requirements. A 90 percent loan guarantee from the Small Business Administration will be of assistance in obtaining a commercial loan.

A franchised operation should have an easier time securing a loan. The franchiser may be unwilling to offer a franchise to an entrepreneur lacking sound financial backing, however.

D. Labor Force

As indicated above, the beauty shop operation is highly labor intensive. At least half of the revenues are returned to the operators as salaries or owner's profit (in the case of an owner/operator). The labor force performance is also the single most important marketing vehicle. Accordingly, selection of a qualified and personable staff is a sine qua non for a successful venture.

The entrepreneur must be sure that each of his operators has met the requirements of the State's board of cosmetology or other regulatory agency responsible for setting standards and issuing licenses for hair stylists. In some States, other shop employees such as manicurists, electrologists, and those who service wigs need licenses.

BIBLIOGRAPHY

Guidelines for the Beauty and Barber Equipment and Supplies Industry, Division of Rules and Guides, Federal Trade Commission, Washington, D.C. 20580.

1963 and 1967 Census of Business, Bureau of the Census, U.S. Department of Commerce, Washington, D.C. 20233.

"Professionalism At Coif Camp," Black Enterprise, November 1970.

Guidance in Buying a Beauty Shop, T. Paul Titus, Milady Publishing Corporation, 3839 White Plains Road, Bronx, New York 10467.

The Beauty Salon, Egon Guttman, Howard University, Small Business Guidance and Development Center Publication, Washington, D.C. 20001.

1969 Industrial Outlook, U.S. Department of Commerce, Washington, D.C. 20230.

Small Business Administration "Counseling Notes" No. 30. Prepared by the Office of Management Assistance, Washington, D.C. 20416.

Employment Outlook for Barbers and Cosmetologists, Occupational Outlook Report Series/Bulletin No. 1550–7, U.S. Department of Labor, Bureau of Labor Statistics. Washington, D.C. 20210.

"Beauty Salons," Small Business Reporter, Bank of America National Trust and Savings Association.

Beauty Salon Management Guide, National Hairdressers and Cosmetologists Association, Inc., 3510 Olive, St. Louis, Missouri 63103.

Personal Care, prepared by the Long Range Planning Service, Stanford Research Institute, Menlo Park, California 94025. Report No. 175, June 1963.

National Beauty Culturists' League (NBCL) (Cosmetologist) 25 Logan Circle N.W., Washington, D.C. 20005, Founded 1919. Members, 10,000. Beauticians, cosmetologists, and beauty products manufacturers. Opposes segregation because of race on State regulatory and licensing agencies. Encourages standardized, scientific and approved methods of hair, scalp, and skin treatments. Sponsors: National Institute of Cosmetology (training course in operating and designing techniques and business techniques); Annual Trade Shows; National Beauty Week; Hall of Fame. Publication: Forecast, semiannual.

National Beauty & Barber Manufacturers Association (NBBMA): 1023–25 National Press Building, Washington, D.C. 20004. Founded 1941. Members, 110. Manufacturers and distributors of cosmetics, equipment, and supplies used in or resold by beauty salons and barber shops.

Associated Master Barbers and Beauticians of America (AMBBA): 537 South Dearborn Street, Chicago, Illinois 60605. Founded 1924. Members, 10,000. Barber and beauty salon owners and managers, school operators, supply dealers, trade magazine publishers, and manufacturers. Publications: Master Barber and Beautician Magazine, monthly.

BOWLING ALLEYS

Section Contents

URBAN BUSINESS PROFILE
Bowling Alleys

(SIC 7933)

I. RECOMMENDATION

The high rate of failure of bowling establishments in the past decade—due primarily to a combination of overreaction to a rising market, underfinancing, and inexperienced management—suggests that a prospective entrepreneur should enter this industry with caution. Individuals should perform thorough market and financial analyses and consult with industry sources (particularly the two large national suppliers of bowling equipment and the association of bowling proprietors) before venturing into the industry.

The key to the success of a bowling operation is the ability of the management to attract and maintain a full schedule of league bowling. Almost 75 percent of all games are rolled during the course of league play. Thus league attraction and league creation are critical to success. Consequently a strategy for league formation at the proposed center should be worked out in advance of facility planning.

Initial capital investment is relatively high. Good management is considered essential, although other labor force requirements are easily met. Sites with high accessibility and large parking areas are highly desirable. Potentially attractive market areas will vary greatly from locale to locale, depending on such factors as popularity of the sport with the target community, availability of competing facilities, alternative forms of recreation and entertainment available, and the potential of a marketing strategy to increase the local demand.

Increasing popularity of the sport among minority groups provides a growing base upon which minority ventures—relatively rare to date—may establish themselves and achieve a profitable level of operations.

II. DESCRIPTION OF THE INDUSTRY

A. Identification

The traditional bowling alleys of the 1940's and 1950's have evolved into the bowling centers of the 1960's and 1970's, which include all the facilities of the earlier establishments plus additional amusements and subsidiary services. Thus, a bowling center is likely to include, in addition to the basic requirements of the sport (alleys, balls, and shoe rental), food and beverage service, bar service, amusement machines (pinball, children's rides, etc.), pool tables, and other miscellaneous recreation (model car racetracks, indoor miniature golf, etc.). The service offered may also extend beyond service and maintenance functions associated with the game of bowling itself to include operation of the above-mentioned recreation and service activities, bowling clinics, meeting halls, child care facilities, and shops for sportswear and bowling balls and accessories. Many of these services may be operated on a lease basis by individuals other than the bowling proprietor.

Establishments whose principal function is to provide facilities for the sport of bowling are classified for statistical purposes as Standard Industrial Classification (SIC) 7933. Four types of bowling are included: tenpin (the oldest, most popular, and nationally played), duckpin, rubberband duckpin, and candlepin bowling. The latter three types of bowling utilize smaller pins and balls and are popular only in a few areas of the country (notably New England, Pennsylvania, and Washington, D.C.). About 95 percent of the bowling done in the United States is tenpin bowling.

In this profile, cost and revenue estimates and corresponding user statistics are based upon tenpin bowling centers. The cost differentials between tenpin bowling establishments and the three less common forms of bowling establishments can be obtained from equipment suppliers. Special market analysis would need to be performed to determine if the area under consideration was suitable for smaller pin bowling enterprises.

B. Dimensions

The popularity of the sport of bowling (as measured by the total number of bowlers sanctioned by the American Bowling Congress) has increased steadily during the past 2 decades. Most rapid growth occurred almost immediately after the introduction of the automatic pinsetter machine by the American Machine and Foundry Company

(AMF) in 1955 and by the Brunswick Corporation in 1957. The number of sanctioned bowlers (that is, bowlers with membership cards in the American Bowling Congress—generally required of all league bowlers) increased from 2½ million in 1955 to 5½ million in 1960 and to over 8 million by 1963.

In response to this rapid rise in popularity, a great surge took place in the number of bowling establishments that were opened to meet the growing demand. The number of certified bowling lanes increased during this same period from 58,200 in 1955 to 108,000 in 1960 and to over 150,000 lanes by 1963. Well over 1,000 new bowling centers opened during this period. While the number of new lanes thus kept pace with the growth in the number of sanctioned bowlers, the new bowlers turned out to be less ardent than their predecessors (as exhibited by a rapid decline in the number of games bowled per lane per day). Hence, there was clear evidence of overbuilding by 1963. This was reflected in a sharp decline in profits throughout the industry after the surge in the late 1950's.

The decline in profits was not due solely to overbuilding, although this was the principal cause. Other factors of importance were poor management and undercapitalization. Many people invested in bowling and became proprietors because they had been bowlers for several years, liked the game, and assumed profits came automatically. They were inexperienced in running these operations and, in the case of absentee ownership, selected other bowling associates—with similarly weak management—to operate the alleys for them. An accompanying problem was that these new entrepreneurs had not fully worked out all the costs of operating a bowling establishment and had based revenue projections on experiences of early years when the smaller number of establishments then in operation were always crowded. Consequently, they lacked the funds necessary to support the operation during the slack period of the middle 1960's.

There are good indications that the bowling industry has now stabilized and that opportunities for profitable ventures are possible with well-planned marketing and operating strategies. The total number of bowling establishments in the United States is now estimated at around 9,000. The Atlantic and North-Central regions of the country continue to have the strongest concentration of establishments, with New York, Ohio, Illinois, and Pennsylvania as the four leading States in this regard. The Mountain and Pacific regions (and particularly California, Washington, Oregon, and Colorado) also have active bowling populations with participation rates above the national average.

C. Characteristics

1. Nature of the Product

While bowling centers offer a wide variety of services in addition to providing facilities for the sport itself, revenues from bowling are by far the chief source of income, accounting for at least half and usually as high as 70 to 80 percent of all revenues generated. In turn, the major source of bowling revenues results from league bowling. A 1968 survey conducted by the Bowling Proprietors' Association of America indicated that 73 percent of all games bowled across the country were by league bowlers (including practice games apart from league action).

This same survey indicated that of the 38 million persons who had bowled at least once in 1967–1968, 30 million were casual bowlers (did not belong to leagues) and 8 million were active bowlers. Of the 1.7 billion annual games rolled, only 27 percent or 0.5 billion were by casual bowlers—the remaining 1.2 billion games were rolled by the 8 million active bowlers. Thus the average casual bowler rolled roughly 15 games per year, while the league bowlers averaged 150 games annually.

The reasons given by survey respondents for starting to bowl did not differ significantly between casual and active bowlers. The dominant reasons given were (1) seeking fun and recreation and (2) encouraged to try sport with friends or family. The reasons for continuing to bowl also did not differ greatly among casual and active bowlers, and were dominated by (1) healthy exercise, (2) challenging activity, (3) fun and relaxation, and (4) a good form of social activity.

The cost of bowling, typically between 50 to 75 cents per game rolled, has not been found to be a serious factor in limiting the market. League bowlers are accustomed to paying considerably more per game, not only to cover their bowling, but also to contribute to cash funds for end-of-the-season league dinners and for cash prizes and trophies. Casual bowlers are likewise relatively insensitive to bowling prices; their participation is probably more limited by the unavailability of alleys at prime time (nonsummer evenings) due to scheduled league bowling than by the cost of the sport.

2. Nature of the Customer

This same 1968 survey indicated that, of persons in the United States 11 years of age and over, some 58 percent had bowled tenpins at least once in their lives and an additional 5 percent had bowled smaller pins. Some 26 percent—of which 6 percent were active league bowlers—had bowled at least once in the past year.

While a greater percentage of metropolitan area residents had tried bowling than nonmetropolitan area residents (62 compared with 47 percent), among those who had tried bowling, the percentage of presently active bowlers was similar in the metropolitan and nonmetropolitan areas (10 compared with 9 percent).

An analysis by age of population reflected the surge in popularity of bowling in its "golden years," 1955 to 1962. While only 34 percent of the population sampled over age 50 had ever bowled, the percent rose markedly to 68 percent from ages 40 to 49, 76 percent from ages 30 to 39, and 79 percent from ages 20 to 29. In the youngest age group, 11 to 19, a total of 67 percent had bowled at least once. Of active league bowlers, the 30 to 39 and 40 to 49 age groups each had 9 percent of their populations represented, while 7 percent of the total population from 20 to 29 were league bowlers.

Statistics broken down by sex revealed that 36 percent of the males sampled had never bowled compared with 45 percent of the females sampled. However, among those who had tried bowling, 10 percent of the males and 9 percent of the females were now regular league bowlers.

As a general rule of thumb, industry sources recommend that a population of at least 1,000 persons per lane is needed to support a bowling center. This figure needs to be adjusted, however, to account for such factors as recent population growth (10 percent growth for the 1960–1970 period is considered a good gauge of increasing market size and potential), proximity to competing bowling centers, neighborhood bowling history (blue-collar areas traditionally have been thought to be better sources of bowlers than white collar areas, although this may be more stereotypical than factual); racial composition (minority community members have only recently begun taking up the sport in significant numbers); accessibility (high-traffic areas—such as shopping centers—are prime locations); and climate (warmer climates favor competing outdoor recreation such as golf and boating). On the basis of these factors, it is clear that each city —and, in fact, each neighborhood within it—must be analyzed separately; there are no simple rules of thumb to pinpoint with certainty a favorable location or to define the local population size needed to support a lane or center.

3. *Staffing Needs*

As indicated above, one of the major causes of failure in the bowling industry has been the absence of sound managerial skills. Accordingly, manufacturers of bowling alley equipment, Brunswick and AMF, have set up management clinics that cover such areas as marketing and public relations, business management, human relations, advertising, and instruction on how to teach bowling to beginners. In addition, they provide assistance in planning of the center as well as in financing equipment and other facilities. The Bowling Proprietors' Association of America (BPAA) periodically organizes conferences and seminars and also publishes a monthly journal, Bowling Proprietor, containing management articles and advice.

Because leagues are the backbone of any successful operation, an owner or manager must be able to work well with league representatives, present his bowling center in its best light, and be able to coordinate the league activities throughout the season. In this regard, managers with intimate knowledge of the sport have a slight competitive edge on managers without bowling background. However, since leagues are always looking around for new arrangements—especially those leagues with bad past season experience—an ability to negotiate skillfully is essential.

The number of employees needed to run the center will depend upon the size of the center and the variety of subsidiary services offered. A rule-of-thumb figure is one full-time employee for every four lanes; these employees may include a manager, an assistant manager, a counter control man (who assigns alleys and collects fees), an alley maintenance mechanic and an assistant mechanic, janitorial staff, and clerical staff. Other employees—depending on the presence of the service—may include a bartender, waitresses, snackbar personnel, a nursery attendant, playroom supervisors, bowling instructors, pro shop attendant, and billiard room manager. Clearly, these latter employees may be paid and supervised by a lessee of the facilities in which they work.

Typical 1970 wage and salary ranges for bowling employees were managers—$8,000 to $16,000 per year, plus percentage of profits; assistant managers—$6,500 to $12,000 per year, mechanics—$7,000 to $12,000 per year, counter control man—$2.50 to $3.50 per hour, and janitors—$2 to $3 per hour. The snackbar and playroom attendants generally earn between $2 and $2.50 per hour. In total, bowling centers spend between 15 percent and 30 percent of their gross income for employee wages. The ratio of male to female employees in the industry is approximately 3 to 1.

4. Competition and Marketing

A bowling establishment faces two levels of competition: (1) competition from other bowling establishments in the area and (2) competition from other recreation and entertainment alternatives.

Competition among bowling establishments for their share of the local bowling market focuses largely on attracting leagues to their respective establishments. Since the basic service offered (reserved lanes, balls, and shoe rental) are rather standard throughout the industry, the proprietors tend to emphasize the availability of adequate parking, the complement of secondary services available (primarily snackbar and bar), and the overall cordial and friendly environment of their respective establishments. Of critical importance is the ability of the establishment to insure that (1) lanes are available on time, (2) equipment failure is minimized, and (3) the facilities are clean at all times. Price-cutting is rare, although some establishments offer reduced rates continually for children and at offpeak hours (weekdays and weekend afternoons) for adults. The establishments often award trophies free of charge to league winners as an inducement for patronage of their alleys. Other promotional features, such as awards for bowling perfect "300" games and rolling a strike when a specially marked pin is in the head position, are sometimes offered at offpeak hours as well. Free group instruction, special group rates at offpeak hours, and introductory promotional games at reduced prices through community Welcome Wagon operations are also used to attract new bowlers. Finally, the sponsoring of prestigious local or national tournaments or special match games with outstanding bowlers is employed to publicize establishments.

In order to increase the overall bowling market, both Brunswick and AMF and the Bowling Proprietors' Association of America conduct nationwide advertising campaigns and provide assistance to local establishments in organizing individual or group advertising efforts. The weekly exposure of large segments of the public to professional bowling tournaments through the television media ("The Pro Bowlers Tour") also stimulates interest in the sport. More subtly, the bowling industry encourages the use of bowling in advertisements for unrelated product lines (such as the use of amateur bowlers in a prime time commercial for life insurance).

5. Ease of New Firm Entry

The relatively high capital requirements needed to start bowling centers have not acted as a major deterrent to the establishment of new bowling facilities. The large number of bowling center failures in the mid-1960's, however, reduced the appeal of the industry as a business opportunity from its earlier high levels. Both the Bowling Proprietors' Association of America and the two national suppliers of equipment encourage new entry, but they are careful to warn the prospective entrepreneur of the risks involved and the need for well-conceived marketing studies and for well-planned and managed facilities.

There is no institutionalized bias against minority firm entry, although the number of minority proprietors is small due to the large initial investment required and the historic absence of minority bowlers. As bowling continues to grow in popularity with minority groups, the need for establishments serving minority neighborhoods should become more pronounced.

The initial capital investment to start a bowling center is considerable. For example, the investment required for a fully equipped 32-lane center with billiard room, restaurant, and lounge can run as high as $1.5 million. Bowling equipment is expensive, although leasing terms are available. AMF and Brunswick both help their customers with financing, but a substantial downpayment is usually required. These two firms will provide continuing assistance to establishments that have bought or leased their equipment.

Finding staff to operate the center is not considered a serious problem, since most required skill levels are low. For the more skilled employees—managers and mechanics—adequate training programs and materials are made available by the BPAA and by AMF and Brunswick.

The breakeven point in the case of a new bowling center is directly linked to its ability to book leagues for the two evening slots (7 to 9, 9 to 11) each week night. Proprietors opening new centers are often surprised at the number of leagues looking for lanes. The newness of the center is a highly marketable feature, as leagues are continually searching for more modern, better equipped centers. A center that can attract leagues away from older establishments and that also conducts a well-conceived program to establish new leagues can become profitable within the first season of operation. More often, centers will not achieve profitable operations until their second or possibly third season of operation.

6. Bowling Center Physical and Capital Requirements

The average bowling establishment contains 15 lanes, although this average is biased downward by the large number of very small bowling facilities at universities, military bases, and clubs with less than 10 alleys. The optimum size recommended by the industry for a full service bowling center is 36 lanes. As indicated above, such a facility together with billiard room, restaurant, and lounge, can require an initial investment of up to $1.5 million.

In general, lanes and automatic pinsetters will cost between $12,000 and $15,000 per lane, excluding installation. Other related basic costs include metal storage lockers ($10 to $14 each), custom seating ($250 per lane), pin finders to indicate pins left standing

($150 per lane), elevator bowling ball returns ($800 per lane), automatic ball cleaners and polishers ($1,500 each), and automatic scorers ($3,000 per lane). Considerable smaller item costs are required for balls, shoes, cleaner, lane duster, pins, scoresheets, spectator seating, and a variety of other supplies and equipment.

The indoor area requirements for a bowling center average about 1,000 square feet per lane. This figure includes additional space for auxiliary facilities, such as snackbars, lounge, playrooms, offices, pro shops, and locker and restrooms. An outside parking requirement of seven spaces (or at least 2,000 square feet) per lane is considered desirable.

Construction costs will vary according to design specifications. A good quality building which includes auxiliary facilities will range from $11 to $15 per square foot. This would include architectural fees. In most buildings, the bowling alley should be soundproofed and the building completely heated and air-conditioned. Approximately one-fourth of the building goes to auxiliary facilities and three-fourths goes to the lanes. The auxiliary rooms and services are:

Pro Shops

The average pro shop produces a little over 5 percent of the gross income. Inventories include the following: bowling balls, priced from $19.95 to $50 (proprietors state the average price for women's bowling balls are $24.95 and for men $27.95); shoes, priced from $5.95 to $14.95, with an average selling price at $9.95; bowling bags priced from $3.95 to $14.95, with an average selling price of $9.95. The markup on items is approximately 40 percent. Most proprietors plan inventory stock according to the economic structure of their communities. An average inventory will range from $2,000 to $3,000.

Rental Shoes and Bowling Balls

Shoe rentals are not highly profitable, but they are very essential. An average of 1 to 2 percent of the gross income is from shoe rental; ball use is included in linage (game) fees. Most bowling shoes are purchased by the operator at approximately $6 per pair. A charge to the customer for shoe rental is 25 cents. Shoes are depreciated over a 2-year period. Balls cost proprietors $15 each, and there are usually five per lane. They depreciate in about a 5-year period.

Cocktail Lounge and Bars

A successful cocktail lounge and bar operation can make as much profit as linage receipts. For a successful operation, liquor costs should not exceed 25 percent of gross receipts from the bar. The key to success is careful cost control. The State controls operations at bowling centers by licensing procedures. This license usually designates the eating areas of the center as a bona fide public eating place, which allows cocktail-waitresses to serve drinks to customers on the lanes. Some proprietors indicate that as much as 79 percent of their bar business is done on the lanes. In order to qualify for this type of licensing the center must have a complete restaurant facility, including a kitchen. This means that there must be service of full meals rather than, or in addition to, an exclusive sandwich operation. This license also allows minors (anyone under 21 years of age) to be on the premises. Other types of licenses may be available, depending on the regulations of the State Department of Alcoholic Beverage Control.

Snackbar-Restaurant

Vending machines for food service can lessen operation cost, but many owners insist upon manual snackbars, and some prefer operated restaurants. The amount of commission to the proprietor from vending machines depends upon the volume and amount of servicing. Items that are not perishable and will last more than a week are possibilities for higher commissions.

Vending machines are advantageous because there are no labor costs, no inventories, no kitchen to equip and supply, and no personnel problems. However, totally automated food service will restrict the type of liquor license available. Full information may be received from the State Department of Alcoholic Beverage Control.

The proprietor who desires a manual operation should spend no more than 40 percent of gross income for operating and food costs. There should be an entrance that is separate from the center in order to attract additional business to the restaurant.

Playroom

Many bowling establishment owners find that supervised playroom service for toddlers and young children will attract women to morning and afternoon league play. No direct income can be earned. Equipment such as cribs, tables and chairs, and a few toys should be estimated at $7 to $10 per lane. Older women in the surrounding neighborhood are often ideal employees for this service because they can work short hours (9 to 12 a.m. or 2 to 4 p.m.) on a part-time basis.

Because of the high initial investment, both Brunswick and AMF offer financial packages for the purchase of basic equipment. A typical schedule requires repayment in 8 years, at an annual interest rate of 5 to 6½ percent on the unpaid balance. Usually, a 15 to 30 percent down payment of the total equipment cost is required.

The payments are usually scheduled to coincide with the peak bowling season. Usually no payments are required during the summer season (June to September), and eight equal monthly payments are required during the peak bowling period.

Accessory equipment may be purchased or leased. For example, the new automatic scorers can be purchased for $11,500 per four lanes outright or financed with 5-year notes. Alternatively, the scorers can be leased for 10 years at a cost of 3 to 5 cents per game rolled depending on volume of usage.

Maintenance of bowling facilities can be estimated at around $500 per lane per year. Equipment is depreciated over a 10-year period in accordance with Federal Government regulations.

7. Profitability

The two major sources of income to bowling centers result from bowling fees and from sales of food and liquor. The larger the center, the greater will be the share of total receipts credited to the latter activity. Thus, for example, a typical establishment with an annual business volume of $65,000 is likely to have generated over 80 percent of this income from bowling fees. On the other hand, a typical establishment with annual volume of $475,000 will have generated only 40 percent to 50 percent of this income from bowling fees. Consequently, the profits of larger centers in particular are related to successful bar and restaurant operations as well as to sound bowling business.

Typical profitable bowling centers show net profits of between 4 percent and 7 percent of sales, after owners' salaries of up to 9 percent. Unprofitable centers may show net losses of similar proportions. Trade sources indicate that slightly over half of all centers fall into the "profitable" category.

8. Market Fluctuation

As suggested by the analysis above, the bowling industry has experienced both a boom period and a subsequent slowdown in the past decade. While there are more bowlers today than ever before, the average active bowler is apparently not as dedicated to the sport as in past decades. Other recreational sports (notably golf, tennis, and boating and fishing) and other leisure activities (notably television and cardplaying) offer strong competition to bowling. Bowling is unlikely to experience another "golden age" like the 1958 to 1962 period. It should, however, be able to continue to compete for its share of the growing recreation market.

III. ANALYSIS OF BUSINESS FEASIBILITY

A. Review of Key Factors

The following factors are essential to successful development of a profitable bowling center:

1. Market

League bowling is the "bread and butter" part of the industry; those centers that can attract leagues to the evening time slots (7 to 9 and 9 to 11 on Monday through Friday and on Sunday) will generally show an annual profit; other centers usually will not.

A general rule is that 1,000 persons without ready access to existing bowling establishments are required to support a lane. This standard must be adjusted to the socioeconomic characteristics of the population, the historic popularity of the sport in the region, and the availability of competing forms of recreation and entertainment.

2. Location

Given the appropriate market, a center should be located in a commercially zoned area with high accessiblity and visibility. A large shopping center complex, for example, is cited by the industry as an ideal location. Highway sites are also popular choices.

3. Site Requirements

The center should be located in a structure providing at least 1,000 square feet per lane. Outside parking in the order of at least seven spaces per lane (2,000 square feet per lane) is also suggested. While second-floor locations are feasible, ground-floor locations are desirable.

4. Complementary Services

At a minimum, a bowling center must provide alleys, balls, shoe rental, service desk, bowler and spectator sitting areas, and restrooms. Some form of refreshment service (vending machines, snackbar, lounge, or restaurant) is considered mandatory. Other services, such as pro shops, child care areas, billiard and/or other game rooms, are considered desirable to enhance the attractiveness of the center to potential clientele.

5. Equipment

Bowling equipment is available from two large national suppliers: Brunswick and AMF. Both have wide ranges of equipment and supplies and are available to assist in planning the center to insure that all needs are met. Several forms of financing are available, although initial capital requirements are still relatively high.

6. Management

A manager of a bowling center should have both familiarity with the sport itself and a good background in bowling center management. Training programs are offered by the two bowling suppliers and by the Bowling Proprietors' Association of America. However, it is considered prudent to receive some additional training in an existing center before undertaking the management of a new center.

7. Work Force

In addition to the management staff, a number of less skilled workers are required to maintain and operate the facilities. Roughly one full-time employee per four lanes is required to run a bowling center. There are certain economies of scale associated with the bowling operation itself (that is, fewer additional employees are required as extra lanes are introduced), but larger centers usually offer additional services as well and hence require more diverse staff positions to operate the center efficiently.

B. Special Factors for New Minority Ventures

It has been only in the past decade that significant numbers of minority group members have begun to bowl on a regular basis. Since that time, however, growing numbers have taken up the sport.

There are no known industry-imposed barriers to the establishment of minority-owned bowling centers. The large initial investment required is the principal deterrent.

The two most inexpensive ways in which minority proprietorships can be obtained are: (1) buying an existing establishment in a racially mixed area from a white proprietor or (2) establishing a new, small center of, say, 11 to 15 lanes in a converted structure. A successful proprietor can at a later date branch out into a larger operation of 30 or more lanes.

C. Projections of Attainable Returns on Investment

Representative projections are furnished for three typical levels of operation: A center with $65,000 annual volume of business (10 lanes), a center with $150,000 annual volume of business (20 lanes), and a center with $250,000 annual volume of business (32 lanes). It is assumed that as the number of lanes increases, an appropriate level of secondary services is offered at the center in addition to the bowling facilities. Proprietorships are assumed in all cases, and the amount of profit shown has not been reduced by the amount of owner's compensation.

Those bowling establishments achieving a smaller level of gross receipts are generally characterized as being less successful in attracting leagues than the profitable centers. The less profitable centers can be characterized as having higher rental and employee costs and greater maintenance costs. Thus, a combination of inability to attract league bowling and less efficient management generally accounts for reduced profits or net losses.

1. *10-Lane Bowling Alley*

Revenues		
Bowling income (8-month season)	$ 46,000	
Bowling income (summer)	5,500	
Food and bar sales	11,000	
Other revenue	2,500	
Total revenues	$ 65,000	100%
Operating expenses		
Employee wages (excluding owner/manager)	$ 10,000	
Supplies and maintenance	4,300	
Rental space, including utilities	10,000	
Food and bar costs	8,000	
Other expenses (advertising, licenses and fees, insurance)	7,000	
Total operating expenses	$ 39,300	60.5%
Gross operating profit	$ 25,700	39.5%
Other expenses (equipment, interest, and depreciation)	$ 15,700	
Net profit before owner's draw and tax	$ 10,000	15.4%

2. *20-Lane Bowling Center*

Revenues		
Bowling income (8-month season)	$ 97,500	
Bowling income (summer)	14,400	
Food and bar sales	31,500	
Other revenues	6,600	
Total revenues	$150,000	100%
Operating expenses		
Employee wages (excluding owner/manager)	$ 30,000	
Supplies and maintenance	9,000	
Rental space, including utilities	24,000	
Food and bar costs	20,400	
Other expenses	14,600	
Total operating expenses	$ 98,000	65.3%
Gross operating profit	$ 52,000	34.7%
Other expenses	$ 34,500	
Net profit before owner's draw and tax	$ 17,500	11.7%

3. *32-Lane Bowling Center*

Revenues		
Bowling income (8-month season)	$125,000	
Bowling income (summer)	23,500	
Food and bar sales	92,000	
Other revenues	9,500	
Total revenues	$250,000	100%
Operating expenses		
Employee wages (includes nonowner manager)	$ 62,500	
Supplies and maintenance	14,500	
Rental space, including utilities	37,000	
Food and bar costs	40,000	
Other expenses	22,000	
Total operating expenses	$176,000	70.4%
Gross operating profit	$ 74,000	29.6%
Other expenses	$ 50,000	
Net profit before owner's draw and tax	$ 24,000	9.6%

IV. ESTABLISHING THE BUSINESS

A. Approaching the Market

A well-conceived market analysis study of the intended locale of the bowling center is highly recommended before commitment to begin construction. Emphasis should be placed on studying existing bowling patterns of the intended client community to determine their present level of interest in the sport and to identify other bowling centers in the area that will provide the major competition to the proposed facility. Estimates should then be made of the extent to which: (1) existing active bowlers can be drawn away from these centers to the proposed center, (2) casual bowlers in the area can be converted to active bowlers, and (3) nonbowlers can be encouraged to take up the sport. Estimates of other possible revenue flows (bar, restaurant, billiards, etc.) should also be made. These figures could then be reviewed with AMF and Brunswick and with other bowling proprietors in the city or region to check and revise as necessary.

While special attractions (introductory discounts, free drawings for prizes, free games for rolling strikes when a specially marked head pin is set up, opening week tournaments, and special match games between regional professionals) will serve to introduce the new center to the target community, the critical factor will be the ability to schedule league bowling. Consequently, the market strategy adopted should have this goal as the top priority item. Existing league representatives should be approached. Potential groups (such as plants in the vicinity, military bases, and community organizations) should be contacted and attempts made to establish a league on a trial basis.

B. Facility Requirements

Both of the national suppliers, AMF and Brunswick, will be more than willing to provide the entrepreneur with alternative plans for designing and equipping the facility. A variety of alternatives are available to suit virtually any type of bowling establishment.

As indicated above, roughly 3,000 square feet per lane of indoor and outdoor space will be required, with two-thirds of it for outside parking. Thus, a 10-lane bowling alley will require a ¾-acre site; a 20-lane bowling center will require a 1½-acre site; and a 32-lane bowling center will require a 2½-acre site. A single-floor structure is ideal, although use of converted first- or second-floor space in an existing multistory building is feasible. The intended area must be properly zoned, both for the bowling activity and for the sale of food and beverages.

The average center will cost about $30,000 per lane to construct and will cost roughly $500 per lane per year to maintain.

C. Financing

Both AMF and Brunswick offer financial packages for purchase of equipment and supplies. A typical schedule requires repayment in 8 years, at an annual interest rate of 5 percent to 6½ percent. Usually a downpayment of between 15 percent to 30 percent of the total amount is required.

Bank loans may also be available. However, in view of the high rate of failure in the industry in the mid-1960's—due primarily to an overreaction on the supply side of the market to an increasing market demand—banks may be hesitant about authorizing loans for bowling center ventures. In some cases, a bank loan of up to $350,000 may be secured through a 90 percent guarantee by the Small Business Administration.

A relatively low-cost method of entry for a minority entrepreneur would be through the purchase of an existing bowling facility. Alternatively, a small center of, say, 15 lanes might be developed first, with the ultimate goal of establishing a base upon which to develop a larger center at a later date.

In some locales, franchise arrangements may be possible. The franchisee will pay as much as half of the original investment. Usually a franchise fee is based upon a monthly royalty per lane plus an initial cost for the franchise.

D. Labor Force

As indicated above, a full-time labor force of roughly one person per four lanes is considered desirable. As the number of lanes increases, certain economies of scale exist in the labor force needed to maintain the lanes. However, other services—such as larger restaurants, lounges, and gamerooms—will consequently increase the total labor force requirement.

A labor force breakdown for a 20-lane bowling operation might include the following.

Owner/manager	1	
Assistant manager	1	
Mechanic	1	Staff costs: $45,000
Maintenance	1	
Food service	1	
	5	

A labor force breakdown for a 32-lane bowling operation might include the following:

Manager	1	
Assistant manager	1	
Mechanic	2	Staff costs: $62,500
Maintenance	2	
Food service	2	
	8	

The managers can receive training from their bowling equipment supplier or from the Bowling Proprietors' Association of America. The monthly trade journal, The Bowling Proprietor, also provides valuable management information. Mechanics will receive training from the equipment supplier. The maintenance and food service staff will be drawn from the unskilled labor force.

The food service operation and the secondary services (pro shop, gamerooms, etc.) can be leased to concessionaires, if desired.

APPENDIX

BIBLIOGRAPHY

Bowlers Journal, 506 South Wabash Avenue, Chicago, Illinois 60605. Monthly. $4 a year. Mostly consumer oriented.

Bowling Magazine. Published by the American Bowling Congress, 1572 East Capitol Drive, Milwaukee, Wisconsin 53211. Monthly. $3 a year. Mostly consumer oriented.

The Bowling Proprietor. Published 11 times a year by the Bowling Proprietors' Association of America, Inc., West Higgins Road, Hoffman Estates, Illinois 60172.

The following publications may be ordered from the Superintendent of Documents, Government Printing Office, Washington, D.C. 20402.

Tax Guide for Small Business. Internal Revenue Service, U.S. Department of the Treasury, Washington, D.C. 20224. 60 cents.

Starting and Managing a Small Business of Your Own. Small Business Administration, Washington, D.C. 20416. 35 cents.

ASSOCIATIONS

Professional Bowlers Association of America (PBA), 1720 Merriman Road, Akron, Ohio 44313. Founded 1959. Members 900. Professional bowlers. Promotes the status of the qualified bowler to the rank of professional and bowling as a major sport. Assists the American Bowling Congress in enforcing its rules and regulations. Promotes better understanding between professional bowlers and bowling proprietors, bowling manufacturers, and the communications media.

American Bowling Congress (ABC) 1572 East Capitol Drive, Milwaukee, Wisconsin 53211. Founded 1895. Members, 5 million. Includes all organized male tenpin bowlers in United States, Puerto Rico, Canada, Canal Zone, Saudi Arabia, and military installations in Europe, North Africa, Japan, Korea, Guam. Sponsors annual tournament competiton. Has State associations (50) local associations (2,995) and sanctions teams (1,268,000). Provides standard rules and tests and approves materials and equipment to be used in sanctioned competition. Publication: Bowling Magazine, monthly.

Billiard and Bowling Institute of America (BBIA), 23 East Jackson Boulevard, Chicago, Illinois 60604. Founded 1934. Members 125. Distributors and manufacturers of billiard and bowling equipment. Publication: BBIA Bulletin, monthly.

Bowling Proprietors' Association of America (BPAA) West Higgins Road, Hoffman Estates, Illinois 60172. Founded 1932. Members 5,150. Proprietors of bowling establishments. Publication: The Bowling Proprietor, monthly.

MANUFACTURERS

American Machine & Foundry Company, Bowling Division, Jericho Turnpike, Westbury, L.I., New York 11590.

Bowl-Mor Company, Inc., Newton Road, Littleton, Massachusetts 01460.

Brunswick Corporation, Bowling Division, 623 South Wabash Avenue, Chicago, Illinois 60605.

BUILDING SERVICE CONTRACTING

Section Contents

URBAN BUSINESS PROFILE

Building Service Contracting

(SIC 7349)

I. RECOMMENDATION

Building maintenance service is one of the fastest growing industries in the United States today. The growth of the service sector of the economy, the increasing urban concentration, and an ever-growing tendency for office building owners to "contract out" their office building cleaning needs combine to support a current industry growth rate of 15 percent. The attractiveness of this market and its relative ease of entry have caused a high level of competition among building maintenance contractors. Firms obtain business largely on the basis of price competition in bidding, though an established reputation for reliability is also important. These industry characteristics, along with the labor intensive nature of building maintenance services, underscore the importance of managerial skills to success.

The building maintenance industry employs a large number of minority workers, and there exists a growing number of such persons with experience in supervisory positions. An experienced maintenance crew supervisor, who acquires independently or through franchiser training practical skill in cost estimating, bidding, and employee management, can earn a moderate return on his time and invested capital in the building maintenance service business.

II. DESCRIPTION OF THE INDUSTRY

A. Identification

Building maintenance services are included in Standard Industrial Classification (SIC) 7349, Miscellaneous Services to Dwellings and other Buildings, described as:

> Establishments primarily engaged in furnishing, to dwellings and other buildings, specialized services not elsewhere classified, such as janitorial services, floor waxing, office cleaning.

Building maintenance contracting is a service-oriented activity providing janitorial and related services to homes, small businesses, commercial office buildings, hospitals, apartment houses, government offices, factories, hotels, motels, schools, etc. Services provided include such things as:

- Dusting, dustmopping of floor areas.
- Other floor cleaning, including vacuuming, floor waxing and buffing, wet mopping, and stripping and machine scrubbing.
- Toilet room cleaning.
- Cleaning of stairways and landings, as necessary.
- Cleaning of walls, woodwork and partitions.
- Cleaning of building exterior.
- Window washing, as necessary.

Sample building maintenance specifications, detailing the required services, are attached as appendix A of this report.

In addition to those services listed above, a building maintenance contractor may provide what is known as the "total maintenance concept." This includes the provision of heating, air conditioning, and electrical engineers, painters, carpenters, yardmen, and garage personnel. Other operations handled under such a contract might include elevator operators and dispatchers, guards and lobby dispatchers, and specialized personnel who might be required by the particular building or institution.

There is a decided trend toward this total concept form of building maintenance. If a building services contractor is not himself equipped to handle all the above-mentioned services, he may contract with the building owner to provide them, then subcontract those services which he himself is not equipped to perform. This tends to make the building maintenance contractor more attractive to his prospective client. A building owner or manager is interested in receiving the best maintenance at the lowest possible cost with the least visibility. This is best provided by the one contractor who renders *all* the services required by the building. In the total concept plan, the contractor in effect serves as the "middle man," presenting the building owner with a completed product—a clean and efficiently run building.

B. **Dimensions**

There were some 9,675 businesses with payrolls in 1967 which provided general building maintenance and janitorial services on a contract basis, according to the 1967 Census of Business of the U. S. Department of Commerce. These businesses earned gross receipts of $884 million and paid wages amounting to over $555 million during 1967. These figures indicate that there has been significant growth in the industry since 1963, when there were 6,949 businesses, $500 million in receipts, and payrolls totaled $317 million.

It is currently estimated that over half of all building maintenance service firms are unaccounted for by these statistics, as they report no payroll in census data. Current figures are unavailable, but, in 1963, 9,414 firms provided contract building maintenance service with no employees in addition to the proprietor and perhaps members of his family. This large number of one-man firms account for only a small fraction of total industry earnings, however. These 9,414 proprietors reported only about $38½ million in receipts in 1963, the last year in which data were collected for these nonpayroll firms.

The structure of the industry is suggested by the accompanying breakdown of all the 1963 reporting firms by size in terms of receipts.

TABLE 1

Dimensions of the Industry—1963

Size of establishment (By receipts)	Establishments (Number)	Receipts ($000)	Payroll entire year ($000)
Total, all establishments	16,363	538,523	316,893
Establishments operated entire year, total	14,074	508,005	301,422
With annual receipts of:			
$500,000 or more	175	N.A.	N.A.
$300,000 to $500,000	140	N.A.	N.A.
$100,000 to $300,000	554	90,554	56,157
$ 50,000 to $100,000	625	43,362	24,040
$ 30,000 to $ 50,000	721	27,178	13,077
$ 20,000 to $ 30,000	852	20,426	8,272
$ 15,000 to $ 20,000	715	12,096	4,218
$ 10,000 to $ 15,000	1,250	14,969	4,195
$ 5,000 to $ 10,000	3,101	20,483	2,980
$ 3,000 to $ 5,000	2,358	8,051	634
$ 2,000 to $ 3,000	2,063	4,126	326
Less than $ 2,000	1,490	1,490	182
New establishments in business at end of year	2,289	$ 20,085	$ 9,940

The current market for building services is over $1 billion. It is estimated by Building Services Contractor (the leading trade publication in the field) that by 1976, more than $2 billion a year will be spent on commercial, institutional, and industrial cleaning services. The same source estimates that over 30 percent of the Nation's office buildings and factories were cleaned by outside contractors in 1968, compared with 15 percent only 5 years before. Combining this growing share of the office building market with the rapid rise in industrial and commercial construction affords a glimpse of the growth potential of this industry.

The trend today is toward greater concentration within the industry. That is, while there are still a great many small establishments, larger establishments are accounting for an ever greater portion of the gross receipts. Most of the building maintenance service establishments are located in urban areas for the obvious reasons. The cities provide the concentration of business, commercial, and government buildings to be serviced, as well as employee availability. In particular, the contractor will find his clients among predominantly urban facilities (in addition to commercial office space), such as railroad stations, department stores, sports stadia, airports, etc. New York City, for example, where over 95 percent of all the large office buildings are cleaned and maintained by service establishments, accounts for one of the largest concentrations of building service contractors in the Nation.

Minority entrepreneurship in this field is relatively scarce. According to industry sources, only about 5 percent of the establishments grossing from $100,000 to $1 million annually are minority owned. However, this figure is above the national average for all businesses of this size. Because a major portion of the work force in this field is now made up of minority group members, there exists a growing pool of minority individuals with some experience in a supervisory capacity who might be able to make the transition from labor into management of building maintenance establishments.

C. Characteristics

1. *Nature of the Product*

The building maintenance contractor serves building owners and/or managers. He provides these clients with a continuing service—a clean and well run building. The reliability of the building service contractor is being purchased as well as his cleaning ability—the assurance that the work will, in fact, be performed. Thus, the product can actually be broken down into two components: quantity and quality of cleaning and other building maintenance functions and the assurance that those functions will, in fact, be performed.

Building maintenance services are usually provided to building owners and managers on a contract basis. Contracts are generally for 1 year, with either party entitled to terminate upon 30 days' notice. Since building maintenance and janitorial services are performed on a continuing basis, the contractual system is the most efficient manner to insure the provision of these services. A sample Professional Building Maintenance Agreement is attached as appendix B.

2. *Nature of the Customer*

The customer of a building services contractor is the building owner or manager. As discussed above, the client *must* have the services provided by the building contractor—that is, he must have a clean, serviceable building. However, in order to achieve this goal, he may have the option of: (1) doing his own janitorial and other maintenance work; or (2) contracting such work to the building services. Which of these options will be chosen depends upon the size and complexity of the building to be maintained and the costs of performing the maintenance work with in-house staff compared to contracting out the work.

Building owners are finding—to a greater and greater degree—that it is more economical for them to contract out their janitorial and building maintenance functions. A firm devoted to maintenance work can afford to use the more advanced equipment being developed and can rely more heavily on specialization of labor. The result is that the contracting firm can usually do a better job for less money. Thus, a building owner will generally include the cost of a building maintenance contractor when computing the overall cost of the building. On an average, if a commercial office building rents space at $6.50 per square foot, it will assume that maintenance costs will be $.50 per square foot per year.

The customer will choose a building services contractor on the following basis:

a) the contractor's ability to provide quality service;

b) the contractor's reliability to assure that such services will, in fact, be provided; and

c) the cost which will be required for these services.

On the other hand, how does the building services contractor decide for whose work he will bid? In undertaking market analysis of potential customers, the building services contractor will take into account such things as: the number of commercial, government, or other serviceable buildings or businesses in his market area; the amount, types, and degree of completion of new construction; the amount of potential business already accounted for; the possibility of providing services to those buildings already accounted for at a less expensive rate (due to the new contractor's lower overhead, lower salary requirement, or greater efficiency), etc.

The number and types of customers of a building services contractor will also depend upon certain characteristics of his own operation. These might include: number of employees on the payroll at a given time; number of potential employees in the market areas; amount of equipment on hand or available; capital required for expansion and possibility of obtaining it.

Major locational determinants include the location of potential customers in relation to the dwellings of the contractor's employees and the location of the customer with respect to the contractor's place of business and storage supply. The contractor must decide if a building is, for example, so distant from the location of the cleaning equipment and the employees needed to do the cleaning that it is impractical for him to service it

All of these factors are included in the contractor's estimating calculations. Cost estimating is one of the major skills required of the building services entrepreneur. He must accurately measure the above-listed factors, decide what weight to give each, and translate these decisions into a price which will be competitive and which will at the same time provide him with an acceptable profit level. These estimating procedures are discussed in greater detail below. An example of one possible estimating procedure is attached as appendix C of this report.

3. *Technology*

Building services contracting has traditionally been a labor intensive business. The main expense item of any contractor is his payroll. In a sense, the contractor is merely a "labor broker" who handles personnel problems for the building owner.

The new or prospective entrepreneur is likely to need a wide range of skills, preferably gained by experience as he develops an enterprise in the building maintenance field. He will probably do much (if not all) of the actual cleaning work at first, as well as the estimating of new jobs and the selling of his services. When the operation expands, the entrepreneur, while still cleaning, estimating, and selling, will have to train his new employees. In addition, growth will bring problems of accounting, inventory control, purchasing procedures. He will have to have a relatively high degree of proficiency to operate a successful establishment.

Once a business has become established, the entrepreneur of a building maintenance service can usually take out as profit 5 percent of the net receipts of the business, according to informed industry sources. The percentage will vary, of course, depending on:

a) the accuracy of entrepreneur's estimating procedures. If the entrepreneur does not estimate properly, profits built into business contracts will be consumed by costs overrun.

b) the extent of the competition on the contract. In some instances the entrepreneur will cut profit margins in an effort to win contracts.

c) the amount the entrepreneur wishes to reinvest in the establishment. This in turn will depend on the desired rate of growth.

The employees of a building services contractor are, for the most part, unskilled. (The major exceptions to this are window cleaners and any engineers provided.) Any training received is usually on-the-job, although some larger contractors are beginning to use classes to supplement this training.

Most employees used by the building services contractor are women, who are used for all but the heavy work. The majority of the employees in this field, particularly in the larger urban areas, are minority group members. Since most of building contract work is accomplished during the nighttime hours, it provides an excellent "moonlighting" job and a source of income for those with little formal training or education.

Wage rates for employees hover around the minimum wage rates applicable. In larger urban areas, wages are usually somewhat higher. In Washington, D.C., for example, with a minimum wage of $1.65 per hour, the wages of building service employees range from $1.75 to $2 per hour, with $1.90 per hour the average rate. Window cleaners' wages are higher, often ranging from $4 to $4.50 per hour and up.

In some locations, wage rates and availability of labor may be somewhat affected by unionization. (The building services industry is covered by the Building Service Employee Union, as well as others for the more specialized employees.) This is mainly true in highly industrialized towns which are in any case predominantly union. Elsewhere, the moonlighting nature of the jobs and rapid turnover among the employees have prevented unionization from taking hold.

One of the main problems of a building services contractor is the high turnover rate among his employees. Industry sources indicate that most remain on the job for a period of 2 to 6 months. This is an annual turnover rate of from 200 to 600 percent. This situation, again due to the moonlighting nature of the job, has caused a premium to be placed on reliability by the building services employer.

The high turnover rate has also led to increasing the screening procedures for potential employees of the building services company. Many job application forms now contain rather pointed questions involving: the reason the applicant desires work; whether or not he is buying a home; how long he has been on his present job, etc. The whole object of such screening is for the contractor to acquire a "solid" employee who will have an interest in working and who will stay on the job.

Equipment required in the building services contractor field has been relatively basic in the past. A sample inventory of equipment is reproduced below:

Sweeper
Buffer
Brushes
Floor pads
Extension cords
Mop bucket—round—oval
Wringer
Mop
Dust mop handle
Dustpan
Trash containers
Water pails
Pushbroom
Strawbroom
Rubber gloves
Uniforms
Smocks
Shirts
Ammonia
Bowl cleaner
Cleanser
Disinfectant
Furniture polish
Liquid detergent
Floor finish
Plastic bags
Sanitary napkins } occasional
Toilet seat covers } occasional
Paper towels } occasional

Recently, technological advances and greater sophistication have affected the equipment used by the building services contractor. In addition to the list of basic items reproduced above, such machines as institutional vacuums, high pressure cleaners, and power sweepers with centrifugal clutch are now available. These technological advances have affected profitability positively and have somewhat reduced labor requirements in the industry.

One major piece of equipment used by the building services contractor is a truck. The new entrepreneur may at first transport machines and supplies in a car or station wagon. Usually, however, the enterprise will develop to the point where one or more trucks are needed. In a survey performed by Building Services Contractor, the average number of trucks in operation per firm surveyed was 4.3.

The same survey noted that 92 percent of building services contractors keep a warehouse of expendable cleaning supplies, with the average firm keeping 54 days of normal consumption on hand. Being able to keep such stock on hand is a problem to be dealt with by any new entrepreneur.

There are definite economies of scale accruing to a building services contractor. These usually begin at annual gross revenues of $500,000 and include savings on supplies, which can then be purchased directly from the manufacturer rather than from the distributor, savings on machines (with fewer having to be purchased for each additional $100,000 of income), and easing of credit binds for the growing business.

4. *Competition*

The largest form of competition the building services contractor has to face outside of his own industry is in the form of buildings which do their own in-house maintenance. This alternative is becoming more and more rare, however, as building administrators realize the advantage of contracting with a maintenance company. The building administrator is relieved of the worry of hiring and firing of maintenance employees, can rely on the contractor's use of more specialized labor, obtains the use of more advanced and complex equipment, and has no inventory problems in this area.

The growing market for the building maintenance services industry does not insure high margins and ease in securing work. However, a great many small contractors in this field assure intensive bidding competition, with the emphasis on shaving prices. Cost of maintenance is a primary determining factor in the choice of a building services contractor, and the building owner will, reputation for quality and reliability being equal, choose the contractor who comes in with the lowest bid for the job required. In this type of price competition, the large contractor has some advantages, the small contractor others. The large contractor may be able to provide equipment and supplies at a less costly rate than his smaller competitor because of economies of scale; the cost of "gearing up" to do a job, especially a large one, may be lower for him. On the other hand, the small contractor may have lower overhead, due to lower direct expenses and less equipment, and may be willing to have a smaller profit margin for the sake of getting the job and developing his reputation.

The problem of estimating must again be stressed. The small contractor, and especially the new entrepreneur, must be particularly careful in his estimating procedures. A net deficit is likely to result from inaccurate decisions about costs and personnel requirements, and although a contractor may be willing to reduce his profit margin, maintaining a loss is hardly a sound business practice.

5. *Ease of Entry*

The ease of entry into building services contracting is attested to by the large number of firms beginning operation each year. There are no licensing requirements in this industry, and many contractors begin with no more than experience in the cleaning field, determination, and a small amount of capital. Because many businesses begin with no more than the owner and operator (and perhaps one other part-time employee), qualified employees do not present an immediate problem for the prospective entrepreneur. At this stage, no office or storage space is required, and a new enterprise can be operated from the entrepreneur's home. Between $1,200 and $1,500 monthly contracts may be sufficient to begin an operation if accurate cost estimation and time allocations have been made. The failure rate of building services contractors is, according to industry sources, higher than the combined rate for all businesses. Some of the reasons for failure cited by trade authorities include: overextension, resulting in inability to complete jobs properly and to the satisfaction of the client; poor estimating procedures, resulting in cost overruns and unprofitable contracts; lack of managerial experience, resulting in higher than usual labor turnover; competitive weakness because of lack of established reputation; and general administrative difficulties.

In addition, industry sources indicate that experience in the building maintenance field is almost essential to the success of an enterprise. The majority of contractors interviewed stated that they had worked for 6 months to 2 years in the field before attempting to branch out into independent operation, and many noted that it was this early experience that helped to insure their success.

6. *Financing*

It is difficult to estimate the capital requirements of a new or prospective building services contractor. Industry sources indicate that a rough rule of thumb is: have available capital in the amount of three times the expected first month's gross income. For example, an entrepreneur who has secured a contract that will produce monthly gross receipts of $1,500 will be able to begin operations with $4,500. This amount will cover the cost of supplies, salary for the entrepreneur and any employees he might require, and working capital requirements needed to carry him through the timelag in payment for past services.

There are no special programs or sources of capital for establishing a building services contractor. The Small Business Administration, however, has been quite active in providing regular business and economic opportunity loans in this field, a large portion of which have been to minority entrepreneurs. The breakdown of these loans is presented below.

TABLE 2
SBA Regular Business and Economic Opportunity Loans: Building Maintenance and Janitorial Services

Number total	White and others	Percent	Black	Percent	Other nonwhite	Percent
60	33	55	23	38.3	4	6.7

Volume total	White and others	Percent	Black	Percent	Other nonwhite	Percent
$750,250	$522,300	69.6	$186,950	24.9	$41,000	5.5

Another form of organization and source of capitalization that is becoming increasingly popular in this field is the franchise arrangement. One of the largest franchise operations provides such assistance as training programs, managerial assistance, continuing counseling support, working equipment, supplies, advertising and promotions for a nominal fixed fee.

7. *Profitability*

As noted above, the reasonably successful building service contractor can expect an average of about 5 percent profit on net receipts. The industry can be expected to grow at about 15 percent per annum.

Factors tending to decrease profitability are: inaccurate cost estimation; the high labor turnover, with resultant costs; frequent theft of equipment and supplies; and overextension of operation.

8. *Dependence on Outside Factors*

The field of business maintenance contracting is less subject to the effects of economic conditions than are many industries or types of business. Building cleaning and maintenance needs exist irrespective of business cycles, and purchasers of these services usually think of them as fixed costs. One effect of the business cycle, however, is the decrease in construction during times of recession, in turn causing a decrease (or, more accurately, a less rapid increase) in the contractor's potential business. The availability of credit would most likely affect the building services contractor less than other areas of the economy.

III. FEASIBILITY ANALYSIS

A. Review of Key Factors

The following factors bear on the feasibility of establishing a building service contracting business:

1. *Management*

The new entrepreneur requires experience in the field of cleaning or building maintenance. At least 1 year working for an established firm will enable him to acquire the technique of accurate cost estimating which is essential to his success. Because personnel management is also vital, the new entrepreneur will need experience or potential in this field as well. If the prospective manager has shown some knack for selling, accounting, and ability to handle inventory, he is enhancing his chances for success.

2. *Market*

The market for his services will determine the new contractor's success. Such a market can be analyzed in part by the following:

a) concentration of office buildings in the area;

b) new construction, noting state of completion;

c) competition;

d) the contractor's own reputation.

3. *Location*

While not crucial at the early stages of operation, the contractor's offices and warehouses should be convenient both to his prospective clients and, if possible, to the homes of his employees.

4. *Labor*

Although availability of labor is usually not a problem, retention and management of this labor can be problems. Employee benefits, profit-sharing and other such methods are often used to hold employees, and careful screening of applicants and training of employees are used to ease the management problem. The building services contractor may benefit from the activities of government-funded manpower programs which screen jobseekers and which provide basic education and pre-vocational training to them. Such programs as JOB 70, the Work Incentive Program (WIN), and on-the-job training under the Manpower Development and Training Act (MDTA O-J-T) would provide a ready source of potential employees in most urban areas. An analysis of the quantity and quality of the work force is essential in assuming the potential feasibility of the enterprise.

B. **Special Factors for New Minority Ventures**

The largest market for a building services contractor is in the urban areas. It is in urban areas, too, that there exists a reservoir of potential employees, many of them minority members. Thus, location and labor will serve as assets to the prospective minority entrepreneur who can also benefit from a continually growing market and the increasing acceptance of minority entrepreneurship.

C. **Projections of Attainable Returns in Industry**

Projections follow for two different types of operations. The first is for a starting independent operation, with three part-time employees. The second is for a new franchise operation for professional building maintenance.

1. *Small, One-Man Operation*

The projections here are based on the following assumptions:

a. A one-man operation, with the prospective entrepreneur having had some experience in the building maintenance field.

b. Three part-time workers, each available for approximately 17 hours per week of employment at $1.65 per hour.

c. An initial investment by the manager of $4,500.

d. A 40-hour work week for the owner, who does both selling and supervising of the operation as well as some actual building maintenance work.

e. Operation out of the home of the manager during at least the first year of operation, using the personal vehicle (car, station wagon, or small truck) for the business.

f. A relatively high cash requirement, since the owner will be unable, as a new operator, to secure his supplies and equipment on credit and will require initial cash outlays.

As the following operating statements shows, such an operation, grossing $18,000 per annum, might provide a net profit of about $9,600. This figure is deceptively high, however. It does not take into account the owner's draw for salary and any amounts to be reinvested in the business.

Gross Annual Revenue		$18,000
Investment	$4,500	
Area served and customer type	7 to 12 buildings 4,000 to 6,000 sq. ft. each 36,000 sq. ft. total	
Production hours	74 hours per week	
Operating location	Works from own home	
Vehicles	Car, station wagon or used truck	
Equipment and material	$3,000	
Distribution of labor		
Owner's function	Management, sales, and cleaning	
Number and type of employees	Owner, 3 part-time employees for cleaning	
Fixed costs		
Vehicle depreciation	$ 500	
Equipment depreciation	750	
Telephone and yellow pages	50	
Rent, office help, supervisory, outside services	0	
Total fixed costs		$ 1,300
Variable costs		
Labor	$4,500	
Advertising, selling expenses	700	
Payroll tax, employee fringes	600	
Vehicle operating cost	1,000	
Liability insurance	300	
Total variable costs		$ 7,100
Net profit before tax and owner's compensation		$ 9,600

If the entrepreneur has had adequate experience in the field, if he is able to sell his services, if his cost-estimating procedures are accurate, and if he provides quality service, a 1st-year operation of this size is feasible. However, unless all of these characteristics are present, as well as a willingness by the new entrepreneur to forego present profits and reinvest heavily in his business, an establishment such as this cannot be maintained for any length of time.

2. *Franchise Operation*

The owner of a typical, but hypothetical, franchise must initially invest $5,000. Of this amount, $1,500 is paid to the franchiser for goods and services, including:

- The licensed use of the franchiser's trademark and training—$900.
- Professional products, business forms, supplies and tools, sales promotion aids, and technical manuals—$500.
- Equipment—$100.

The training provided by the franchiser is particularly geared to servicing buildings, offices, and plants under contract. Because of such possible benefits as the established name of the franchiser, cost-cutting centralized purchase of supplies, advertising provided by the franchiser, and continuous consultation and advice, the franchisee may possess advantages over the independent operator. In addition, special financing is occasionally provided by the franchiser, making it easier for an individual to begin a business.

New operation—Husband and wife or part-timer

Investment	$5,000
Area serviced and customer type	22,000 square feet 4 to 10 commercial buildings 4,000 to 6,000 square feet each

Operating location—works from home
Vehicles—one truck, probably used
Equipment—primarily supplied by franchiser

Distribution of labor

Owner's functions—housekeeping, sales and management
Number and type of employees—owner and wife, with one part-time employee

Gross Annual Revenue		$15,000
Fixed costs		
Vehicle depreciation	$ 500	
Equipment depreciation	50	
Telephone and yellow pages	100	
Rent, office help, outside services	50	
Manager's administrative salary	1,000	
Total fixed costs		$ 1,700
Variable costs		
Manager's production salary	$7,500	
Labor (part-time)	1,750	
Sales expense (advertising—paid by franchiser)	- 0 -	
Vehicle operating cost	1,200	
Franchising fee (percentage of gross income—here, 7 percent)	1,050	
Liability insurance (paid by franchiser)	- 0 -	
Total variable costs		$11,500
Total costs		$13,200
Profit before tax		$ 1,800
Net to owner		
Manager's administrative salary	$1,000	
Manager's production salary	7,500	
Profit before tax	1,800	
Net to owner before taxes		$10,300

ESTABLISHING THE BUSINESS

A. **Approaching the Market**

If he is planning an independent, one-man operation, the prospec- ve building services contractor should have his market fairly well lefined. In addition, he should have already secured contracts assur- ng him of $1,500 monthly gross revenue. These agreements are made through previous contacts while working in the field. Ability to secure these contracts will indicate to the entrepreneur that his bidding has been price competitive, and if his performance is of acceptable quality, he should be able to maintain an independent operation at this level for at least 1 year.

The franchisee, on the other hand, does not require an initial knowledge of the cleaning industry. The franchiser trains him to be an expert professional cleaner. The franchiser also generally provides the new owner with an advertising and sales promotion program, other assorted sales aids, and instructions on their use. These benefits, added to the use of the franchise brand name and the advantage of its reputation, will ease the franchisee's approach to the market.

B. **Plant Requirements**

The small, one-man operation requires minimum space and can comfortably be operated from the entrepreneur's home. The only room needed is a storage room for equipment and supplies; a garage or basement area will certainly suffice for the 1st year of operation at this level. The same is true for the beginning franchise.

Growth of the establishment will require office space and more storage space than can be adequately provided in the home. At this point, the entrepreneur will seek a location close to the buildings which he is servicing and as close as possible to the location of his employees. Office space may range from about 1,000 square feet for an establishment with 15 to 40 full- and part-time employees, to 22,000 square feet of office space for a 900-man operation. In addition, storage space may run 500 to 13,000 square feet, accordingly.

C. **Financing**

The basic investment involved in building services contracting is the purchase of equipment and supplies. Although some financing arrangements may be made with equipment suppliers, expendable items such as chemicals, cleaning agents, and paper products will require a cash outlay. In addition, enough capital must be kept on hand to meet 1 month's payroll requirements, supplies, and rent.

(This is necessary because of the timelag between contractual agreement and actual payment.)

Because the initial capital requirement is relatively low, the building services contractor can often begin operation with his own savings or other private sources. If a franchise operation is contemplated, the franchiser is often willing to provide special financing arrangements. And it may be possible to secure a loan from the Small Business Administration. Unless the individual entrepreneur has an independently stable credit reputation, it may be difficult to secure conventional bank financing for this type of operation.

D. **Labor Force**

The labor force used by a building services contractor is, for the most part, unskilled. Although the wages are low, recruitment of employees is rarely a problem. The new entrepreneur, probably needing only two or possibly three part-time employees, will be able to recruit them through his previous business contacts or through the standard advertising methods.

As the enterprise develops, however, maintaining a reliable and efficient labor force will require special effort. Such an effort might include such things as profit sharing, bonuses for outstanding work, and other employee benefits. Raising the wage rate as much above the minimum wage as possible is probably the best method of securing and maintaining personnel.

BIBLIOGRAPHY

SMALL BUSINESS ADMINISTRATION, Washington, D. C. 20416
Small Business Administration, Office of Planning, Research, and Analysis, *Selected Industry Profiles,* August 16, 1968.

Guide to the Assessment of Minority Business Opportunities.

BUILDING SERVICE CONTRACTOR, 101 West 31st Street, New York, N. Y. 10001.

Trade magazine, published bimonthly. Each firm engaged in contract cleaning, maintenance services, and allied operations may obtain one copy bimonthly without charge, by a written request to the publishers. To all others, the subscription price is $6 annually —$10 for 2 years. Single current copies are available at $1 per copy; back copies available at $2 per copy.

FORMS FOR THE BUILDING SERVICE CONTRACTOR, National Association of Building Service Contractors, 2215 M Street, N.W., Washington, D. C. 20037. 1970.

Representative samples of forms used in building service contracting businesses throughout the country.

1967 CENSUS OF BUSINESS—BC67-SA1, Bureau of the Census, U. S. Department of Commerce, Washington, D. C. 20233.

1963 CENSUS OF BUSINESS, Bureau of the Census, U. S. Department of Commerce, Washington, D. C. 20233.

TRADE ASSOCIATION

The trade association serving building service contractors is the National Association of Building Service Contractors. This association has over 550 members, primarily engaged in contracting of building maintenance service and janitorial cleaning. Associate members are manufacturers of cleaning supplies and equipment.

NABSC is located at 2215 M Street, N.W., Washington, D.C. 20037. It was founded in 1965 and serves as a representative voice of building services contractors. In addition, NABSC conducts studies in areas of interest to building services contractors, such as costs and ratios, industrial relations and personnel, marketing and sales, contract improvement, materials and supplies sources, etc.

APPENDIX A

Typical Specifications For Custodial Services

1. *Waste Paper—Ash Trays—Daily*

   Waste baskets and ash trays shall be emptied daily. Ash trays shall be wiped clean. Trash generated by normal daily office routine shall be emptied into trash containers. Trash removal shall be provided by the *contractor or building owner*. If by contractor, he generally subcontracts.

2. *Dusting—Daily*

   All furniture, file cabinets, and horizontal surfaces which can be reached while standing on the floor shall be dusted daily with a chemically treated cloth.

3. *Dust Mopping—Floors—Daily*

   All noncarpeted floors shall be dust mopped with a treated yarn dust mop daily with special attention being given to areas under desks and furniture to prevent the accumulation of dust and dirt. Dust mopping shall be done after furniture has been dusted.

4. *Toilet Rooms—Daily*

   a. Wash all mirrors.

   b. Wash hand basins and hardware.

   c. Wash urinals.

   d. Wash toilet seats using disinfectant in water.

   e. Wash toilet bowls.

   f. Damp mop floor using disinfectant in water.

   g. Damp wipe, clean, and disinfect all tile and other surfaces. Spot wipe and clean where necessary. Walls and partitions are to be free of handprints and dust.

   h. Replenish hand soap, towels, and tissue. These expendable items shall be furnished by the building owner or contractor. In 90 percent of contracts, provided by the contractor.

   i. Toilet bowl brush shall be used on toilet bowls, and care shall be given to clean flush holes under rim of bowl and passage trap.

   j. Bowl cleaner shall be used at least once each month or more often if necessary.

5. *Stairways and Landings—Daily—As Necessary*

   All stairways and landings shall be dust mopped with a treated yarn dust mop daily. Railings, ledges, and equipment shall be dusted daily. Spot cleaning of doors and walls shall be done as necessary. These floor areas shall be damp mopped, scrubbed, waxed, and buffed as necessary.

6. *Vacuuming—Daily*

   All rugs in office areas and public spaces shall be vacuum cleaned daily. Hard-to-get spots and corners shall be cleaned with necessary tools.

7. *Floor Waxing & Buffing—Daily and As Necessary*

   All noncarpeted resilient floors shall be waxed with Underwriter Laboratory approved materials. The frequency of the waxing shall be governed by the amount of wear due to weather and other conditions. The floors and traffic areas shall be waxed so as to maintain a uniform appearance throughout the entire building. Corridors and elevator floors shall be buffed daily.

8. *Wet Mopping—Daily and As Needed*

   All waxed floors shall be damp mopped when dirt can not be swept or dusted, and spots shall be removed daily.

9. *Stripping and Machine Scrubbing—As Needed*

   This operation shall be accomplished as frequently as necessary, depending on the need to remove dirt-embedded finishes, stains, spillages, and wax buildup.

10. *Water Coolers—Daily*

    All water coolers shall be cleaned and polished daily.

11. *Spot Cleaning—Daily*

    Walls, doors, painted woodworks, and interior glass shall be kept free from handprints and smudges which can be removed with cloth and neutral cleaner. The type of cleaner to be used shall be appropriate for the wall material.

12. *Ash Receivers—Daily*

    Ash receivers shall be cleaned and sanitized as necessary.

13. *Lighting Fixtures—Semiannually—Annually*

All lighting fixtures shall be dusted every 6 months and washed annually.

14. *High Dusting—Quarterly*

Pipes, ledges, mouldings, etc., shall be dusted every 3 months.

15. *Venetian Blinds—Daily*

A sufficient number of venetian blinds shall be dusted or damp wiped daily so that all blinds shall be dusted every 90 days. Draperies shall be straightened and vacuumed.

16. *Walls, Woodwork, and Partitions—Quarterly*

All walls shall be brushed down every 3 months with approved wall duster or a vacuum cleaner.

17. *Glass Partitions and Doors—Monthly*

All glass partitions and doors shall be damp cleaned monthly.

18. *Window Washing—Quarterly*

All windows shall be washed inside and outside once every three months. [Often contracted out, because of high insurance risks, labor skills required, etc.]

19. *Air-Conditioning Grills—Monthly*

All areas around air-conditioning and return air grills shall be cleaned once each month.

20. *Elevators—Daily*

The interior surfaces and fixtures of the elevators and the elevator lobby doors shall be dusted daily and damp wiped as necessary.

21. *Polishing—Daily—Monthly*

All doorplates, kick plates, brass and metal fixtures within the building shall be wiped daily and polished monthly.

22. *Toilet Rooms—Daily* [This involves day laborers.]

Maid and/or porter shall make periodic checks of toilet and rest rooms, and shall replenish supplies, clean fixtures as necessary, empty waste cans, etc.

23. *Policing Floors—Daily* [This involves day laborers.]

Corridors, lobbies, and other public areas shall be kept free of wastepapers, cigarette butts, matches, etc.

24. *Entrance Lobby—Daily*

Entrance lobby shall be serviced daily. Lobby glass shall be washed and cleaned as necessary. Particular attention shall be given floor and glass doors during inclement weather.

25. *Building Exterior—Daily*

Entrance shall be swept clean of litter. Sidewalk shall be kept clean and free of snow and ice. Salt or other ice-melting material shall be furnished by the building management.

26. *General—As Necessary*

   a. Employees of contractor shall report to the building superintendent any conditions such as leaky faucets, stopped toilets and drains, broken fixtures, etc., or any other unusual happenings in buildings.

   b. Employees of contractor shall check windows and turn off all lights when night cleaning is finished.

   c. Employees of contractor shall have proper identification during hours of employment.

   d. Employees of contractor shall not disturb papers on desk, open drawers or cabinets, use telephones, televisions, radios, drink, or gamble while on duty. They shall report any open safes and cabinets to the building guard force or building management.

   e. Day employees shall be under supervision of the building superintendent. The duties and work schedule shall be agreed upon by contractor and building management.

   f. Daytime employees of contractor will wear uniforms. They will be neat and clean in appearance.

   g. No cleaning services shall be provided on legal holidays.

APPENDIX B

Sample Professional Building Maintenance Agreement

AGREEMENT made on ______[date]______ between ______[contractor]______ and ______[client]______

NOW THEREFORE, the parties agree as follows:

1. Beginning on ______[date]______, Contractor will provide and perform for the Client the services described in the work schedule [see appendix A], in the buildings and areas to be serviced therein set forth.

2. All personnel furnished by the Contractor will be employees of the Contractor, and the Contractor will pay all salaries and expenses of, and all Federal social security taxes, Federal and State unemployment taxes, and any similar payroll taxes relating to such employees, and will carry workmen's compensation insurance for such employees. The Contractor will be considered for all purposes an independent contractor, and will not at any time directly or indirectly act as an agent, servant, or employee of the Client.

3. The Contractor will provide all proper safeguards and shall assume all risks incurred in performing its services hereunder.

4. The Contractor shall provide the insurance coverage agreed upon, include comprehensive liability coverage and workmen's compensation coverage.

5. Without limiting the responsibility of the Contractor for the proper conduct of its personnel and the cleaning of the areas to be serviced hereunder, the conduct of the cleaning personnel hereunder is to be guided by rules and regulations as agreed upon from time to time between the Client and the Contractor, and such additional special written instructions as may be issued by the Client to the Contractor from time to time through its designated agent.

6. The Contractor is responsible for the direct supervision of its personnel through its designated representative, and such representative will, in turn, be available at all reasonable times to report and confer with the designated agents of the Client with respect to services rendered.

7. The Contractor agrees that the cleaning services to be provided hereunder shall be performed by qualified, careful, and efficient employees in strict conformity with the best practices and highest applicable standards. The Contractor further agrees that upon the request of its Client, it will remove from services hereunder any of its employees who in the opinion of the Client are guilty of improper conduct or are not qualified to perform the work assigned to them.

8. It shall be understood and agreed that during the term of this agreement and for ninety (90) days thereafter, the Client will not, directly or indirectly, hire any person employed by the Contractor.

9. In exchange for performance of services hereunder, the Client shall make payment to the Contractor for services rendered hereunder at the rate of ________ per month. The Contractor will give the Client at least thirty (30) days notice of any price change for services rendered hereunder, and the Client will notify the Contractor of any changes in the use of the areas covered by this agreement and any additions to or changes in the furnishings or floor, wall, or ceiling surfaces forming a part of the Client's premises.

10. The Contractor will perform all services required hereunder, except when prevented by strike, lockout, act of God, accident, or other circumstances beyond its control.

11. This agreement shall continue in effect for 1 year from the date services are to begin, but may be terminated by either party by giving thirty (30) days written notice by registered mail addressed to the other party.

APPENDIX C

Estimating A Single Job*

Assume that the building maintenance contractor is pricing the maintenance of 50,000 square feet of office space. The work is to be done each weekday evening after employees leave at 5 p.m. Calculations indicate that three men and a supervisor will be needed on a regular 40-hour week. The estimate should look like this:

MATERIALS AND EQUIPMENT
(Approximately 15% of total labor costs)

Materials (per month)	$ 160.00	
Prorated equipment depreciation	60.00	
Equipment repairs and maintenance	10.00	
		$ 230.00

LABOR COSTS

Number of men	Monthly hours	Wage rate	Monthly payroll	
3	480	$2.25	$1,080.00	
1 supervisor	160	$2.60	416.00	
			$1,496.00	
Vacation, sickleave, overtime factor, etc.—10%			149.60	
				$ 1,645.60

TAXES AND INSURANCE

**Social Security—5.2% of monthly payroll $1,496.00	$ 77.79	
State and Federal employment taxes 2% of monthly billing	30.71	
Insurance cost (prorated for total monthly billings on all accounts serviced by firm)	30.00	$ 138.50
SUBTOTAL (70% of bid price)		$ 2,014.10

To arrive at total price, divide subtotal by 70%

$2,014.10 ÷ 70% = $2,877.28

15% of monthly contract for overhead =	$ 431.59	
15% of monthly contract for profit =	431.59	$ 863.18
TOTAL MONTHLY CONTRACT		$ 2,877.28
TOTAL YEARLY CONTRACT		$34,527.36
PER SQUARE FOOT PER YEAR		69¢

(National average ranges from 50¢ to 80¢ per square foot for maintenance)

*Adapted from Building Services Contractor for April 1968.
**As of July 1971.

CHILDREN'S AND INFANTS' WEAR

Section Contents

URBAN BUSINESS PROFILE

Children's and Infants' Wear

(SIC 5641)

I. RECOMMENDATION

Entry into the dynamic industry of children's and infants' wear sales is recommended only for those who are experienced retailers, who have experience in following apparel fashion trends, and who have access to at least $80,000 of risk equity capital from personal savings or investors. The children's and infants' wear industry has become an increasingly important part of total apparel industry sales, with a dollar volume of approximately $500 million in 1969. Yet the children's and infants' wear retail trade had a failure rate of 49 firms out of every 10,000 in 1968, according to Dun and Bradstreet, making its industry failure rate higher than average for the retail field.

The dynamic changes that are continually taking place in the industry can, however, offer rewards to the retailer who knows both his local market and the trends in children's fashion to which the buyer is increasingly sensitive. The minority entrepreneur who meets the above qualifications and who is able to locate so as to take best advantage of his desired market segment will be in a position to capitalize on growth trends in the industry.

II. DESCRIPTION

A. Identification

Standard Industrial Classification (SIC) 5641 defines children's and infants' wear stores as those stores stocking and selling a variety of clothing sized and designed especially for children from infancy to the age of 12 years. An assortment of children's furniture, toys and accessories is also included.

B. Industry Dimensions

Trends within the industry indicate a movement toward fewer but larger stores. The number of specialty stores decreased from 4,879 establishments with payroll in 1963, to 3,556 in 1967, while the average annual sales per store went from $79,960 in 1963 to $92,700 in 1967. The typical selling space in a specialty store has increased from 1,800 to 2,500 square feet in the same time period. These trends have continued since that period.

Industry sources indicate that several other trends have become apparent. Departments devoted to infants' and children's wear have proliferated in department stores on an increasingly subdepartmentalized basis, breaking merchandise down into increasingly narrower age groupings, such as preteen or teen. This has also been the case in specialty stores where emphasis has been on merchandising to children by breaking them into age categories. There has also been growth in the selling of children's and infants' wear in men's and women's shops, supermarkets, drugstores, and variety chains, resulting in increased competition for those specialty and department stores that base their market appeal on greater convenience and lower price. Sales of suburban retailers are also increasing at a faster rate than downtown, reflecting, in part, demographic patterns and the convenience and increased appeal of shopping centers.

C. Industry Characteristics

1. Nature of the Product

The infants' and children's wear industry is designed to satisfy clothing needs of children to the age of 12, including diapers, underwear, nightwear, day wear, coats, shoes, and accessory needs. The apparel is increasingly styled for adaptability to children's activities, ease of care, and durability. These items may thus be considered both staple and impulse and are for the most part repeat sale items.

Infants' and children's clothing and accessories are available in a wide range of prices. Price range bears a functional relationship to quality and, therefore, to the nature of the particular merchant's target market. "Big ticket" products may include those items which are specially designed or novelty creations or which are sold as accessories to children's wear such as jewelry and toilet items.

The marketing or sales approach is very much dependent upon the type of store and the target market. It may reflect a higher price, high quality, and service orientation, as does the department or specialty store, or a lower price, less quality conscious, self-service approach characteristic of the discount or drugstore. Higher price department stores and discount stores currently lead the children's wear industry in terms of growth in sales volumes.

2. Nature of the Customer

Despite the fact that children are the ultimate wearers of the merchandise sold by children's and infants' wear stores, adults are usually the purchasers. Adults develop preferences toward a particular seller on the basis of price, quality of merchandise, service, selection, style, and goodwill.

Children's wear retailers have found the most profitable locations for business to be those areas with a heavy concentration of families, with adequate housing facilities for future growth, and with business and commercial activity capable of sustaining local population growth. Locational determinants to be considered in the selection of a particular site include the extent of customer traffic (including pedestrian) and the nature of the existing stores in both the immediate vicinity and in the community.

3. Competition

Infants' and children's wear stores may take any of several organizational forms—proprietorships, corporations, franchises. No single form predominates, though the growth in the number of department stores that include infants' and children's wear departments and the trend in the industry toward larger size and multiple stores suggest increasing use of the corporate form. One of the most significant features of the industry from the competitive aspect is the large variety in the types of business operations which stock and sell infants' and children's wear; outlets include everything from department stores and specialty stores to discount operations, supermarkets, and mail order houses.

Fashion consciousness has become more and more significant in the industry, particularly at the higher quality outlets. Department stores and specialty shops in particular have based their approach on quality and fashion, competing with each other largely on the basis of price and service. The low-end price lines tend to be "fashion followers" and are handled primarily by stores such as discounts, chains, mail order firms, supermarkets, and varieties which depend on high turnover for success. Use of a merchandise buying service may offer the smaller retailer a source of information about price changes, new merchandise, best sellers, and other trade features on which success in his chosen market is based.

There are three major types of buying services which an infants' and children's wear retailer may use. All fulfill the same function, market representation for the stores served, but differ from one another in the matter of ownership. Wholly owned services include Allied Purchasing Corp. and the May Company; association buying offices (owned and operated by members and stockholders) include Associated Merchandising Corp. and the Specialty Stores Association; and privately owned independent buying offices include Kirby Block & Co. and Youth Fashion Guild. Unless the prospective entrepreneur is very experienced in the trade, he should investigate affiliation with an established buying service.

4. *Promotional Techniques*

Every infants' and children's operation needs sales promotion to attract customers. But too often, store owners equate merchandise promotion with reduced prices alone. This is usually a mistake. Unless the store is purely a bargain operation, it has other things to offer—values, assortment, service, and fashion. Some of its promotional efforts should, therefore, be keyed to these themes.

The major methods for promotion used in the industry are newspaper advertising, direct mail, and store window displays. While newspaper advertising gets its major share of the large store's promotional dollar, smaller stores with smaller budgets have tended to avoid the newspaper because they cannot afford professional advertising staffs. However, some smaller stores have found that running small ads regularly keeps the store's name before the public, and that the extra cost of professional advertising help is often offset by the extra sales for which the ads are responsible.

With respect to direct mail, this technique has the virtue of being available to any store, no matter how small the amount it can invest. A mailing list should be developed from customer records, supplemented by birth lists and school rosters.

Perhaps the most economical form of promotion is the store window display, and specialty stores have found this to be the best way of attracting customers. Effective windows tell a story, and each item displayed should be an integral part of that story, with no extraneous merchandise present.

5. *Ease of Entry*

The industry is characterized by relatively easy entry, the one restrictive factor perhaps being the trend toward bigness and the consequent financing problems. Licensing is usually required at the local level, but this, as a rule, does not pose a serious or costly problems.

In a major city, a specialty store with an $80,000 or more annual sales volume and with a selling area of 20 by 100 square feet requires a minimum capital investment of about $45,000. This figure by 1970 standards represents a rather small initial investment. Once a general area has been selected in which to locate, feasibility planning should be done on the basis of available store space, sources of supply, and licensing and capital requirements. One means by which a businessman new to infants' and children's wear may become better acquainted is by joining an infants' wear and children's wear merchandising group, such as Youth Fashion Guild and the National Retail Merchants Association.

6. *Capital Requirements*

Financing in the infants' and children's wear business today must be thought of only in "big" terms. Insufficient financing at the outset is extremely dangerous. In 1967 an estimated capital investment of $35,000 was required to finance a 20 by 100 foot shop capable of generating a sales volume of $80,000 in the first year, with $15,000 to $18,000 going for fixturing, $17,000 for inventory, and $3,000 for other expenses. Capital needs for almost all types of shops have since climbed. In 1970, a recommended minimum capital investment for an infants' and children's wear store was about $45,000. However, this figure will vary considerably with the particular store's situation—rents, anticipated price and quality level of the merchandise, and amount of service offered.

Determination of the initial capital needs may be accomplished through a valuation of opening merchandise inventory, a summation of projected fixture and equipment costs, and an estimate of such operating expenses as credit costs, payroll size, and startup expenses such as licensing and advertising.

Other important factors to be considered in determining the capital investment required in infants' and children's wear retailing include the intended markup on the merchandise to be carried and the expected annual turnover of inventory. The children's and infants' wear trade average of three stock turnovers per year (calculated by dividing annual net sales by average monthly inventory) is lower than is usually found in men's and women's wear sales and is the main reason for a relatively high initial capital requirement in children's and infants' wear stores. This turnover rate will often vary by specific items within the store's stock, and successful stores are adept at stocking these high turnover items.

7. Profitability

Trade data on infants' and children's wear stores throughout the U.S. indicate the following operating ratios for the "average" children's and infants' wear store:

1969

Item	*Percentage*
Net sales	100.0
Cost of goods sold	61.0
Gross margin	39.0
Total operating expenses	36.8
Owner's compensation	10.4
Employee wages and benefits	8.2
Occupancy	8.4
Advertising	1.8
Depreciation, fixtures	1.5
Buying expenses	1.0
All other expenses	5.5
Net profit before taxes	2.2
Inventory turnover (annual)	2.9

Gross margins in the industry have improved from 32.5 in 1957 to 39.0 in 1969, and the annual turnover rate has risen slightly from 2.6 in 1957 to 2.9 in 1969. These figures should not be taken to indicate an industrywide strengthening of margins, as they are suggestive primarily of the growing market strength of the department store outlets at the upper end of the market.

8. Outside Factors Affecting Business Success

The seasonal cycles exert a strong influence on the apparel business in general, and children's and infants' wear stores are no exception. There is generally slower activity in the winter months, a gradual upswing into the spring, a leveling off during the summer months, and an upswing in the fall lasting through Christmas. A notable feature in this industry is a general insensitivity to economic downturns, particularly in the discount lines and their outlets. This is an important factor in the projection of sales and turnover rates and offers a favorable margin of stability to this industry.

III. BUSINESS OPPORTUNITIES IN THE INDUSTRY

A. Success Determinants

There are several features of the industry which affect the probabilities for business success.

- The requirement for substantial display and selling square footage is high, due to the necessity for a large stock assortment both in depth and breadth of styles, sizes, and colors.

- There is a relatively large amount of "detail" work in the business due to the breadth and depth of the stock assortment which must be carried. This also requires greater buying and inventory control skills.

- An average annual turnover which is slower than men's and women's wear entails a relatively large initial capital investment.

- During economic and business downturns this industry is less affected than many retail industries since customers seem to continue spending on their children.

- Considerable departmentalization now characterizes the businesses in the industry since fashion considerations have become more essential to selling and since both children and parents are increasingly interested in and aware of clothing. Children prefer to find their clothing broken down by age groups, and their growing interest and awareness has tended to increase their influence on parents' buying habits.

B. Examples of Returns Attainable in the Industry

1. Small Suburban Shopping Center Partnership

Two partners open an infants' and children's wear store in a shopping center centrally located with respect to several middle income housing developments consisting primarily of young families. This location affords 8,000 square feet of selling space, good pedestrian traffic, and convenient parking facilities. The merchandise to be carried is in the medium price range. There is a weekly regional advertiser available. The initial capital investment is $80,000, $70,000 of which is financed by a long term bank loan with a 90 percent Small Business Administration guarantee, with the remaining $10,000 provided by the owners. The business is established as a proprietorship by obtaining a license from the county at a nominal cost. The two proprietors expect to hire additional sales clerks necessary to provide a high level of customer service. First-year sales are good, with operating results as follows:

Sales		$300,000	100%
Cost of goods sold		183,000	
Gross margin		$117,000	39%
Operating expenses		$ 94,600	
Fixtures	$15,000		
Wages and benefits	36,000		
Rent	3,600		
Interest	5,000		
Advertising	5,000		
Buying expense	3,000		
Owner's compensation	26,000		
Depreciation	1,000		
Net profit before taxes		$ 22,400	7.4%

2. Downtown Specialty Shop

A proprietor opens a small downtown children's wear shop featuring relatively low prices and self-service. High volume is expected to provide enough revenue to cover relatively high operating costs. It is expected that advertising will be important to the operation, and advertising space is bought in the local newspaper. Only 4,500 square feet of selling space is available; display area fixtures are crowded but arranged for maximum traffic. The assortment in terms of style, color, and size is somewhat limited. The strategy is to achieve a faster turnover than is generally found in the industry through lower pricing catering to the lower income level of the majority of the pedestrian traffic. Sixty thousand dollars of financing is needed to open the store; capital sources include:

$20,000	Bank loan (5-year, 10%)
10,000	Owner's equity
10,000	Grant, local urban development foundation
20,000	Loan, MESBIC (10-year, 8%)
$60,000	

First-year operating results for the store:

Sales		$161,000	100%
Cost of goods sold		112,700	
Gross margin		$ 48,300	30%
Operating expenses		$ 46,280	
Fixtures and equipment	$18,000		
Wages and owner's compensation	12,880		
Rent	4,800		
Advertising	3,220		
Buying expense	1,980		
Depreciation	1,800		
Interest costs	3,600		
Net profit before taxes		$ 2,020	1.3%

In the first example, the market was segmented predominantly on the basis of price, quality, and service. A middle-income area offers good consumer spending potential at the level associated with a higher price range, since this income level is in a position to demand and to pay for a certain quality and to expect service when a purchase is being considered. The second example portrays a store oriented more toward a market based on daily commercial center traffic. Pricing policy is aimed at capturing impulse sales from passers-by and from respondents to the media advertising which emphasize price specials. Depth of selection and service are sacrificed for the lower-priced levels.

IV. ESTABLISHING THE NEW BUSINESS

A. Establishing the Market

The first step in starting a new children's and infants' wear store is to determine the market which the store is intended to serve. The prospective entrepreneur must identify the general type of consumer he wishes to cater to. He may wish to locate downtown, for example, and make his appeal to inner-city residents; or he may take a location in a suburban shopping center and cater to the suburban population.

Whatever the decision, it will affect where the new store is to be located, what it's total market is, and what kind of merchandise it should carry. If the market is an upper income one, willing to pay higher prices, it will require higher quality merchandise, dressing room space, merchandise displays, and gift boutiques. The entrepreneur who wishes to cater to this market will have to invest considerably more in a wide range of merchandise, store fixtures, and in trained sales staff than the discount operator.

The general procedure to be followed in selecting a store location begins with the identification of several potential locations where space is known to be available, the computation of the number of potential customers within the shopping area of each location (statistics from the local school system may be of value), and determination of the amount of annual expenditures on children's wear. An analysis of competition from department stores, discount operations, and other children's wear stores will suggest where underserved markets exist.

B. Securing Capital

A number of cities have organizations which specialize in assisting minority entrepreneurs to secure capital. A prospective entrepreneur should seek out these sources and go over his plans with them.

The local Small Business Administration office or OMBE affiliate may help to put the prospective entrepreneur in touch with sources of capital and to provide the names of banks which have made minority loans. Minority-owned banks may also provide capital.

BIBLIOGRAPHY

Walker, Herbert S., Nathaniel H. Mendleson, *Children's Wear Merchandiser,* National Retail Merchants Association, New York, 1967.

Infants' and Children's Wear Store, Small Business Supplement No. 22—State of New York Department of Commerce.

1969 Key Business Ratios, Dun and Bradstreet, Inc.

Sloane, Leonard, "Boy's Wear Market Termed High Risk," New York Times, January 13, 1971.

Retailing, Small Business Administration, Washington, D.C. 20416. Small Business Bibliography No. 10. Revised March 1969. Reprinted November 1969.

Discount Retailing, Small Business Administration, Washington, D.C. 20416. Small Business Bibliography. No. 68, Revised April 1968. Reprinted 1970.

TRADE ASSOCIATIONS

Infants', Children's and Teens' Wear Buyers Association: 45 West 35th Street, New York, New York 10001. Founded 1942. Members, 500. Buyers, merchandisers, and owners of stores selling infants', children's, and teenage apparel. Supplies market information and statistics. Publication: Bulletin, monthly.

National Retail Merchants Association (NRMA): 100 West 31st Street, New York, New York 10001. Founded 1911. Members, 14,000. Department, chain, and specialty stores retailing men's, women's and children's wear, shoes, dry goods, etc. Conducts conferences and workshops; provides extensive group of manuals, bulletins, promotion materials, and advisory services on all phases of retail merchandising including budgeting, credit, increasing sales, style changes, visual selling, etc. Publications: 1) Stores, monthly; 2) Retail Control (Controllers Congress), monthly; 3) Personnel Service, bimonthly; 4) New Bulletin (Store Management Group).

BIBLIOGRAPHY

TRADE ASSOCIATIONS

CONTRACT CONSTRUCTION

Section Contents

URBAN BUSINESS PROFILE
Contract Construction

(SIC Division C—Major Groups 15 and 17)

I. RECOMMENDATION

Entry into the contract construction industry is recommended only for those who have some technical knowledge of the construction process and, more importantly, a sound background in business management. For although it is estimated that the volume of construction will continue to rise at the rate of 10 to 15 percent per year, the failure rate has been high and the industry has been justifiably characterized as "high risk/high gain." Considering the number of uncontrollable factors that bear heavily on the ultimate profitability of a contract (weather, the state of the economy, etc.) it is extremely important that the contractor or manager be able to manage effectively those factors that can be controlled, such as cash flow, scheduling, estimating and bidding.

The industry can, however, be attractive to the minority entrepreneur. Contract construction is characterized by ease of entry and allows operation at a wide range of scales including relatively small volume levels. Compared to other forms of business, the capital requirements for starting in the construction business are not great. Overhead can be kept to a bare minimum (operation out of one's residence is not uncommon), and the minimum amount of money needed would be one third of the value of an anticipated contract plus a minimal overhead level. (It takes an outlay of one-tenth to one-third of the contract cost before payments to the contractor begin.) Thus, despite the risks that may be involved, a prospective entrepreneur with the required business skills would be well placed to capitalize on growth trends in the industry.

II. DESCRIPTION

A. Identification of Industry

As defined by the Standard Industrial Classification (SIC) Manual of 1967, contract construction activity is included within the following broad categories:

Major Group 15: Building Construction—General Contractors. This group includes building contractors primarily engaged in the construction of dwellings, office buildings, stores, farm buildings, and other projects of a similar character.

Major Group 16: Heavy Construction Contractors. This group includes contractors primarily engaged in the construction of other than buildings—highways, streets, bridges and tunnels, docks and piers, dams and water projects, etc. This group will not be considered in this profile.

Major Group 17: Construction—Special Trade Contractors. Included in this group are contractors primarily engaged in specialized construction activity such as plumbing, painting, electrical work, carpentry, etc.

(Operative Builders who build on their own account for resale or lease and investment builders who build structures on their own account for rental are classified in Major Group 65, Real Estate. Establishments so classified are not included in this profile.)

B. Dimensions of Industry

Construction represents a major component of the United States economy. During peacetime periods, this industry accounts for 10 to 11 percent of the total gross national product. For 1969, the total gross investment in construction reached $90 billion. Approximately one-third of this investment represented public construction while the remaining two-thirds was split about evenly between private residential and nonresidential construction.

A 1968 Small Business Administration (SBA) report estimated the number of establishments in the industry at approximately 500,000 "visible" (an established place of business or at least one paid employee) firms plus about 250,000 independent operators.

Minority ownership in the industry, however, is disproportionately low, both with respect to total population and with respect to minority ownership in business as a whole. The 1968 SBA report estimated that about 3 percent of all U.S. businesses are owned by nonwhites, while no more than 8,000, or 1.6 percent of the visible construction businesses, are nonwhite owned. Nonwhites, however, are better represented among the independent operators, comprising 10 percent or more of this group. Given the anticipated growth of the construction industry and various programs to overcome the traditional problems of the minority contractor, the 1968 Small Business Administration report foresaw the possibility of increasing the number of minority-owned firms to 70,000 or 80,000 by 1978.

C. Characteristics of the Contract Construction Industry

Contract construction involves the agreement on the part of an establishment to perform a specified series of operations resulting in a new or modified physical structure. As an industry, contracting contrasts with other industries in a number of ways.

Unlike other industries, the product of the contractor does not lend itself to standardization. Each job produces a different product and is unique. Other conditions surrounding the production process, such as payment terms, location, and financing availability and arrangements, also are not generally standardized.

The contractor takes a new and unique risk with each contract he signs. Another significant difference between contracting and other forms of industrial activity lies in the fact that it is one of the few industries in which a price is usually fixed before the product is produced. Upon signing a contract, the contractor is legally bound to perform and cannot curtail production to minimize loss without doing irreparable damage to his business reputation.

Additional problem areas which confront the contractor are highly competitive bidding on projects, a market that is dependent on the state of the economy, seasonality of work, unpredictability of weather, labor relations, interest rates, and complex purchasing and unavoidable dependence on others (on owners for payment, on other contractors and subcontractors for performance as specified and scheduled).

Because the industry is so varied, there are certain advantages to the prospective contractor. There is operating room within the industry for a variety of activities at a wide range of scales. The bulk of the firms are small, but the bulk of business goes to the larger firms. Entrance is relatively easy and growth potential great. Although construction activity is cyclical and uneven, growth for the industry in the long run is virtually assured (approximately 10 percent a year is currently estimated).

1. The Actors in the Contract Construction Industry

One of the difficulties for the construction contractor is the number and variety of participants in the construction process with whom he must deal. These actors and their roles are briefly defined:

a. *Contractors* are those who enter into agreements to perform certain building operations. They are of two types:

General Contractor—The general contractor provides overall supervision of the job, including obtaining and coordinating the subcontractors, and is responsible for satisfactory completion of the job as specified by the contract. The general contractor may perform the subcontractor's function (i.e. the specialty trades), but usually not for more than one or two specific construction operations. The contractor receives payment from the owner as specified by the contract, and is responsible for payment to subcontractors and suppliers.

Specialty Contractor—The specialty contractor specializes in one specific construction operation such as plumbing, painting, or electrical installation. He may work directly for an owner or serve in a subcontractual role for a general contractor. He is dependent on the general contractor for payment.

b. *Owner*. The owner is the individual who contracts for the job and makes the payment. He determines the price range, accepts bids or contract offers, fixes the payment schedule, establishes the desired work schedule and completion date, and provides plans and specifications, often through an architect or engineer. The owner also determines acceptability of the completed job, subject to legal settlement in the event a dispute arises.

c. *Architect or Engineer*—The engineer develops the plans for the project and specifies materials and installation methods to be used. He often provides a preliminary cost estimate and approves progress estimates before payment is made to contractors. He also provides supervision and passes judgement on acceptability of the final job.

d. *Materials Suppliers*—Materials suppliers provide job materials and, by deferring payment for a short period of time, serve as an important source of temporary credit. (A poor payment record to a supplier may result in a contractor being placed on a collect-on-delivery basis. This hampers the contractor by necessitating greater amounts of working capital.)

e. *Labor Force*—The labor force performs according to the direction of the builder/contractor. As a key cost and quality factor, the relationship between the contractor and his labor force is a critical job component.

f. *Bond Companies*—Owners often demand bonds of contractors, and contractors in turn often require them of subcontractors. They are a legal requirement for all public work. Bonding companies provide bonds for a certain percentage of the contract price. There are three main types of bonds:

(1) *Performance* bonds assure completion of the job according to plans and specifications. If the contractor defaults, the bonding company steps in and hires another contractor to complete the job.

(2) *Payment* bonds guarantee that all subcontractors, materials suppliers, etc. dealing with the bonded contractor will be paid off so that the owner can receive the finished product free of all liens and claims.

(3) *Contract* bonds guarantee both completion of the job and the payment of all liens.

Bonding companies have preferential rights over other creditors if they must step in and perform. They are generally conservative institutions and may be reluctant to bond new contractors. Because of their stake in contractor performance, bonding companies are usually willing to provide valuable advice and assistance.

g. *Financial Institutions*—These institutions, usually banks, serve as an important source of short term financing for contractor and owner alike. They generally require strong evidence of the contractor's ability to perform as a prerequisite for a loan. Like bonding companies, they may be a source of sound business advice for the contractor.

2. *Competition in Contract Construction*

Competition in the industry serves to keep net profit margins low. Dun and Bradstreet reported a 1969 industry return on sales (ROS) of 1.23 percent, although there is some evidence that smaller firms are able to report a higher figure by understating the value of the proprietor's contribution to his firm's revenues. The smaller contractor, for example, may keep his own books in the evening at no "cost" to the firm.

These figures suggest that a large portion of the contracting firms operates at a subsistence level. Whereas only six of 68 manufacturing industries included in a Dun and Bradstreet survey operate at a lower net worth to sales ratio than do general contracting, low overhead costs permit such operations to exist.

With a large number of smaller firms, many of which would have to be classified as marginal, competition in the industry is keen. This high level of competition is a prime cause of the low level of profit margin. Competition in the construction industry is largely price competition. While price is the predominant variable by which contracts are awarded, the business reputations of the competitors are also important. Even though the owner can protect himself against failure on the part of the contractor (by requiring a bond and/or through court action), delays caused by contract failure can be costly to the owner in terms of time and money. Therefore, an owner is likely to award a contract to the contractor who has demonstrated a capability of executing the contract expeditiously and on time. Also, although all bidders are competing to produce the same product, not all workmanship is of the same quality. A reputation for producing quality work as well as one for efficiency is therefore beneficial to the contractor.

The high level of competition in the construction industry is further evidenced by its high rate of failure. The 1968 Dun and Bradstreet report on business failure shows failures among construction firms comprised 17.3 percent of all business failures, or twice as many as the industry's portion of total business activity suggests.

3. Profitability

Construction contractors normally operate on a small margin of net profit. Below is a graph showing the trend in average net profits on net sales, or return on sales (ROS), for general building contractors since 1958.

GENERAL BUILDING CONTRACTORS
AVERAGE NET PROFITS ON NET SALES (ROS)
1958-1969

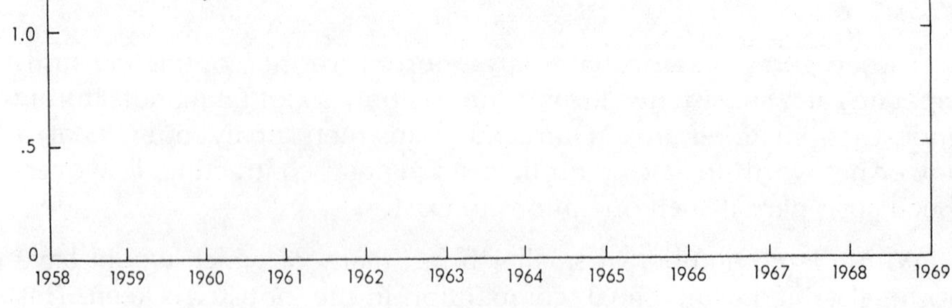

Specialty contractors typically generate a somewhat higher ROS than general building contractors. Whereas the latter group showed average net profits of 1.23 percent in 1969, plumbing, heating, and air-conditioning contractors averaged 1.71 percent and electrical work contractors 2.36 percent in 1969.

4. *Problem Areas for the Construction Contractor*

A number of specific problem areas can be isolated as causes of the high industry failure rate.

a. *Estimating and Bidding*—Estimating job costs is a complex operation that is crucial to a successful contracting business. Winning a contract with a bid based on an inaccurate estimate can be fatal to the contractor. Contractors will commonly bid against the competition rather than on the basis of the anticipated cost of carrying out the contract. The combination of underestimation with a low profit margin is an invitation to disaster.

Careful, realistic bidding not only insures against loss but aids in the execution of the contract since it requires that forethought be given such key job components as materials, scheduling, financing, and subcontract costs. Estimating for a specialty trade contract involves careful determination of all cost factors (labor, materials, etc.). Bidding is based on cost estimates plus the overhead and profit factors. To the degree that the general contractor subcontracts specialty work, he fixes his cost by legally binding the subcontractor to perform the specified work for the specified price. Cost overruns become the responsibility of the subcontractor. The resultant loss is his, not the general contractor's, and not the owner's. The general contractor will bid based on his own estimates for specialty work he performs, the bids submitted by the various subcontractors, and his own overhead and profit margin.

b. *Cash Flow*—Because prompt payment is critical to continued availability of credit and the contractor's reputation, it is vital that cash balances and transactions be carefully planned so that necessary payments can be made on time. Contractors and subcontractors must be sure that sufficient capital is available to meet payrolls and costs that come due before payment is received for work completed. Critical scheduling binds can occur if supplies can not be paid for and outside credit is not available. A discussion of the various types of contract agreements and contractual payments can be found in the appendix.

c. *Buying*—For specialty contractors, some inventory of supplies is necessary. However, there are problems of cost, spoilage, and storage that are sometimes overlooked in purchasing these supplies.

Overbuying is especially costly when it involves unstable materials such as paint and plaster. Bargain buying can result in more loss than gain.

To assure quick delivery and favorable discount and credit terms, good relations with suppliers are something to be coveted. Better customers receive preferential treatment from suppliers. High-volume, established customers might receive 40-day 15 percent discount terms, while the smaller newer customer might get only C.O.D. or 15-day terms with only a 10 percent discount.

Large expenditures for equipment are best avoided when the equipment cannot be put to steady use. Such special equipment can be rented or leased when needed. Renting avoids the problem of having to take marginal jobs just to pay for equipment and to keep it in use.

d. *Record Keeping and Cost Control*—Improper estimating and other financial problems are usually related to poor record keeping and cost control. A common and potentially serious problem for the new contractor is the confusing of accounts among the various components of one job, accounts for several jobs, and funds relating to business with personal funds. Good records help to provide a solid base for estimating, better job supervision, elimination of material and labor wastage, and a better basis for computing taxes and reserve accounts.

e. *Bonding*—All public construction, virtually all private Federal Housing Administration (FHA)-insured construction, and much private construction, especially larger jobs, requires that the contractor be bonded. General contractors will often require bonds of specialty subcontractors. Bonding companies are very cautious about writing bonds, especially for small contractors. One official of a contractors' association states that yearly volume of $100,000 is a virtual prerequisite for bonding. Yet most contractors do not operate at this volume, and certainly the newcomer to the field will not fall into the $100,000+ category. In order to land the larger more lucrative contracts, therefore, the novice contractor must prove himself to the bonding companies by successful performance on a series of smaller contracts which do not require bonding.

The bonding problem is particularly acute for minority contractors. Bonding companies will not bond contractors unless they are reasonably certain that the contractor has the experience, organizational, and financial capacity to undertake and satisfactorily complete the project. While some government programs and private sources have alleviated the problem of insufficient capital to an extent, it remains difficult for the minority contractor to gain the experience and to prove managerial capability sufficient to gain the approval of bonding companies. It becomes a vicious cycle; the minority contractor cannot get bonding without large job experience and cannot gain large job experience without bonding. While this is a problem for anyone venturing into the contracting business, the development of experience and managerial capability is more difficult for the minority individual who has been denied access to the construction trades. This has deprived the minority member of the entry at the first step in a normal process of advancement in the construction industry: skilled craftsman to foreman to small contractor to large contractor. Aware of the bonding difficulties of minority contractors, FHA has waived its bonding requirement on all FHA-insured projects of less than $500,000. However, the lending institution or owner of the project may still require a bond, as may the contractor for his subcontractors.

The Housing Act of 1970, signed into law in January 1971, authorized the Small Business Administration to utilize an existing revolving fund of $10 million to underwrite the bonding of small construction contractors by assuming 90 percent of the loss of the bonding company should a loss materialize. (This is the same fund that also supports a lease guarantee program.) There is a fee to the bonding company for this loss insurance. Projects so underwritten are limited to those of less than $500,000 and may be either the private or public sector. The intent of this program is to diminish substantially the bonding risk of surety companies so as to allow smaller contractors to obtain the bonds necessary to compete successfully for the larger contracts necessary for business growth.

f. *Overextension*—It is understandable why businessmen are reluctant to turn away business. Accepting work beyond one's capacity, however, can lead to problems, especially in management. Capacity is a function of capital, equipment, personnel, past experience, and business know-how. A heavy workload requires business skill, financial strength, careful cost control, and coordinating skill. These are capabilities which come from business experience, not technical experience. The skilled craftsman first venturing into the business end of the industry should be wary of business overload. Another danger is overextension beyond one's financial capabilities. With insufficient capitalization for the workload, an otherwise small or minor cost or payment problem can be disastrous. One rule of thumb says that incomplete work should not be valued at more than 10 times the working capital.

III. RETURNS ATTAINABLE IN THE CONSTRUCTION INDUSTRY

Presented on the following pages are hypothetical annual financial statements for three representative contracting businesses. The profit levels projected are neither excessive nor meager, given the assumed scale of operations. These cases assume no extraordinary problems of operation. It must be stressed that circumstances and/or mismanagement could easily alter these figures to erase the profit shown.

Situation I

Two electricians have established themselves as a partnership to perform electrical subcontract work. The projection is for their second year of business. They do a total volume of $50,000 in business, almost half of which is one large contract for the electric work on a 40-home subdivision. Additionally, they perform the electrical work on a small shopping center and carry out a series of smaller jobs plus some repair work.

Labor costs for the partnership come to $20,000 for the year, half of which goes to the partners themselves working as craftsmen in the execution of their contracts. Additionally, they draw $1,500 for the year from the firm, and show a yearend profit of $6,000. Therefore, in self-generated wages, draws and profits, the partners divide $17,500 for an income, before Federal income tax, of $8,750 each.

SALES			
40 home subdivision @ $600/home	$24,000		
Small shopping center	10,000		
Small jobs	12,000		
Repair work	4,000		
Total		$50,000	100%
COSTS OF PRODUCTION			
Materials	$15,000		
Labor	20,000*		
Total		$35,000	70%
GROSS PROFIT		$15,000	30%
OVERHEAD EXPENSES			
Wages (clerical help)	1,000		
Rent	1,000		
Interest	250		
Taxes	1,000		
Bad debts	100		
Repairs	900		
Depreciation, amortization	1,250		
Other (licenses, vehicle costs, tool losses)	2,000		
Payments to partners and bonuses	1,500		
Total		$ 9,000	18%
NET OPERATING PROFIT BEFORE TAXES		$ 6,000	12%

* Half to partners working as craftsmen

Situation II

A medium-sized general contractor does a business volume of $120,000 for the year. This work includes the construction of three stores, substantial remodeling of five homes and two stores, and a series of smaller jobs (such as finishing an unfinished basement or adding a room to a home).

On this volume, the contractor retains a gross margin of one-quarter or $30,000 which, after overhead is deducted, yields an income for the year of $8,800 before payment of Federal income taxes.

SALES			
New construction—3 stores	$60,000		
Remodeling—5 homes	30,000		
Remodeling—2 stores	10,000		
Small jobs	20,000		
Total		$120,000	100%
COST OF PRODUCTION			
Materials	$25,000		
Labor	20,000		
Subcontracts	45,000		
Total		$ 90,000	75%
GROSS PROFIT		$ 30,000	25%
OVERHEAD EXPENSES			
Salaries	$ 7,800		
Rent	900		
Interest	750		
Taxes	2,000		
Bad debts	250		
Repairs	2,000		
Depreciation, amortization	3,000		
Other	4,500		
Total		$ 21,200	17⅔%
NET OPERATING PROFIT BEFORE TAXES		$ 8,800	7⅓%

Situation III

A well established homebuilder has reached an output of 20 homes per year which sell for an average of $30,000. The sale of these homes yields a revenue level of $600,000. Production of the homes costs the developer/contractor $520,000. His gross profit, therefore, is $80,000. From this is deducted his overhead cost to yield a before-taxes income of $30,000.

This high income is accompanied by a high risk factor. Acting as a developer, the contractor is not assured of his money upon completion of the project. Nor does he receive compensation throughout the production process. Should production costs be underestimated and/or competition and market factors preclude the sale of the homes at the planned asking price, the developer/contractor could end the year with substantially less than an income of $30,000. Also, should several homes remain unsold for longer than anticipated, increased expenses could result in unexpected losses.

SALES—20 homes at $30,000			$600,000	100%
COSTS OF PRODUCTION				
	Per unit	20 units		
Materials	$ 6,000	$120,000		
Labor	5,000	100,000		
Subcontracts	10,000	200,000		
Land—Raw	3,000	60,000		
Developed	2,000	40,000		
	$26,000	$520,000	$520,000	86⅔%
GROSS PROFIT			$ 80,000	13⅓%

OVERHEAD EXPENSES				
Financing expenses				
Interim financing, construction loans	$ 1,600			
Fees, commitment, origination or standby	600			
Interest on notes and mortgages	400			
Land development loan expense	0			
Discounts on mortgages (points)	800			
Closing costs paid for customers	0			
Hazard or builders risk insurance	400			
Other financing costs	200			
Total		$ 4,000		
Marketing expenses				
Salaries and commissions	$ 6,200			
Advertising	5,100			
Sales office expense	1,350			
Model home expense	600			
Model home maintenance	0			
Sales showroom expense	450			
Sales training expense	550			
Consultant fees—marketing	0			
Other marketing department expense	750			
Total		$15,000		
General and administrative expenses				
Salaries	$15,000			
Office expense	6,000			
Depreciation and amortization	3,000			
Taxes	1,500			
Insurance	2,000			
Professional fees	3,000			
Travel and entertainment	250			
Contributions	150			
Other	100			
Total		$31,000		
Total			$ 50,000	8⅓%
NET OPERATING PROFIT BEFORE TAXES			$ 30,000	5%

IV. GUIDANCE IN STARTING A CONSTRUCTION BUSINESS

A. Growth Ladder for Contract Construction

The nature of the contracting business within the construction industry implies a series of steps by which an individual would logically start and grow in the industry. These are as follows:

1. Craftsman
2. Subcontractor/craftsman
3. Subcontractor
4. Contractor/subcontractor
5. Contractor
6. Developer/contractor
7. Developer

While entrance into the industry can be and is made from without (from other forms of business, architecture, law, finance, etc.), this series of steps represents a continuum for growth wholly within the construction field. As the individual establishing a contracting business progresses from one function to a higher one, he generally will play a dual role, assuming both the function from which he is progressing and that to which he aspires. Thus, the craftsman turned subcontractor will continue to perform as a craftsman as he builds his business as a subcontractor. Likewise, the smaller contractor will perform more as his own subcontractor than will the larger. Often a higher function on the continuum is assumed to increase the level (or assure an even level) of business or activity at the lower level. For example, the contractor develops a subdivision in order to increase or assure business for his contracting operation. For each function, a volume level is reached where it makes better business sense to assign lower level functions to other firms or individuals.

It is significant that as one progresses through this continuum, the degree of responsibility for project completion and the potential for financial gain (or loss) increases. Also, the need for technical construction skills decreases as the need for business skills increases.

B. Starting a Contracting Business

For the skilled craftsman desirous of becoming a contractor, a logical first step is to establish himself as a small subcontractor in his construction specialty. As such, his technical knowledge would be of value. As his business grows, he should be able to pick up the more sophisticated business skills that would be required. With a thorough knowledge of his technical specialty and a familiarity with the construction "community" in the geographic area of operation, the new contractor would be in a fair position to secure business. Geographic identity is important because working friends and acquaintances will serve as primary sources of contacts and leads from which contracts are secured. This is often a necessity since the new contractor has only his skill and reputation as a craftsman to recommend him for higher levels and types of work.

Establishment as a small subcontractor need not be a "formal" event. Extensive investment in offices and equipment is not necessary to begin in business and might obligate the new businessman to a level of business which may not be obtainable. Because an individual starting a subcontracting business will often continue to work for others as a skilled craftsman while building up his own business, he may be able to begin his own contracting firm more deliberately by working for himself only when when real opportunities appear.

General contracting requires more business skill than technical skill (although technical skill is needed to determine if subcontractors are performing as specified by contract, and also to oversee any of the specialty work which the contractor performs for himself rather than by hiring a subcontractor.) Estimating is less critical to the degree that the contractor uses estimates prepared by subcontractors (to which they may be contractually bound). Scheduling, however, is a major responsibility for the contractor. Keeping to a schedule is crucial to completing a job at the predetermined contractual cost, and a delay by any one of the many subcontractors, suppliers, and others whom the contractor is co-ordinating can force a major reorganization of the job schedule with a concomitant loss in time and money. Subcontractors branching out into general contracting should be aware of the additional managerial requirements which such a venture entails. Just as the successful skilled craftsman does not necessarily make a successful subcontractor because of the difference in required skills, the successful subcontractor is not necessarily ready to become a general contractor.

Similarly, expanding one's operation from contracting to developing requires a number of new skills. Principal among these are finance and marketing. A contractor is relatively certain of payment for his work. If his estimate is well prepared and his bid allows for a safe margin, barring any unforeseen circumstances, the contractor can be somewhat sure of his profit. The developer, on the other hand, is taking a greater risk. He operates on a profit margin that is based on an assumed product price. The developer is vulnerable on two counts: cost overrun and forced sale at a discount. Also, he must invest substantial amounts of capital, either his own or that of investors or of a lending institution.

The contractor will encounter jobs which he feels are attractive but which are clearly beyond his capacity. Beyond the obvious attractions of additional work and profitability, the larger job offers the contractor an opportunity to learn, to broaden his experience, and to prepare himself for even larger jobs in the future. When confronted with an attractive job opportunity beyond his capacity, the contractor should be wise enough to seek a joint venture with other firms. Firms band together for a specific job because they are unable, as individual units, to handle it. Together they may possess the financial, technical, and managerial resources and experience to compete for the job. By participating in such joint ventures (which usually dissolve at completion of the job), the smaller contractor gains exposure to larger jobs. Building upon this, he may develop the experience and, equally important, the credibility to progress to larger jobs on his own.

A similar aid to growth for the homebuilder is an arrangement with a prefabricator. Prefabricated homes simplify the rather complex homebuilding process, and suppliers of prefabricated homes, having a stake in their builders, offer valuable advice and assistance in marketing, management, and financial matters.

C. Requirements for Establishment of a Contracting Business

1. *Capital Requirements*

Compared with other types of business, capital requirements for construction contracting are not great. Many a small contractor will operate out of his own home, possibly with a separate room as an office and with a separate telephone (though even this is not a necessity). The degree of capitalization required to begin in business is primarily based on the size of anticipated contracts. Approximately one-tenth to one-third of the value of a contract is sufficient to carry the contractor until payment begins and a cash flow can be established. For financing, however, some evidence of a personal stake by the contractor is necessary. An official of the National Institute of Home Builders suggested that $20,000 would be sufficient to establish oneself in business. The skilled craftsman with a good reputation in the field, however, may be able to start as a part-time subcontractor with even less capital, slowly building a capital reserve with his reputation as a competent subcontractor.

2. *Equipment Requirements*

At a minimum level, little in the way of expensive equipment is required, especially for the general contractor. A truck will be the major expense, although small operators may get by with a station wagon which doubles as a family car. Skilled craftsmen who will be hired for contract execution provide their own tools. Major pieces of equipment need not be purchased, as they may be rented until such time as the volume of business warrants purchase. Specialty contracting, on the other hand, has greater equipment requirements, although the needs vary from field to field. A small carpentry contractor may get by with a few hundred dollars in hand and some power tools, whereas excavating or demolition work requires expensive heavy machinery.

3. Physical Space Requirements

For general contracting at a smaller operating level, little physical space is required. As stated, many smaller general contractors operate out of their own homes. For the specialty trades, physical space is needed to the degree that equipment and supplies must be stored. Many smaller specialty contractors will also operate from a private residence using a garage for storage of supplies and a driveway for vehicle parking.

4. Licensing Requirements

Licensing requirements vary greatly among the States. Massachusetts, for example, has no licensing requirement, and New Jersey requires no license except in the case of certain types of electrical contracting. Delaware and New Mexico, on the other hand, require a license of all contractors for both public and private work. Many States require a license for only contracts above a certain dollar value (varying from $100 to $30,000). Maryland requires a license based on an annual dollar volume of work. The State of Washington requires both a license and a surety bond of contractors. A summation of the licensing requirements by State appears in the appendix.

Although a license may not be required, many States require "prequalification" of contractors bidding on public works above a certain dollar value. This will usually involve completion of a form that requires information about the contractor's financial resources and liabilities, equipment, past record, personnel, and experience. It is generally limited to highway work, but may be required for larger public jobs.

Detailed information about licensing and prequalification requirements, as well as tax information, may be found in Summary of State Regulations and Taxes Affecting General Contractors, published annually by the American Insurance Association, 85 John Street, New York, New York, 10038.

5. Labor Requirements

The availability of construction labor varies from skill to skill and from one geographic area to another. Steamfitters, carpenters, electricians, and plumbers are most in demand, and the potential entrepreneur would do well to review the availability of local skilled labor in those fields prior to selecting a site for his business.

A key decision for a contractor is whether to use union or nonunion labor. There are advantages either way. Union labor is available on relatively short notice, and by virtue of union membership, a certain level of proficiency is assured. Furthermore, training is not the responsibility of the contractor, but the union. The contractor need not carry a full-time crew for fear of losing good men as he might with nonunion labor. However, for these advantages, the contractor pays the price of higher wages (nonunion wages are about 85 percent of union wages) and the possibility of union disputes. For example, with a crew of a certain size, the union business agent may insist on a foreman that the contractor considers unnecessary. These kinds of problems do not arise with nonunion labor.

Many contractors come from the skilled trade unions and because of their loyalty and personal experience will use exclusively union labor. In some areas of the country, particularly the Northeast, the West Coast, and major metropolitan areas, the unions are strong, and union labor is used for virtually all construction. In such areas, the contractor has no choice but to use union labor.

6. *Education Requirements*

While there are no specific requirements for formal education for contract construction, certain minimal business skills are needed for even a small business. There is evidence that higher levels of formal education and larger-size operations are directly related. Below is a table showing the education level by size of operation based on a response of almost 9,000 home builders in a 1969 survey of the National Association of Home Builders.

Educational Level by Size of Operation for Homebuilders, 1969

Educational level	All sizes %	Small (1-25 units) %	Medium (26-100 units) %	Large (101+ units) %
Less than high school	7.2	7.9	5.4	3.1
High school	25.2	29.1	21.5	14.1
Vocational school	4.3	4.6	3.3	1.4
Some college	27.2	27.2	28.0	22.6
Associate degree	2.3	2.1	2.5	3.1
Bachelor's	29.3	25.6	34.3	45.5
Master's	4.0	3.1	4.6	8.6
Ph.D.	0.6	0.4	0.4	1.6

While the above table implies that the larger the business, the higher the level of formal education, it also indicates that large operations can be and indeed are being run by individuals without a great deal of formal education. According to the survey, there are at least 1,500 home builders producing over 100 buildings each with only a high school education or less. Formal education is thus useful, but not essential, to success in contracting.

BIBLIOGRAPHY

Industry Trends and Data

Construction Industry Trends, 1958–1968, Dun and Bradstreet, 99 Church Street, New York, New York 10007.

Cost of Doing Business, Corporations, Dun and Bradstreet.

Cost of Doing Business, Partnerships and Proprietorships, Dun and Bradstreet.

County Business Patterns, 1968, U.S. Department of Commerce, Bureau of the Census, Washington, D.C. 20233.

1969 Key Business Ratios, Dun and Bradstreet.

Profile of the Builder and his Industry, National Association of Home Builders, January 1971.

Business Guidance

The Accounting System for All Builders, National Association of Home Builders, August 1965. (Directed to the homebuilder; an addition modifies the system for the apartment developer.)

Basic Principles of Business Management in Home Building, National Association of Home Builders, 1966. (A volume programmed instruction self-study course.)

"Bonding Minority Contractors," G. Douglas Pugh in *Black Economic Development,* William F. Haddad and G. Douglas Pugh, editors, pp. 138–150.

"Bonding Problems of Black Contractors" Senate Congressional Record, Volume 155, No. 16, January 24, 1969.

Center City (A Study of Boston), pp. 63–64, Urban Research, Inc., 1968.

Contract Construction and Related Industries Outlook, 1968–1978, Small Business Administration, Washington, D.C. 20416, 1968.

The Contracting Business, the Small Business Reporter, Bank of America, Small Business Advisory Service, Bank of America, San Francisco, March 1960.

How to Job Cost Estimate, National Association of Home Builders, 1968.

How to Schedule and How to Purchase, National Association of Home Builders, 1968.

Minority Business Opportunities, Department of Housing and Urban Development, Washington, D.C., 20410, pp. 38–65.

Profit Planning for Home Builders, National Association of Home Builders, 1968.

Summary of State Regulations and Taxes Affecting General Contractors, 1970. American Insurance Association, 85 John Street, New York, New York 10038.

"The Unbondables," Gilbert B. Friedman, The New Republic, 6 July 1968, pp. 27–29.

TRADE ASSOCIATIONS

Associated General Contractors of America (AGC) 1957 E Street, N.W. Washington, D.C. 20006. Founded 1918. Members, 8,100. General contractors engaged in construction of factories, office buildings, warehouses, highways, bridges, dams, railroads, and municipal utilities.

Construction Industry Manufacturers Association (CIMA) 135 South LaSalle, Chicago, Illinois 60603. Founded 1949. Members, 240. Manufacturers of construction machinery, allied equipment and components; industry suppliers and publications producers.

Council of Mechanical Specialty Contracting Industries (CMSCI): 610 Ring Building, Washington, D.C. 20036. Founded 1950. Members, 250. Electrical, heating, air-conditioning, plumbing, and ventilating contractors, architects and engineers on interindustry matters, codes, bidding and contracting procedures, and legislative matters. Publication: Councilator, monthly.

Mason Contractors Association of America (MCAA): 208 South LaSalle, Chicago, Illinois 60604. Founded 1950, Members, 1,850. Masonry construction firms. Publication: Masonry, monthly.

Mechanical Contractors Association America (MCAA): 666 Third Avenue, Suite 1464, New York, New York 10017. Founded 1889. Members, 1,100. Contractors who furnish and install piping systems used for air-conditioning, plumbing, sprinkling, heating, other purposes. Publication: Mechanical Contractor, monthly.

National Association of Home Builders of the United States (NAHB): 1625 L Street, Washington, D.C. 20036. Founded 1942. Members, 43,000. Homebuilders and others associated with homebuilding (architects, mortgage lenders, manufacturers of building products, subcontractors, engineers). Publications: 1) NAHB Journal of Homebuilding, monthly; 2) Washington Scope, weekly.

APPENDIX

Following is a description of the various types of contract agreements and several methods of contract payment.

Contract Agreements

The most common type are *lumpsum* and *cost-plus.* Under the *lumpsum* contracts, the owner agrees to pay the contractor a specific amount for completion of the job, no matter what the ultimate costs are to the contractor. With *cost-plus (fixed-fee)* contracts, the owner agrees to pay direct costs, plus a specified amount (either dollar amount or percentage) for profit and overhead.

Other contract types include *unit price* (a specified amount for each measurable unit completed) and *guaranteed maximum cost* (a guaranteed ceiling price for owner and sometimes a fixed fee for contractor).

Payments

On most larger jobs, monthly progress payments—based on percentage of job completion or estimated dollar value of work performed—are made. Many jobs provide for payment as various stages of the job are completed. *The money flows from owner to general contractor to subcontractor to material supplier.* Each link in the chain depends on payments from above.

One important payment feature is retainage. On most large jobs, the contractor receives only about 85 percent to 90 percent of his estimated costs for each billing period. The rest is withheld in retainage, payable under most contracts 35 days after the job is completed and accepted by the owner. *Any mechanics' liens for unpaid labor or material bills normally must be filed within a given number of days, usually about 30, after acceptance.* It is vital to become familiar with State lien laws and procedures to afford protection when needed.

Since retainage often exceeds profit, the contractor has a considerable amount of potential working capital tied up in retainage, especially if he has many jobs in progress. This problem is especially acute for contractors who finish their work on a job early, but must wait many months before the job is completed and accepted. Of course, if there is a conflict concerning acceptance, no matter whose fault, all the contractors have their retainage held up. The effect on subcontractors is often more serious because they usually bear the main material and labor costs. Some have worked to cut down the retainage percentage.

Another payment method is common with 30- or 60-day private jobs. In these situations, ⅓ payment is made upon delivery of material and start of work, ⅓ at completion, and ⅓ 30 days after completion. Contractors often attempt to get down payments of around 10 percent.

On some small jobs of less than 30 days, the contractor receives full payment upon completion. This practice is not too common, however. And even in these cases, the general contractor may withhold retainage from the subcontractor until acceptance.

Licensing and Prequalification Requirements, by State

State	License Required for:	Prequalifications Required for:
Alabama	All projects over $20,000	Highway projects only
Alaska	Not required	Not required
Arizona	All projects	Highway projects only
Arkansas	All projects over $20,000	Highway projects only
California	All projects over $100	State projects over $50,000
Colorado	Not required	Highway projects only
Connecticut	Not required	Highway projects only
Delaware	All projects	Highway projects only
D.C.	Not required	Not required
Florida	All projects	Highway projects
Georgia	Not required	Not required
Hawaii	All projects	May be required on public projects
Idaho	Public projects over $1,000	License serves as prequalification
Illinois	Not required	Highway projects only
Indiana	Not required	State work over $20,000, except State colleges and universities
Iowa	Not required	Highway projects only
Kansas	Not required	Highway projects only

Kentucky	Not required	Highway projects only
Louisiana	All projects over $30,000	May be required for highway projects
Maine	Not required	Not required
Maryland	Registration for $5,000 volume per annum	Highway projects only
Massachusetts	Not required	State Department of Public Works projects over $50,000
Michigan	Registration for residential projects	Highway projects only
Minnesota	Not required	Not required
Mississippi	All projects over $10,000	All public projects over $25,000
Missouri	Not required	Not required
Montana	Public projects over $1,000	Highway projects only
Nebraska	Not required	Highway projects over $2,500
Nevada	All projects	Highway projects only
New Hampshire	Not required	All public projects
New Jersey	Electrical contractors only	All State projects
New Mexico	All projects	Highway projects only
New York	Not required	Not required
North Carolina	All projects over $20,000	All State projects over $20,000
North Dakota	All projects over $5,000	Highway projects only
Ohio	Not required	Highway projects only
Oklahoma	Not required	Highway projects only
Oregon	Not required	All public projects over $10,000
Pennsylvania	Not required	Highway projects only

Puerto Rico	Not required	Not required
Rhode Island	Not required	Not required
South Carolina	Registration for projects over $30,000	Highway projects only
South Dakota	Not required	Highway projects only
Tennessee	Registration for projects over $10,000	Highway projects only
Texas	Not required	Highway projects only
Utah	All projects	Projects under State Road Commission or State Building Board
Vermont	Not required	All State Highway Department projects; highway and bridge projects over $50,000
Virginia	Registration for projects over $20,000	State highway projects only
Washington	All projects	Highway projects only
West Virginia	Not required	Highway projects only
Wisconsin	Not required	May be required on public projects
Wyoming	Electrical contractors only	Highway projects only

CONTRACT DRESS MANUFACTURING

Section Contents

URBAN BUSINESS PROFILE
Contract Dress Manufacturing
(SIC 2335-Pt.)

I. RECOMMENDATION

Entry into contract dress manufacturing involves relatively little investment, but considerable knowledge of the industry. The principal managerial requirements are production planning and supervision and contacts within the trade to secure business. The availability and productivity of the labor force are the key variables affecting profitability.

Investment requirements are limited because dress manufacturing contractors can generally lease the required machines or purchase them on credit. Manufacturing plant requirements are minimal, and plants can be established in almost any type of vacant building which has heat, light, and plumbing. Since the materials being processed are owned by others, no investment in inventory is required.

The cost of labor is the major cost of doing business, and success or failure will be determined by the ability to achieve a high rate of labor productivity relative to the cost of wages. This can be accomplished by successful recruitment and training of the work force, good labor relations, and highly effective production planning and supervision. Care should be taken to make certain that foremen and supervisors are experienced and capable, since attempts to establish production with inexperienced management, inexperienced supervision, and inexperienced labor have been disastrous. There is, however, no reason why contract dress manufacturing should not be suitable for the minority entrepreneur with some experience in production planning and supervision.

II. DESCRIPTION OF THE INDUSTRY

A. Identification

Women's and misses' outerwear is a segment of a major manufacturing group known as Major Group 23, Apparel and Related Products, a group sometimes known as the needle trades. Women's and Misses' Dresses are classified as Standard Industrial Classification (SIC) 2335, the code which covers establishments primarily engaged in the manufacture of women's, misses' and juniors' dresses, including ensemble dresses, whether sold by the piece or by the dozen. There are further subclassifications by fabric (i.e., cotton, wool, and manmade fabrics) and by price.

The apparel production industry is characterized by three major types of establishments: (1) regular factories known as "manufacturers"; (2) apparel jobbers; and (3) contractors. The manufacturer purchases fabric, employs production workers to cut and sew garments, and sells the finished product. The apparel jobber buys the raw materials, designs samples, and markets the finished product, but he does not manufacture the garments. Instead he arranges with outside factories (contractors) to perform the manufacturing operations. The apparel contractor employs production workers in his own establishment to process materials owned by others (either jobber or manufacturer), makes products to specification, and does not become involved in the sale of the finished garment. In many instances, the jobber will employ his own cutters, and thus the contractor need only sew the various pieces together. In other instances, the contractor will perform both the cutting and sewing operations.

B. Dimensions of the Industry

The needle trades are the second largest employer in nondurable goods manufacturing, surpassed only by the food manufacturing industry. In 1967, more than 1,357,000 persons were employed by the industry. Value added by manufacturing was over $10 billion. There were more than 26,000 establishments, 48 percent of which had over 20 employees.

Women's and misses' dresses are the largest single type of employer within the Apparel and Related Products Group, with 5,225 establishments in 1967, of which 59 percent had over 20 employees. The total number of employees was 209,900, with value added by manufacturing exceeding $1.5 billion. The industry has been constantly growing as it keeps pace with the growth in population and the general rise in the national standard of living. Value added increased at a rate of approximately 6 percent annually between 1963 and 1967, and at a rate of over 4 percent annually between 1958 and 1967. Employment has also increased steadily, but at a somewhat slower rate of about 1.5 percent annually between 1958 and 1967.

Within the women's and misses' dresses group, contractors are the most numerous type of employer, having 2,642 establishments in the United States, of which over 77 percent have more than 20 employees. They also account for the largest segment of value added, $588 million compared to $523 million for manufacturers. Contractors are not growing at as fast a rate as manufacturers, however, with the value of their product having grown at a rate of only 2 percent annually in the 1963–67 period compared to a manufacturers' value-added growth rate of more than 15 percent annually during the same period.

Most dress manufacturing contractors are located in the New York area, with significant numbers in Pennsylvania, New Jersey, and California. North and South Carolina, Georgia, Florida, Illinois, Texas, Massachusetts, and Connecticut also have noticeable concentrations in the industry. There is a trend in location of contractors toward the South and West. In 1963, 75 percent of all contractors were in the three States in the Mid-Atlantic Region (New York, Pennsylvania, and New Jersey). In 1967 this percentage had dropped to 69 percent. Concentrations of contractors are increasing in and around metropolitan areas such as Dallas, Los Angeles, St. Louis, and Miami.

C. Characteristics of the Industry

1. Organization

The dress manufacturing contractor performs a relatively simple function. He receives textile goods from a jobber or occasionally a manufacturer. This fabric may or may not have already been cut to the desired patterns. He then proceeds to sew the sections together to make a finished garment, presses it, and ships it back to the jobber. The contractor performs a useful function because styling and fashion play such an important part in the overall industry and are so volatile and unpredictable that flexibility in manufacturing is highly desirable. Thus, the jobber traditionally employs a designer to design a seasonal "line" for him. He then makes samples and displays them to the trade. Certain items will turn out to be popular, while others will be ignored. He then must purchase the goods and get relatively quick production of certain numbers of large quantities. Access to a number of contractors greatly increases the jobber's ability to expand or contract his deliveries to meet changing markets.

While there has been a trend among many segments of the industry to go into integrated manufacturing on a larger scale, the traditional roles of jobber and contractor are still highly important, and are expected to remain that way, particularly for higher-priced dresses, where production runs are small and style is all-important.

The jobber pays the contractor for each dress produced. The contractor develops his cost on the basis of his piecework and hourly rates for labor, his overhead, trucking costs, and his profit.

2. Labor

Apparel manufacturing is highly labor intensive; for the contractor, his operations are almost totally labor intensive, with the wages of production workers accounting for almost two-thirds of the total value of contractors' shipments in 1967.

About one-half of all production workers are sewing machine operators, and women represent more than 95 percent of the sewing machine operators. There are two types of systems used in production: (1) the singlehand system of sewing in which the operator performs all or most of the operations needed to produce a finished garment, and (2) the section system, in which each operator performs only one or two of the operations required to complete the garment. As might be expected, singlehand operators get paid more and are usually employed on more expensive garments. Slightly more than half of the sewing machine operators are employed on the singlehand system of sewing.

Other production workers are hand and machine pressers, hand sewers, cutters and markers, final inspectors, thread trimmers, and work distributors.

For all jobs, the ratio of women to men workers varies among areas. For example, women outnumber men 10 to 1 in Miami and in the Wilkes-Barre-Hazleton area in Pennsylvania, while the proportion is only 3 to 1 in New York City.

About 60 percent of the production workers are paid on a piecework basis. Sewing machine operators and pressers are typically paid on this type of incentive program. Time rates usually apply to cutters and markers, inspectors, thread trimmers, and work distributors.

Most workers in the industry are unionized, and nearly all agreements are with the International Ladies Garment Workers' Union. However, there are considerable variations. For example, only one-eighth are unionized in the Los Angeles area and less than one-tenth in Miami and Dallas. However, in New York and Pennsylvania, virtually every shop is unionized.

Average hourly earnings in 1968 ranged from $3.27 an hour in New York City to $1.90 an hour in Miami. However, there are a great many variations within areas, because so many of the workers are on incentive plans, with the faster and more skilled operators earning considerably more than those who are slower. Most of the shops in the higher-paying areas use the singlehand system, while most of the shops in the lower-paying areas use the section system.

Most shops work a 35-hour week except in the Los Angeles, Dallas, and Miami areas, where the schedule is 40 hours a week. Paid holidays are common, and employees receive health, welfare, and vacation benefits. Unionized employees are also provided supplementary unemployment benefits and retirement plans.

3. Competition

Competition is very intense, as might be expected where entry into the industry is relatively easy and where there are many firms producing an undifferentiated product.

The major form of competition is in pricing and a difference between competitors of a few cents on the cost of processing can result in the loss of business. Contractors are always trying to cut costs, and the more profitable operators are highly sensitive to cost items.

Contractors are also selected on the basis of quality and service. The jobber wants his contractor to be reasonably convenient and able to produce acceptable work on a reliable basis. During the rush seasons, it is relatively easy for a contractor to get work, because all of the jobbers are hard put to find enough contractors to fill their orders. During the slack season, the jobber will look around very carefully for the best price.

4. Ease of Entry

As indicated above, there are no special licensing requirements or other restrictions barring entry into the business. The individual desiring to establish himself as a contractor need only find some space, order some machines on time, line up some business, and employ a work force. If sufficient business has been lined up in advance, and the manager is capable of producing the work within the quoted price, there is no reason why a new firm should not be profitable from the start.

When starting a plant in an area where the labor force is not experienced, allowance should be made for an additional startup cost to train the labor force. If local job-training resources are not available to assist in training, an average of about $1,000 per worker should be allowed for training inexperienced employees.

5. Capital Requirements

Capital requirements for a contract dress manufacturing business are relatively small. Listed below are the basic machinery and capital requirements for the smallest size business feasible, as well as for an average shop.

	Smallest	**Average**
Weekly production	800 medium-priced dresses	2,500 medium-priced dresses
Building size	2,500 square feet	7,000 square feet
Single-needle regular machines	20	55
Special machines	4-6	15
Pressing irons	2	5
Steam boiler	1	1
Racks	6	12

If cutting is done internally, the plant will require a cutting table, spreading machine, two cutting machines, and one drill.

Payments on equipment and fixtures	$5,000	$12,000
Rent deposit	300	1,100
Operating capital	4,000	10,000
Miscellaneous supplies	100	200
	$9,400	$23,300

Most equipment is purchased from a machinery dealer or from the factory. To start an operation, the best method is to purchase rebuilt machines on a time payment plan. Other capital will have to be secured from personal resources or from a financial institution.

The factory space is usually leased. In some cases, where operations are being started in areas where no factory buildings are available, local development corporations will construct factory buildings and lease them to a manufacturer. This situation is more likely when the proposed tenant is an established business, not a new entry.

6. *Profitability*

Profitability on sales is very low due to the intense competition and the very keen pressure to keep costs down. Mounting imports are also keeping a downward pressure on prices. The intense unionization of the industry tends to make it difficult for individual entrepreneurs to reap profit from low wage rates. Whatever advantages accrue to businesses in low wage areas are often counterbalanced by high shipping costs, high training costs, or simply increased competition from other new factories established in the low wage areas.

On the other hand, the low capital investment permits a relatively high return on investment. The 1964 profit ratios for all dress manufacturers are shown as follows:

	Upper Quartile	**Median**	**Lower Quartile**
	%	%	%
On sales	1.74	0.76	0.16
On total net worth	20.64	11.03	2.33
On net working capital	23.76	12.15	3.20

7. *Dependence on Outside Factors*

The individual contractor is dependent to a considerable degree on the seasonal factors. Business is at its best from January to May, while fall styles are being produced, and from June to October, while spring clothes are being made. There is relatively little activity during the other months. The seasonal aspect should be kept in mind when starting a new business, so that entry into the business can coincide with heavy seasonal activity and the opportunity to secure orders from busy jobbers.

To a certain extent, the contractor is also dependent upon how well his jobbers are doing. If he limits his work to a few jobbers, he may find himself without orders if the jobbers happen to guess wrong on styles for a particular season. The likelihood that such an event will happen can be reduced by keeping contract with a large number of jobbers.

The women's dress industry itself tends to fluctuate with styling changes. Although there has been a steady growth over the years, there are rather heavy variations in business from season to season or year to year depending in part on how well new styles are going over in the trade and on the state of the economy in general. These factors are largely out of the control of the contractor, and he must provide for them by conserving his profits during the good seasons to keep him solvent during the poor seasons.

III. BUSINESS OPPORTUNITIES IN THE INDUSTRY

A. Important Factors Affecting Opportunities

1. Labor Supply

The most important factor in locating a factory and insuring its successful operation is the availability of a good labor supply in relationship to its cost. The test of whether a labor supply is good is the ability of the labor force to turn out acceptable quality at a competitive cost. This can sometimes be accomplished with a work force that is relatively low-wage but of only average efficiency, or it can be accomplished with a highly efficient work force receiving higher wages. If the relationship between the skill of the work force and what it costs is favorable, many other factors of operation, such as distance from markets, rent, even in some cases inefficient management, can be overcome.

2. Production Management

The management of production is related to the efficiency of the labor supply, and thus becomes highly important. Key factors are the layout of the plant, production scheduling, training of the labor force, supervision of the work force, and labor relations.

3. Sales and Cost Estimating

The successful contractor must have good contacts within the industry, particularly among jobbers who have confidence in his ability to turn out acceptable quality when promised. The jobber cannot afford to take a chance on unknown firms, because if the goods are unacceptable or are not delivered on time, the entire sale may be lost because the season is missed. Equally important is the ability to do good cost estimating. A price which is too low will result in a loss on the sale. An overestimated price may lose the sale.

4. Overall Management

The management of a successful dress contractor requires not only the skills of production management, sales ability, and good estimating, but general business skills and care. Management must know how and when to borrow money at the lowest cost and must insure proper maintenance of his machines so that malfunctions do not interrupt production schedules.

5. Cutting Operations

A typical consideration which management must take into account is the decision about whether or not to have a cutting operation. This will depend to some extent on whether his jobbers want to do their own cutting or not. There are a number of advantages to having a capacity to perform the cutting operation: it is somewhat more profitable; the contractor can have better control over quality; and as material can be saved, the contractor can cut extra dresses to sell on his own.

6. Contractors' Associations

Another consideration is whether or not to join a contractors' association. It is generally deemed advisable to do so. These associations are located in all regions of the country, and they can help in obtaining business from jobbers. However, one of their prime functions is to conduct negotiations with the unions on behalf of all contractors.

7. Location

It is best for a contractor to be located at least within overnight trucking distance of the garment center where his customer-jobbers are located. This factor is more important with regard to medium and higher-priced dresses. Lower-priced dresses are not quite as subject to sudden shifts in style, and the savings in labor costs which can be achieved by moving further away from the garment center become more important as the overall price of the garment drops, assuming an adequate supply of labor remains available.

B. Problems and Potentials for Minority Entrepreneurs

1. Problems

A minority entrepreneur should not experience any special problems in the dress manufacturing industry, except in the sense that social contact with jobbers and within the industry may be limited. There are not very many minority jobbers, and the opportunity to develop sales contacts through mutual friendships and at social gatherings will be somewhat limited. This could be a serious handicap, since so many of the people within the industry already know each other. Many contractors have worked previously as cutters or foremen for other contractors and manufacturers; others have been salesmen within the industry and they have a wide range of contacts. The entrepreneur who does not have access to the "trade" in this respect will have some problems, and these should be carefully considered in advance. One way to overcome them is to get some assurances in advance that help will be forthcoming from someone who is widely regarded in the industry and who can be helpful in opening doors and setting up opportunities to bid on work.

Training the labor force can be a serious problem and one requiring extra capital. Unfortunately, virtually all Federal manpower training programs are unavailable for training operators in apparel manufacturing. Some years ago, the unions successfully convinced the Federal Government that such training programs would give new manufacturers an unfair advantage over those already in existence. While it is possible in some instances to secure State and local help in training a labor force, this type of help tends to be more prevalent in the Southern and rural areas where local development authorities are interested in persuading existing manufacturers to relocate. The prospective new entrepreneur should check carefully with local authorities to see whether or not some assistance would be available with training costs. Lacking such assistance, it may be wiser to rely on using already skilled operators who are available within the local labor force. This will require some preliminary study on the extent of their availability and on their willingness to become employed within the proposed new firm. A high rate of wastage or unacceptable work can be caused by inexperienced operators. This would clearly be detrimental to the new entrepreneur and might be the cause of a business failure.

2. Potentials

On the other hand, the extent to which a minority entrepreneur can develop rapport with the available labor force and secure good productivity from them can be an advantage, particularly in urban areas. Black and Spanish-speaking Americans constitute a highly underemployed labor force in most American cities. A minority entrepreneur who can recruit, train, motivate, and properly supervise a good labor force within the city will have certain advantages in the dress contracting business. It is possible to overestimate this factor, since attaining a productive labor force is more likely to be a function of good managerial skills than it is a function of the racial affinity between the manager and the work force. Nevertheless, it may be reasonable to assume that a given level of competence within management may produce better results with a labor force whose value-systems it understands and can identify with.

A minority entrepreneur may also have access at present to sources of capital and other assistance which might not be available to other entrepreneurs with equally limited means. For example, the Singer Company is committed to trying to help minority entrepreneurs get a start in the apparel industry, and, under certain conditions, it has made machines available on highly favorable terms and assisted in securing business. Bank loans may be available under guarantees from the Small Business Administration, which is committed to helping in the establishment of minority businesses.

C. Hypothetical Projections

Hypothetical operating projections for the smallest-sized operation considered feasible and for an average operation are shown below. Considerable care should be utilized in using the figures shown in these examples, since individual operations may vary considerably on the basis of local and special factors. The examples shown below should be used as rough guides in formulating projections for a specific project.

	Smallest	Average
Annual sales	$125,000	$375,000
Number of employees	30	80
Investment (no cutting)	$ 7,500	$ 20,000
Production wages and benefits	79,000	237,000
Materials, containers, trucking, etc.	7,900	23,700
Utilities	1,500	4,000
Rent	3,600	7,000
Overhead, owner's salary, office expenses	20,000	65,000
Interest and depreciation	4,000	8,000
Total expenses	$123,500	$364,700
Profit before tax	$ 1,500	$ 10,300
Profit percentage on sales	1.2%	2.7%

IV. GUIDANCE IN STARTING A NEW BUSINESS

A prospective entrepreneur who has no experience in the dress contracting business should discard any notions of entering until such experience has been attained. It would be wise to seek employment with an existing contractor or jobber as a production employee or supervisor, or as a salesman to the trade. While the apparel trades are not particularly complex, there are a great many aspects of the business that are really known only to insiders or to those who have had considerable exposure to its operations. A minority individual or group seeking to establish a dress manufacturing business as an economic development project for the inner city would be well advised to find a manager for the new business from among the supervisory or administrative employees of existing firms.

The first step in planning the new business is to determine the general area of location and to visit jobbers in the vicinity to determine the extent to which a new dress contractor would be able to count on business after establishment. While it is recognized that no commitments are possible in advance, the operator of the new business ought to have some feel for whether or not his services will be welcome among jobbers. Moreover, it is not enough to rely on vague assurances given in an effort to "get rid of a salesman." The potential new entrepreneur should have some feel for the amount of work which might be available, the conditions under which it will become available with regard to cost and time, and other special considerations affecting the market.

In discussions with jobbers, it may be advisable to determine exactly what segment of the business the new firm might specialize in. All other things being equal, if available labor is experienced and the proposed location is in an urban area or within 100 miles of one, specialization in higher quality dresses (above $10.75 to $16.75 wholesale) is desirable, since margins are slightly better at this level. However, if the labor force will not be experienced, lower-priced lines should be sought.

After an appraisal of the market and a preliminary examination of the types of financial resources which would be available, a visit should be made to a machinery manufacturer or jobber to determine what machines are available and at what cost. As indicated above, one of the major machinery manufacturers in the country has a program to help minority enterprises, and the availability of this help should be checked. A representative of the chosen machinery manufacturer may also be helpful in determining the amount of space needed and the plant layout.

Steps should next be taken to ascertain the type of factory space available on a lease basis. Most city locations have vacant factory space available, and a trip to an industrial realtor can save time. Considerations to be taken into account in arranging for space include the following:

1. Convenience to labor force; if it is too far from public transportation, many potential workers will not be interested.
2. Truck loading space.
3. Light and heat.
4. Safety and convenience for employees.
5. Total space.
6. Cost.

Arrangements need to be made for an efficient production force. This must include middle-level production supervisors, as well as overall production control. Where the owner is competent in these fields, he can settle for less-experienced help, but if the owner is not going to be able to spend time on the floor supervising production, it is essential that he be able to employ a reliable and experienced person who can.

A decision must be made about the extent to which training will be required for the work force. All other things being equal, it is better for an inexperienced entrepreneur to plan for an experienced labor force. The pitfalls which await the inexperienced entrant into a new business who must deal with an inexperienced work force will guarantee bankruptcy unless sufficient funds are available to compensate for the mistakes. Where an experienced labor force is not available, the inexperienced entrepreneur should start in as small a way as possible and gradually build his own experienced labor force.

The potential entrepreneur should consult with local employment officials and those responsible for local manpower programs to determine the extent of assistance available for training. If a wholly experienced work force cannot be employed and if training subsidies are not available, it would be wise to include sufficient funds for training in the initial startup costs.

The main purpose of training is to give piecework operators sufficient experience with the machines to gain proficiency. If they are too slow, management must generally make up the difference in order to give them the minimum wage. Moreover, careless or inexperienced operators can ruin material, and the contractor will have to compensate the jobber for the loss.

If the proposed new business is to be located in an area where union shops predominate, it would be wise for the new entrant to contact the union for advice on the labor force, methods of recruitment, and leads to experienced supervisors. The International Ladies Garment Workers Union is well-established and has a large array of experts in many facets of the business. The local contractors' association should also be visited and assistance secured as appropriate.

Other assistance can be secured from local organizations offering special programs to help potential minority entrepreneurs. In many cities these organizations are affiliated with the Office of Minority Business Enterprise, U.S. Department of Commerce. Some of these organizations may be able to put the potential entrepreneur in touch with a retired dress manufacturer who is interested in public service. If such a person is available, he can generally be extremely helpful in contacts with jobbers and in production control methods.

A final step prior to operations will be securing capital. If preliminary investigations have been complete, the prospective new entrepreneur should be able to prepare some simple projections indicating the amount of business he expects to do the first year, the amount of equipment he will need, what his costs of operation will be, and how much money he will need to get through the first year. Many of the organizations mentioned above have personnel or access to personnel who can help in this procedure if the entrepreneur himself has secured the necessary basic information.

When capital needs have been estimated and supporting documents carefully prepared, a visit should be made to a local bank which is interested in helping minority businesses or to the local office of the Small Business Administration. There may be other local sources interested in helping minority business ventures, and it may be advisable to check with them in order to secure the best terms.

V. SUMMARY

Dress manufacturing on a contract basis is a volatile business that is highly competitive and labor-intensive. While it is readily entered with comparatively little capital investment, management should have contacts and experience in the field.

Key factors in determining profitability are the productivity of the labor force in relationship to its cost, the production planning and supervision ability of management, and the ability of management to secure business from jobbers.

For potential minority entrepreneurs who have some experience in the apparel fields and who can develop contacts with jobbers, dress manufacturing on a contract basis could prove to be a desirable field in which to establish a new business.

BIBLIOGRAPHY

U.S. Bureau of the Census, Census of Manufactures, 1967, INDUSTRY SERIES, Women's and Misses' Outerwear, MC67(2)-23B, Superintendent of Documents, U.S. Government Printing Office, Washington, D.C. 20402.

Industry Wage Survey, Women's and Misses' Dresses, August 1968, U.S. Department of Labor, Bureau of Labor Statistics, Washington, D.C. 20210.

The Appalachian Location Research Studies Program, Report No. 3, The Apparel Industry, December 1966, Appalachian Regional Commission, Washington D.C. 20235.

Trade Association

American Apparel Manufacturers' Association, 2000 K Street, N.W., Washington, D.C. 20006. Founded 1933. Members, 600. Manufacturers of infants', children's, boys', girls', men's and women's wearing apparel with annual volume in excess of 6 billion dollars at wholesale value. Publications: 1) AAMA Apparel Management Letter, monthly; 2) AAMA Newsletter, monthly, and other publications that are related to the apparel industry.

CONVENIENCE STORES

Section Contents

URBAN BUSINESS PROFILE

Convenience Stores

(SIC 5411)

I. Recommendation

The convenience store is a fast-growing segment of the retail food business which provides an attractive opportunity for independent business ownership and management. The industry is relatively easy to enter, and with some training and experience in foodstores, an individual has adequate opportunities to achieve business success. Although certain aspects of the business are complex, a new store owner or manager can secure help in buying and in resolving managerial problems through franchise operation, membership in a cooperative, or affiliation with a voluntary wholesale organization. While convenience stores have expanded rapidly throughout many suburban areas, their growth has not been as great within the inner city, and appropriate locations in these areas offer minority entrepreneurs a favorable opportunity to establish themselves in the industry.

II. Description of the Industry

The National Association of Convenience Stores describes the convenience store as a shop oriented towards convenience goods, located to serve a neighborhood, occupying 1,000 to 3,000 square feet, and with space to park five to 15 cars. Most convenience stores operate for long hours—usually from 7 a.m. to 11 p.m.—and some stores operate 24 hours per day. Convenience stores provide a service supplemental to other types of retail firms, such as supermarkets and discount centers specializing in fill-in items. Convenience stores stock only those frequently demanded items needed by the housewife between major supermarket shopping trips. However, convenience stores are classified as retail grocery stores, Standard Industrial Classification (SIC) 5411.

Table 1 gives some of the characteristics of the convenience store:

TABLE 1

Convenience Store Characteristics, 1967

Characteristics	Mean	Range
Gross area of building (square feet)	2,400	2,000 to 4,000
Investment (excluding inventory)	$50,000	$40,000 to $120,000
Inventory (number of items)	2,500	1,500 to 3,000
Employees	2.5	2 to 7
Hours open per day (7 days per week)	15	12 to 24
Parking spaces available	11	5 to 15
Sales per customer	$1.25	
Average customer shopping time	4 minutes	2 to 12 minutes
Customer trips per week	4 to 5	2 to 6
Percent of customers living within half a mile	50%	30 to 75%
Percent of customers living more than 1 mile away	20%	0 to 40%
Percent of customers who drive to store	85%	
Weekly sales	$3,000	$1,700 to $5,000
Gross margin	25%	20 to 30%
Income before tax	3.5%	2 to 6%

A brief glance at the table indicates that the convenience store is a very small scale operation, requiring only minimal investment. While operating with sophisticated sales and stocking techniques, the store is, in fact, based on a rather simple concept and can be adequately controlled by one person with some training. Some businessmen have seen the convenience store as a return to the "mom and pop" days of food shopping. However, this is not the case, since the only resemblance is in size. In all other characteristics the convenience store now closely resembles the supermarket, although there are important differences. It will be noted that the inventory is on the average only one-fifth the size of that of a supermarket. Weekly sales are being compared to the smallest supermarkets, but gross margins and income are higher (income as much as two to three times higher). This may be attributed to the charging of higher prices for the high degree of convenience offered by the long business hours and the elimination of waiting time. Convenience stores are usually more personal, friendly, and neighborly than supermarkets. Employees are usually recruited from the neighborhood served by the shop. On the average, 50 percent of the customers live within half a mile of the shop and pass it three or four times per day on other trips. Above all, the convenience store is convenient.

III. Industry Growth

The convenience store is undoubtedly filling a wide gap in the retail food market, and the growth has been spectacular. Industry statistics indicate that the number of convenience stores increased 600 percent in the 1960's.

TABLE 2

Growth of Convenience Stores in the U. S., 1957-70

Year	Number of shops	Total sales	Average sales	Percent of U.S. grocery sales
1957	500	$ 75,000,000	$150,000	.2
1960	2,500	375,000,000	150,000	.7
1962	3,500	525,000,000	150,000	.9
1965	5,000	750,000,000	150,000	1.1
1967	8,000	1,300,000,000	151,000	1.7
1968	9,600	1,625,000,000	169,000	2.1
1970	13,600	2,673,000,000	196,500	3.0

The convenience store started its growth in the late 1950's in Florida and Georgia as a drive-in store with an open front. Since then, the phenomenon has spread to all regions of the United States as convenience store chains have developed and thrived.

The enormous gap in average customer shopping time between the supermarket (22 minutes) and the convenience store (4 minutes) is the key to the success of the convenience store. The higher prices, margins, and income available to the convenience store are, therefore, a function of this changing trade-off between time and money. In addition, the convenience stores are discovering new opportunities for selling to the male customer when he shops for cigarettes or beer or is running a one-item errand for his wife to supply the missing ingredient in the dinner she is cooking at the time. (It has been estimated that two-thirds of the items bought in convenience stores are used within 2 hours, and 50 percent of the customers are male.)

IV. Location

Convenience stores are oriented towards single-item or fill-in merchandise with a very short trip time. They are, therefore, highly neighborhood-oriented, even in the suburbs, and can often be found on single-store sites, on street corners, or in small convenience-type shopping centers in company with a barbershop, a drycleaning outlet, and a carryout. In the urban areas, convenience stores have not flourished as much as they have in the suburbs, largely because there tend to be convenient places in which to shop already located in urban neighborhoods. These are the small "mom and pop" grocery stores which stay open 7 days a week, long hours each day, and have no waiting line. Moreover, there are the difficult problems of urban areas associated with rundown neighborhoods, high insurance costs, high crime rates, and the like. Inner-city convenience stores experience two or even three times the pilferage rates of the suburban store, for instance, and net profit margins are necessarily affected. Nevertheless, as the traditional small grocery store phases out of the city, and as new neighborhoods are created through urban development and low income housing, opportunities are presented for minority entrepreneurs to establish convenience stores. Almost any city neighborhood of 10,000 to 15,000 people not having a convenience store or a convenience store substitute could be a potentially good location. An existing supermarket need not be a problem, but care should be taken to make sure there is no significant competition from chain drugstores selling beer, cigarettes, and some food items.

V. Investment

The total investment needed for a convenience store is small relative to that required for a supermarket or grocery store. Total investment required will depend heavily on the cost of the facilities, if an established business, or of the land and building, if a new venture. Land may cost $40,000 to $50,000 in an urbanized location, and the building investment will probably be between $35,000 and $40,000. New equipment costs usually range from $10,000 to $20,000. If the building is already built and equipment can be leased, building and plant costs can be markedly reduced. The cost of the 2,500 items of inventory considered to be about average for a convenience store would range from $12,000 to $15,000. Operating licenses cost about $500, and cash needs may be $2,500 at the commencement of business. If the new owner/manager decides to become a franchisee of one of the larger national chains, the initial investment would be raised by about $10,000. A common financing plan for the new independent convenience store uses about $40,000 of owner's equity investment to secure a bank loan of from $60,000 to $100,000 of long term debt.

Inventory constitutes a large proportion of total investment (15 to 20 percent), and the choice of items is, therefore, very important both in terms of getting the best investment for one's dollar and in terms of the future operating ratios of the store—in particular its profitability.

Nationally advertised brand name items predominate. Because the store is small and is catering to convenience, the operator must adhere to a policy of stocking only the most frequently demanded items of the family grocery budget, with the constraint that the items have a speedy turnover and a high unit margin. Surveys of some of the chains show the proportion of items carried in each subcategory.

TABLE 3

Types of Items Carried

Convenience Store (Typical)

Total		2,000 to 3,000 items
Grocery	48 to 53%	
Nonfoods	19 to 23%	
HaBa *	12 to 15%	
Baked goods	2 to 4%	
Dairy	3 to 5%	
Meat	1 to 3%	
Frozen goods	1 to 3%	
Produce	1 to 2%	

* HaBa = Health and beauty aids.

TABLE 4

What Convenience Stores Sell

Product	% Handling	Product	% Handling
Bread	100%	Ladies' hosiery	75%
Butter	100	Soft goods	70
Cheese	100	Ice cubes	60
Eggs	100	Radio tubes	60
Milk	100	TV tubes	60
Soft drinks	100	Pet rack	60
Lunch meats, pkg.	100	Greeting cards	60
Health and beauty aids	100	Produce, packaged	55
Tobacco	100	Garden supplies	45
Frozen foods	98	Gourmet foods	45
Light bulbs	98	Records	40
Stationery	95	Fresh poultry, pkg.	35
Beer	90	Wine	27
Baked foods	90	Fresh red meats, pkg.	25
Produce, bulk	87	Liquor	18
Toys	87	Fresh seafood, pkg.	15
Frozen seafood, pkg.	85	Small appliances	15
Housewares	82	Fresh poultry, service	4
Frozen poultry, pkg.	75	Fresh red meats, service	4
Frozen red meats, pkg.	75	Fresh seafood, service	4
Candy, boxed	75		

Over 80 percent of the items are in the following categories: "grocery," "nonfoods," and "HaBa." Most of these items are delivered to the store prepackaged, and goods handling and preparing is cut down to a minimum in order to save on labor costs. This is the basic reason why so few produce, meat, baked and frozen items are carried in convenience stores. Perishables involve higher costs both in labor and equipment, and profit contribution is generally not worth the extra cost involved in carrying them. Even when perishables are carried, they are usually prepackaged at the warehouse or central distributing plant.

On the average, a supermarket has four to five times as many items as a convenience store, the quantity varying in difference from as much as 15 times more in the produce section to one to five times as much in the nonfoods section. Thus, the choice of inventory is a critical one for the convenience store and one which requires much skill and judgment, both in terms of the item's contribution to net profit and as it relates to the tastes and values of the neighborhood customers.

The details of contribution of items to total weekly sales are interesting. A 1967 study published in Progressive Grocer reveals the figures in Table 5 and Table 6. The grocery department contributes over 60 percent of the sales dollar for only 50 percent of total items, while the dairy department, with 12 percent of total sales, makes up only 5 percent of total items.

TABLE 5

Contribution to Total Sales (Weekly)

Total Store (Average)	$3,292.5	100.0%
Grocery	$1,995.9	60.7%
Dairy	385.6	11.7%
Baked goods	272.0	8.3%
Meat	178.5	5.4%
Produce	29.0	.9%

However, it should be kept in mind that soft drinks are included in the dairy department, and there is no breakdown of grocery items, which includes beer and nonfoods, for instance. The actual "Top 10" best sellers, contributing 64 percent of total sales, were as follows:

TABLE 6

"Top 10" Best Sellers

Beer (all brands)	$ 561	
Cigarettes	399	
Soft drinks	206	
HaBa	175	
Milk	160	
Candy	159	
Bread	153	
Snacks	135	
Ice cream (etc.)	107	
Sandwiches	73	
Total	$2,128	64% (80% of total profit)

VI. Operating Information

Convenience stores operate on more generous margins than do supermarkets, largely because they can charge higher prices for the convenience component of their sales; while the range of margins on products in supermarkets is 5.5 percent to 34.8 percent, the range in convenience stores is 23.8 percent to 42 percent. The price differentials between convenience stores and supermarkets are varied but, if prices differ, they are almost always greater in convenience stores. The range is as follows:

TABLE 7

Range of Price Differentials—Convenience Stores and Supermarkets

	Convenience stores	Supermarkets	Differentials
Coffee (regular) (lb.)	99¢	79¢	20¢
Ice cream (gal.)	—	—	10¢
Ice cream (qt.)	—	—	10¢
Cola (6-pack, 10 oz.)	59¢	49¢	10¢
Flour (2 lb.)	43¢	31¢	12¢
Baked beans (16 oz.)	25¢	19¢	6¢
Cigarettes (king, filter)	35¢	30¢	5¢
Bread (regular)	29¢	27¢	2¢
Milk (qt.)	31¢	31¢	—

Margin comparisons reveal quite startling differences. Table 8 shows these in terms of "penny profits" per dollar ($) of sales, per item sold by major departments:

TABLE 8

Penny Profit Differentials

	Convenience stores	Supermarkets	Differentials
Frozen foods	17.0¢	9.7¢	+7.3¢
Dairy	10.9¢	6.1¢	+4.8¢
Nonfoods	13.2¢	17.3¢	—4.1¢
Produce	9.4¢	5.4¢	+4.0¢
Baked goods	7.1¢	5.4¢	+1.7¢
Meat	16.6¢	15.1¢	+1.5¢
Grocery	7.8¢	6.3¢	+1.5¢
Average	8.9¢	7.4¢	+1.5¢

The operating ratios for a typical convenience store are thus somewhat different than for the supermarket. These data are derived from Progressive Grocer's 1968 Annual Retail Survey. The survey shows the following:

TABLE 9
Operating Ratios for Convenience Stores

	(Averages)	
Total annual sales	$150,000	
Average gross margin	25.4%	
Operating expenses (costs)	—20.2%	
Other overhead	— 1.5%	
Net other income	+ .3%	
Total income before taxes	= 4.0%	
Taxes	1.8%	
Net income	= 2.2%	($3,300)

Measures of productivity are less important in these small scale operations than in supermarkets. In general, labor productivity is low because of the long business hours involved. The typical store requires at least 250 man hours per week to operate; sales per manhour are seldom more than $4. Sales per square foot average between $1 and $2, again much lower than in the supermarket industry. Sales per transaction average about $0.90 to $1.25, again a low figure compared to supermarket averages. An interesting comparison, however, is in terms of sales per customer shopping time in the store. For supermarkets the average time is 22 minutes, and average purchases equal $5.75, 26 cents per minute. For convenience stores the average time is 4 minutes and $1.07, an average of 27 cents per minute, almost identical to the supermarket.

VII. Ownership and Franchising

Of the approximately 14,000 convenience stores now in operation, about 15 percent are owned by individual small companies (with less than 10 stores each), 65 percent by corporations (mostly large chains) and 20 percent are franchised. Because of reduced risk and higher profitability, the trend is towards franchise and away from corporate ownership; almost all the large chains are turning toward the franchising method.

One typical chain is corporation-owned, highly neighborhood-oriented, with stores of fairly large size (up to 6,000 square ft.) which are open 7 days per week for 16 hours per day. The average manager is 36 years old. He has between three and six employees. Supervision by the corporation is exercised by intensive training of the manager, a target of "profitability after 1 year," and a long-range goal of $250,000 sales per year. Monthly goals are also set. Strict productivity orientation is typical.

A major franchising operation features store sizes of 50 feet by 50 feet with 12 parking spaces. The stores carry an inventory of 3,000 nationally advertised items. These stores are open from 7 a.m. to 12 midnight and return an average profit of 3½ percent (net before taxes). The firm reports that a typical franchisee makes $17,000 per year from his operation. Total franchisee investment is about $25,000 (though only one quarter of this has to be in the form of a cash down-payment). The franchising costs after the initial investment are:

> 1% of gross sales for royalties;
>
> 2% of gross sales for services (legal, accounting, supervision, business training and help);
>
> 1% of gross sales for advertising (including a grand opening and the distribution of 2,000 hand-bills per week in the neighborhood).

Another franchising operation operates on a similar basis. However, in this case, the typical franchisee investment is $13,400, which is broken down as follows:

Inventory	$11,000
Deposit	1,600
Cash register	200
Supplies	400
License	200
Total	$13,400

In this case the company does not supply the equipment, which must be provided by the franchisee.

Experience in food retailing is a valuable ingredient in the profitable convenience store. A new entrepreneur may find that, for $3,000 to $10,000 in basic franchise fees, he can enter in partnership with a successful food retailing operation. It is strongly recommended, however, that the prospective entrepreneur obtain actual store management experience before entering into a franchise agreement or acquiring a store of his own.

VIII. Starting a New Operation

The individual attempting to start a new convenience store operation in the inner city should attempt to find an appropriate location first. An elaborate statistical survey is not absolutely necessary, but inspection of the proposed neighborhood should be made to learn:

a. The number of people within a short walking distance of the proposed location;

b. The amount of competition, particularly from stores that will be selling the same kinds of items during the same hours of operation;

c. The quality of the competition, in terms of number of items carried, appearance of store, number of hours open, etc.

Small commercial space which might be available in connection with new housing in the inner city may be ideal for the establishment of a convenience store.

The potential businessman should investigate the various franchising, cooperative, and voluntary wholesale organizations he might join. A careful study should be made of the advantages of each, the special services each provides, and the cost.

Before deciding whether or not to affiliate with an organization, he should determine detailed financing requirements, particularly for franchise fees, equipment, and inventory. If a lease guarantee is required this should be noted, too. This material, along with a detailed analysis of the proposed site, should be assembled and discussed with local banks or development organizations specializing in providing financial and technical assistance for the purpose of promoting minority enterprises. Many of these organizations can help direct qualified applicants to sources of financing. Potential applicants can demonstrate their qualifications by the care and thoroughness with which they prepare their preliminary studies and estimates and by the amount of their own funds they are willing to invest in the proposed venture.

It should be recognized by the new entrepreneur that successful convenience stores usually require 6 to 12 months to break even and about 2 years for profitable operations. Enough financing is needed for the new store so that initial operating losses can be adequately covered without impairing service.

BIBLIOGRAPHY

Convenience Store Journal

September	1968	pp 6+	"Trade Winds"
September	1968	pp 14+	"The State of the Industry"
September	1968	pp 18+	"The People Pleasing Pedens"
September	1968	pp 26+	"A Mini-Study: Non-Foods"
September	1968	pp 32+	"Movement"
September	1968	pp 34+	"Advertising"
January	1969	pp 15+	"The Shopulation Study"
April	1969	pp 1+	"The State of the Industry"
August	1969	pp 6+	"Convenience Store Franchising"
August	1969	pp 10+	"Trade Winds"
August	1969	pp 18+	"Beer Merchandising"
August	1969	p 24	"Personalized Service for the Affluent"
September	1969	pp 4+	"Trade Winds"
September	1969	pp 10+	"Food Distribution Conference Emphasizes Convenience"

Progressive Grocer

Annual	1967		Chapter III—2nd Book of Progress "Convenience Stores Carve Out Larger Niche"
October	1967	Reprint	"Inside the Convenience Store"
November	1967	pp 62+	"The Billion-Dollar Part-Time Shopper"
May	1968	pp 78+	"Push Button Convenience Store Offers Grocery Shopping Plus Car Care"
April	1969	pp 55+	"U.S. Grocery Sales Reach $77.73 Billion, up 7.3% Over Previous Year"
April	1969	pp 88+	"Convenience Stores Show Continued Strong Growth"
May	1969	pp 190+	"Shopping in the Round Part of 'Difference' at Park-It Market"
June	1969	pp 46+	"The Supermarket"

Supermarketing

May	1969	pp 25+	"Marsh—Coming of Age in Indiana"
May	1969	p 37	"Retailing Diversifies to Satisfy Customer Needs"
May	1969	pp 44+	"Retailers Find Happy Hunting in Bantamland"
June	1969	pp 13+	"Food Industry Reviews 1968 Performance"

United States Government, U.S. Department of Commerce, Business and Defense Services Administration, Washington, D.C. 20230. *U.S. Industrial Outlook*. "Grocery Stores," 1969.

Bank of America Small Business Reporter, "Convenience Food Stores," San Francisco, 1970.

Convenience Food Stores, Research Brochure No. 25, Stanford Research Institute, Menlo Park, California 94025. October 1969.

"The State of the Industry," 1970. Convenience Store Journal.

TRADE ASSOCIATION

The National Association of Convenience Stores
1835 K Street, N.W.
Washington, D.C. 20006.

CUSTOM PLASTICS PROCESSING INDUSTRIES

WARM THERMOFORGING
COLD STAMPING
CASTING
FOAMED PLASTICS
FABRICATING (THERMOFORMING)

Section Contents

URBAN BUSINESS PROFILE

Custom Plastics Processing Industries

(SIC 3079)

I. RECOMMENDATION

The plastics industries comprise one of the fastest growing areas of manufacturing in the national economy, and plastics processing can provide a handsome profit, fast growth, and an opportunity to be creative. However, it is essential that the prospective entrepreneur have a great deal of ingenuity and creativity in order to perceive the market for plastics products. An affinity for design and its problems, and considerable experience in the industry, are absolutely essential prerequisites for business success, whether these qualities are possessed by the entrepreneur, his partner, or his production foreman. Some form of partnership is important if the entrepreneur is to rely on another person for these skills.

Capital needs are minimal ($50,000) for entry into the industry via the five processes recommended in this report. However, swift growth is a characteristic of plastic processors who are successful, and within 2 to 3 years working capital requirements in the range of $250,000 may be necessary at this expanded level of operation. The entrepreneur should be fully conscious of these future capital needs at the outset. Technical knowledge sufficient to assess the right plastic to use for the job and the right production process to choose so as to deliver the item at the lowest cost also becomes more important with growth. This expertise is difficult to hire in the plastics industry, and good "production engineers" are rare. The owner, therefore, must from the outset be prepared to learn a great deal as he progresses.

The plastics market can accommodate new small firms, and competition on the frontier is not too severe—it only becomes formidable at the larger sizes. The field is recommended for a team of entrepreneurs who collectively have experience in plastics technology and managerial background, who have access to risk capital, and who possess a flair for creativity and ingenuity.

II. DESCRIPTION OF THE PLASTICS PROCESSING INDUSTRIES

A. Introduction

1. *General*

The plastics industries comprise a very large, amorphous, fast-growing, and heterogeneous group of businesses that sprang into prominence during World War II and have grown at an average annual rate of 10 to 15 percent ever since. They divide into three large categories: (1) the plastics materials manufacturer who produces the basic plastic resin or compound; (2) the processor who converts plastic into solid shapes; and (3) the fabricator and finisher who further fashions and decorates the plastic. This report deals only with plastics processing and fabricating. Resin producers are multimillion dollar organizations who must produce 100,000 tons a year to remain competitive. They need large plants and enormous capital investment, research, and technology. Plastic materials manufacturing is an industry entirely unsuited to the capacities of the small businessman.

Standard Industrial Classification (SIC) 3079 covers the whole of the plastics industries. Plastics processors and fabricators make up over 90 percent of the companies in the industry, and they collectively produce hundreds of thousands of individual items from a total of 4,000 available individual plastic materials (divided into 40 "families").

2. *The Processes*

There are many different methods of processing plastic raw material. The major methods are useful for developing a wide variety of products, and the choice of method will revolve around the cost per item produced and whether it is more economical to invest a lot of capital in an automatic machine requiring relatively little labor or whether it is better to buy an inexpensive machine requiring more labor. There are also different levels of technological expertise needed to operate the processes economically.

The major methods that have particular promise are briefly described below. Additionally, cost, technology, level of required investment, and market orientation will also be compared for each, using specific data derived from field and publication research, oriented towards the establishment of a small business. Those processes suitable for small, urban industrial ventures include:

a. *Injection Molding*—Injection molding is the principal method of forming thermoplastic materials (those plastics that become soft when exposed to sufficient heat and harden when cooled). The process depends on forcing heated fluid plastic material into a cool, closed mold where it solidifies.

b. *Compression Molding*—Compression molding is the most common method of forming thermosetting materials (those plastics that will not soften when reheated). The process involves squeezing the plastic material into permanent shape by the simultaneous application of heat and pressure.

c. *Warm Thermoforging*—A technique originally developed for the production of metal items, which is now being adapted to plastics. Warm thermoforging involves heating a sheet to moderate temperatures and forging particular parts from this sheet.

d. *Cold Stamping*—Another technique developed in relation to the production of metal items, cold stamping involves cutting complex shapes out of sheet or forcing sheet into simple shapes by vertical pressure exerted over an appropriate die.

e. *Casting*—In casting, the plastic material is heated to a fluid mass, poured into a mold, cured, and then removed from the mold. The essential difference between casting and molding is that no pressure is used in casting.

f. *Foamed Plastics Processing*—Most foamed plastic parts are produced by casting and compression molding, with a "foaming agent" added to the raw plastic material. On heating, this agent forms a gas that is distributed through the mix in small bubbles.

g. *Fabricating (Thermoforming)*—This process uses plastic sheet as its raw material. The sheet is then softened for subsequent forming over a mold by the vacuum principle.

Other processes, not recommended for small businesses, are briefly described in appendix B.

B. **Dimensions of the Plastics Processing Industries**

1. *General*

According to the 1969 annual Survey of Manufactures, the resin (the raw material of the processing industries) output of the U.S. has increased 15 percent during the last decade and is now approaching 20 billion pounds. By 1967 there were about 5,000 plastics processing companies with revenues totaling $5 billion, an average of $1 million per company. Since then, output has increased. Total output for 1970 is over $7 billion, although the number of firms is unknown. In general, however, (according to the 1967 Census of Manufactures) the number of establishments is growing at a much lower rate than the value of shipments (the latter at over 15 percent per year). This is the fastest growth rate in U.S. manufacturing at this level of generalization.

There were many small firms numbered among the 5,000 processing establishments in 1967. For instance, 41 percent of the establishments had less than 10 employees, but they produced only 2.8 percent of total output. The bulk of the product was produced by the group of firms with 100 to 250 employees averaging 9.5 percent of the total establishments, 29 percent of the total employment and 29 percent of the total output. Firms with more than 250 employees constitute only 3.2 percent of all establishments, and they had 25 percent of all employment and about 36 percent of total revenues.

The national distribution of the industries is heavily weighted towards two main regions. The Mid-Atlantic region (New York, New Jersey, and Pennsylvania) had over 1,300 companies in 1967; and the East-North-Central region, centered in Chicago, contained 1,310 establishments.

Access to the market is an important factor in the location of these industries, but transportation costs tend not to be critical because the output is usually light in weight and of fairly high value. A location in or near a major population center is, however, generally favored. Nevertheless, detailed location patterns are somewhat confused. A location in a fairly cheap rent area with freeway access nearby, on the edge of, or in the old industrial center of the large cities, seems to be the most common feature.

Some companies tend to be oriented toward a special market, and their location reflects this. Detroit has a large number of companies because they sell to the auto industry. Michigan is also beginning to develop a plastics processing industry oriented around the furniture industry.

2. *Types of Processors*

Plastics processors can be divided into three major groups, although the custom processing industry is the facet of the business that is most attractive to the small businessman.

Captive Processors	—firms engaged in fabricating their own plastics products as components for their main output, e.g., General Motors produces plastics components for some of its automobile lines.
Custom Processors	—"independent" processors, who provide a service to other companies, producing plastic parts to order, specifically designed for the customer. Almost all of the output of custom processors is further processed or handled or assembled as a component of the client's main product before reaching the market.
Proprietary Processors	—firms which produce a patented, licensed, or unprotected item for sale. Usually this activity grows out of a custom processing plant, and can involve either products sold to other manufacturers (e.g., drawer clasps to the furniture industry or sheet rod and billet for further processing) or end-use products sold direct on the market, or via distributors to the consumer (e.g., plastic pens).

The *Modern Plastics Encyclopedia* (1969-70) lists 1,622 custom processors in the United States (Table 1 in appendix A). Over 40 percent are primarily in the injection and/or extrusion business, and many are small in size. Modern Plastics estimates indicate that there are more custom operation molding companies than captive ones. Moreover, over 60 percent of the total monthly output (25 million pounds) comes from custom molders. Despite the fact that captive processors are growing in number, in machine capacity, and in resins processed, at a faster rate than are the custom molders, the latter still predominate. Trends indicate that there is a process of elimination of smaller producers in the custom molding field, and output is becoming concentrated in fewer and larger custom molding shops. Nevertheless, most custom molders are still fairly small (Table 2 in appendix A) with 5 percent possessing less than 10 molding machines, 38 percent still in the category of 10 to 24 machines, and only 5 percent with 25 machines or more. In terms of employment, the situation is similar, with 57 percent of captive operations employing less than 25 workers on average, and 57 percent of custom processors employing less than 50 (average).

C. **Business Characteristics of the Plastics Industries**

1. *Markets*

The market for plastics products is a vast one. Literally any item now fabricated out of wood, steel, nonferrous metal, or textiles can be considered a potential substitution market for plastics. There are hundreds of thousands of plastic product types, and each week hundreds more are developed.

Table 3 in appendix A is an attempt at projecting the total market for the plastics industries among various types of customers through 1980. At present, most of the total plastics output is in building and construction, and in the packaging industry. The electrical industry and the transportation industry also consume large portions of output. Most categories are expected to grow at the general rate for the plastics industry, about 15 to 40 percent per year, which means that all plastic markets are phenomenal growth areas. The packaging industry and plastics in transportation are expected to grow at rates in excess of these general rates.

This level of detail is, however, an inadequate basis for making decisions as to which markets have the most potential for a prospective business. Within each of the broad categories there are many other submarkets which spring up each year and often grow in excess of 100 percent per year. The production of recreational vehicles (snowmobiles) and the small boat industry (glass-reinforced polyester) are two examples. However, predictions of the plastics market are not particularly reliable because of the high rate at which new materials become available and new products (and markets) are created. The market for plastics in furniture, for instance, was almost nonexistent in 1960 (other than P.V.C. as a leather substitute) and now consumes over 1 billion pounds of raw materials per year in such product classes as polyesters, methanes, and vinyls. It is very difficult to predict ahead with any accuracy, and the exercise is not particularly valuable since opportunities in markets are more a function of the initiative of the businessman than the availability of a ready market.

One important aspect of the market is the degree to which the output tends to be captive as opposed to custom or proprietary. The automobile industry, for instance, might seem to be the fastest growing and most lucrative market to get into. The average Detroit-produced car had 40 pounds of plastics in it by 1963, and over 100 pounds by 1970, while figures of 200 to 300 pounds per car are projected for 1980. Yet, the auto industry relies on very large-scale production on a scale at which very few custom molders are capable of operating. The investment for serving such a market is very large, and changes in design are frequent. Recognizing this, the auto companies are setting up their own plastics-molding shops, producing as many items as possible in-house. In some ways, the furniture industry also seems to be headed in this direction.

Another feature of the plastics market of particular interest to the small businessman is the fact that entry into a market needs to be as early as possible in the product life cycle. A small business with low amounts of capital investment cannot hope to compete with companies of high capitalization enjoying well developed markets with immense production runs. The small business must enter the process early, producing new products at reasonable cost which will later be produced much more cheaply by bigger companies on more expensive machines as the market grows to a point where really large-scale production is feasible. Expanded operations can be successfully kept within the business if the firm is able to respond quickly with required capitalization. Alternatively, the originating business can take out patents and develop a proprietary line from which future income is assured regardless of by whom the product is manufactured.

The speed of product development is peculiar to the plastics industry. This process often takes less than 1 year for a given product.

Another approach to the plastics market is that of the custom processor who offers a service to plastics designers, and fabricators attached to other companies and other industries. In a sense, this avoids the real market, and relying on others to conceive of the product, design it, and carry the cost of failure if it does not sell. There is a developed market for this kind of service, but the potential client is difficult to identify and cultivate. Almost any company in any industry, other than plastics, may need a plastic component for its finishing product. This is increasingly so as industrial engineers and designers become aware of the advantages of plastics in their particular fields. The ability to offer a complete service is important in this sort of business. All the skills of engineering and product development and an adequate range of machinery—including extrusion, injection, casting, spraying, and thermoforming are needed to take care of all the client's needs. This represents a sizable capital investment and puts the newcomer to the custom processing field at a disadvantage, since capital requirements will probably limit him to only one or two methods of processing.

The custom processor is thus marketing both products and services, and he is likely to succeed best in those situations where he is not close to the end-user but produces an item as a service to a client who then markets it as an entity or combines it with other components of his product. Throughout the plastics processing industry it has been estimated that 70 percent of individual products are not for end use but are components of goods which another company markets. The custom processor stands at a distance from the market in this situation, protected somewhat by his client from the effects of market fluctuations.

2. *Processes Suitable to Small Investments*

In this section an attempt will be made to describe possible plastics processes available to the small businessman by applying the three following criteria:

a. Investment needed must be less than $150,000;

b. The degree of sophistication and technological expertise needed must be low;

c. The process must be capable of producing a profit at extremely low production "runs" of less than 1,000 items which are sold at competitive prices.

It is the application of these criteria which provides a more sound basis for deciding between alternatives than do the market considerations discussed above. Each of the processes described earlier will be dealt with in turn. Market comments are added where appropriate.

a. *Injection*—Injection technology is the basis of plastics processing. Injection machinery is expensive, however, and, depending on capacity, one production line will cost from $40,000 to $200,000. Molds average $5,000 per item. These two components make medium-sized runs essential to spread costs over many items. The lower range of run length is perhaps 3,000 items. Technology is fairly complex, and the machines have many variables in their operation. A minimum-sized shop of two 1602 injection machines plus all peripheral equipment would need $150,000 investment. *Partially recommended for beginning small business.*

b. *Compression Molding*—This is a less expensive process (in terms of investment) than injection molding and has a very fast cycle time. A shop with two or three presses and peripheral equipment would cost about $100,000. The technology is simpler than in either injection or extrusion, and because of the lower investment and faster cycle time it is more suited to small business. A disadvantage lies in the limited kinds of output feasible, namely small sized thermosets. This restricts the market applications. *Partially recommended for beginning small business.*

c. *Warm Thermoforging*—Warm thermoforging of plastic sheet can be accomplished with machinery of $100 to $150 per ton capacity so that (at 1 ton per square inch) a 12-inch by 12-inch machine might cost $14,000 to $20,000. Warm thermoforging is economical with thick and large surface area parts, but materials costs and operating costs are high, while low cycle times mean low labor productivity. *Recommended for beginning small business.*

d. *Cold Stamping*—Cold stamping, using metal stamping machinery, is highly feasible because of very fast cycle times, giving high productivity. The machinery is inexpensive and the technology has been well-developed and simplified in the metalworking industry. A four-cavity machine would cost $40,000 compared to an injection machine equivalent of $160,000. So cold stamping is relatively cheap and fast. Disadvantages include the lack of available cold sheet and billet in sufficient variety as yet. However, this picture is changing. *Recommended for beginning small business.*

e. *Casting*—Technologically the simplest process, casting requires low levels of investment, is suited to very low production runs, but is not competitive at high runs. By itself, or in combination with reinforcing by glass fiber, it is a simple method but has high per part cost due to its hard production character. Dispersing equipment, molds, tables, and so on would not cost more than $5,000 for parts up to 3-foot by 3-foot. For bigger parts (including boat hulls, for example) sprays are still cheap, but molds become expensive. This method has many applications, particularly when used with foamed plastics. *Recommended for beginning small business.*

f. *Foamed Plastics*—Foamed plastics have a wide variety of applications, and products can be produced in foam by all of the above methods at no extra cost (except materials cost). Foaming agents and dispensers are not expensive. Urethane spray equipment for casting fine furniture, for instance, costs $12,000 and is economical at low production runs. *Recommended for beginning small business.*

g. *Fabricating (thermoforming)*—The industry sees this activity as fabricating because the raw material used is preformed stock such as sheet. Technologically simple, this method is also inexpensive to set up, and many small processors build their own equipment. A thermoforming machine merely heats the sheet and (via a pump) creates a vacuum, causing the sheet to take the shape of the mold. Machines of 6 by 6 by 4 feet capacity are available at less than $3,000 and can be built for half this price.

The slow cycle time makes cost per item expensive and labor productivity low. However, it is economically feasible for "runs" as low as 300 to 400. Moreover, injection machines cannot yet produce items as large as thermoforming machines can, while thermoforming can reproduce any injection molded item. An investment of $10,000 to $15,000 would cover two lines. *Highly recommended for beginning small business.*

The above methods all meet or partially meet our three criteria. However, among the methods that are fully or highly recommended are methods which are high in terms of cost per part because of their relatively high labor input. They are economical in comparison to partially recommended methods only because the latter need high runs to be feasible. The use of lower cost per part methods entailing a higher investment is essential once the business has a high demand and larger production runs. Otherwise labor costs will be too high and productivity too low, thereby impairing the business' ability to compete. Other processes, which do not meet the above-mentioned criteria, are discussed in appendix B.

The inverse correlation between cost per part and the price of equipment/technology is an important relationship. The processes above, then, can be viewed in terms of different scales of output as follows:

	Average run size	Investment	Annual revenue
Fully recommended	up to 3,000	less than $50,000	$ 50,000
Partially recommended	3,000 to 80,000	$100,000 to $150,000	$300,000

3. *Costs*

Costs in the plastics processing industry vary with the type of process used. In practice, the most critical controlling factor is the M.H.R. (machine hour rate). The calculation of this rate, composed of labor costs, machine (power) operation costs, amortization of investment, depreciation, and mold or die replacement costs, is critical to the pricing of the final product. In simple terms:

Raw materials + M.H.R. cost per item + Cost of production.

This formula can give the item cost of production and can be used to make decisions about when to move up to more productive processes at higher levels of investment. Most of these costs are under the control of the firm. Power and labor may not be. Power costs are negligible (5 percent), and labor costs can vary between 30 percent and 50 percent depending on the process and the degree to which the firm makes its own molds and dies and maintains a toolroom.

The Society of the Plastics Industry *Survey of July 1970* shows that the average plant operates 120 hours per week, on a two- or three-shift, 6- or 7-day basis. This relatively high level of operation is due to the need to keep expensive machinery in operation in order to spread the investment costs.

Wage rates are quite varied throughout the country. About half the plants are unionized and are working on a 2- to 3-year contract with several different labor unions. There are only two unions which exist specifically for plastics industry workers. The following are averages presented in the July 1970 study referred to above.

Per Hour Wage Rates in the Plastics Industry

	Compression	Injection	Blow	General	Premold workers
Foreman	$3.78	$3.40	$3.36	$ —	$ —
Setup man	—	—	—	3.17	—
Molders	2.65-3.04	2.27-2.51	2.50-3.07	—	1.85-2.91
Other					
Process operator			$2.51		
Extrusion operator			3.10		
Shipping/Receipts			2.59		
Packers			2.43		
Truckdriver			2.94		
Millwright (foreman)			3.86		
Electricians			3.86		
Foreman toolroom			4.40		
Toolroom:					
Mold/Die designer			4.47		
Moldmaker			4.68		
Mold repair			3.80		
Apprentice			2.82		
General helpers			2.36		

Wage rates are fairly high by national standards, and critical wage rates such as those for moldmakers can be as high as $6 to $7 per hour in some areas at times of scarcity. Most plastics processing firms are highly dependent on moldmakers, since almost all products require either a mold or die in their production. There is currently a critical shortage of good moldmakers in the industry and this is impeding growth somewhat. The shortage of workers in other areas is not so critical, but nonetheless difficult, and wages continue to rise as the shortage persists. First-line supervisor foremen, for instance, are paid $1,100 per month in some areas of the country, since their control over the processes is a critical one to production.

The need for high productivity once operations begin to require more than four or five employees is obvious, since it is critical to cost control on a per item basis. The plastics processing industry will be requiring highly skilled men in the future who are ultimately either operating highly sophisticated and automated machinery or are producing highly accurate molds and dies.

Costs of materials are fairly standardized. They are cheapest in pellet tons and are sold by weight. In general, materials costs are slowly declining as new and more efficient methods of producing the material are discovered. Some examples are as follows:

Material	Price per lb. in cents			
	1964	1966	1967	1969
ABS	35	36	32	31
High density polyethylene (injection)	20	17	18	19
Polypropylene (injection)	25	20	20½	19
Polystyrene (high impact)	22	18	18	18

However, delivered costs are a different matter, and there are large savings available for high bulk transfer by both road and rail. Small processors are taking advantage of this by cooperating in their raw material needs, ordering collectively in bulk. Several raw material companies are offering a file-correlation service to allow buyers to coordinate their needs, thus saving on shipping costs.

4. *Productivity*

Generalized measures of productivity in the industry are not based on enough experience to be useful. However, according to a survey conducted by Plastics Technology in 1970, productivity in the plastics industry compares favorably with productivity in other industries. Nevertheless, the rate of increase in productivity levels has slowed down considerably over the past 10 years. Between 1958 and 1969, all manufacturing increased 3.4 percent per year, chemicals 5.7 percent per year, and plastics 6.6 percent per year. Percentage increases in the last 5 years, though, reveal that all manufacturing grew at 3 percent, chemicals grew at 4.4 percent, and plastics grew at only 3.7 percent per year.

Further statistics from this survey indicate that in 1967 value added per man hour of production was $7.15, up from $5.07 in 1958, a growth of 5 percent per year. Value added per employee grew from $7,987 to $11,796 per annum over the same period, a growth rate of 3.4 percent per year.

Payroll in 1967 was 48 percent of value added, a figure unusually high for what is normally thought to be a capital intensive industry. Thus, productivity grows at a moderate rate on the production floor, but administration, sales and other labor costs are causing output per employee to grow only at 3.4 percent per year. This is an indicator of the high cost of the nonproduction activities in this industry.

As might be expected, the Plastics Technology survey showed that productivity has improved differently in each major processing area. In general, the overall emphasis is on tooling, better major equipment, better resins, automation, and control. Tooling and major equipment were rated as most critical productivity factors for injection molding, and control and major equipment were selected for thermoforming. Unfortunately no data were available for the other major processing areas.

5. *Profitability*

Manufacturing profitability depends greatly on run size and the demand (expressed in price terms) for the final product and, accordingly, projection of the profits attainable from a particular plastics process requires assumptions about these factors. Some feeling about the profitability of custom plastics processing can be gained, however, from *Survey No. 9 of Custom Processors,* conducted in 1970 by the Society of the Plastics Industry, Inc. Figures have been rounded slightly for ease in reading.

Revenues			100%
Expenses (as percent of revenues)			94%
	Mean	Range	
Materials	37%	30-50%	
Production labor	15	13-22	
Administrative expense	8	7-10	
Factory overhead	28	20-31	
Selling expense	6	3- 8	
Net profit before tax			6%

Gross margin in the industries is difficult to assess from these very generalized ratios, but it usually lies between 10 percent and 30 percent. A fairly high proportion of processing costs are indirect, centering around administration, depreciation, rental, and other costs.

Profit before tax in the above table is a very generalized figure which masks great ranges of profit. Profit may run as high as 25 percent in some areas of the industry, particularly among small custom processors who have just developed a new proprietary product or have just moved into a field not yet penetrated by plastics where prices charged for output are low in terms of the substitution value to the customers but very profitable in terms of costs of production. Such high margins are not average but are certainly available in a situation where a small business creates its own market. They tend to vanish as other producers begin to compete, bidding down the price to levels more closely related to the costs of production. This feature of operating on the frontier does represent an important phase in the growth of small plastics processors and the high profit can often be used to finance expansion into larger capacity and new processes.

6. *Capital Requirements*

Startup capital requirements depend on the scale of initial operations. Most businesses are launched at a level below $50,000 investment, and, at this level, capital procurement can often be a great difficulty, particularly for the minority businessman. The problem revolves around the market. It is difficult for a potential lender as investor to be assured that a market exists for the output of the proposed business. Indeed, success often revolves around the ability of the entrepreneur to create a demand for a product by his ingenuity in perceiving that articles now made of wood or metal can be made more cheaply and effectively out of plastics, leaving a high gross margin of profitability. The beginner often starts by producing a plastic substitute for an item with which he already has some familiarity in former occupations. The production of sound-absorbing plastic doorstops helped one company. Another entrepreneur perceived that a wooden sorting tray used by a large state institution could be better made in plastics and won a large contract by taking his plastic substitute into the purchasing agent's office.

This kind of ingenuity is vital to success, and hopefully is likely to show up in the ability of the entrepreneur to obtain capital. If the prospective businessman can persuade the banker that he has a marketable operation based on his ability to create demand and his ability to offer a components production service for clients, he is likely to succeed in the business.

As the company grows, however, larger amounts of capital are essential. When the business reaches 10 to 20 employees, capitalization may be necessary at a level one to three times greater than the initial amount. This can be a formidable barrier to growth.

III. ANALYSIS OF BUSINESS FEASIBILITY

A. Factors Influencing Performance

1. The conceptual ingenuity of the plastics entrepreneur, particularly in relation to marketing and sales, is perhaps his most important skill. Thinking up a product is a process for which there are no established guidelines or training programs. The ability to perceive a need is important and can be developed by bringing to the business some experience in another material for which plastics may be substituted.

2. Experience in some aspects of the plastics industry, even as an employee, is useful and perhaps even critical. The entrepreneur himself can manage without it, but if this is the case, it is essential that he has working with him a good, experienced machinist who can make simple molds, design and build simple equipment, and who has a thorough knowledge of a number of the plastics, wood, or metal fabricating processes. Successful ventures in plastics processing generally have a good all-around mechanic who is used to producing the simple hardware needed to make simple plastic products. Such a man can learn the operating skills involved in a particular machine and transmit those skills to others.

3. If the entrepreneur does not have these skills and experience, a partnership with an ex-plastics-producing foreman or toolroom man, for instance, would be invaluable. Failing this, the hiring of such a man as an employee, probably costing $800 to $1,200 per month, is very important.

B. Projection of Attainable Returns for Five Plastics Processes

This profile has discussed several different plastics technologies, and has recommended seven as being suitable for new small businesses. Of these seven, two (injection and compression molding) were only partially recommended because of the size of the initially required capital investment. This section will compare the investment, operating costs, and returns associated with the five fully recommended processes. These processes are:

(a) Warm thermoforging
(b) Stamping
(c) Casting
(d) Foamed plastics
(e) Fabricating (thermoforming)

They also have the advantage of being highly comparable. Parts produced by a casting technique are often made into foamed plastic items or a casted part can be cut and stamped into intricate shapes.

This flexibility, at low levels of capital investment, is gained only because we are accepting low labor productivity (except for warm thermoforging), and a relatively high price per part. This restricts the market potential to runs of less than 1,000 pieces each except on very simple parts where parts made with these processes can be made economically at very large runs (particularly with warm thermoforging which competes effectively with injection molding at 50,000 parts and above). For the most part, however, the processes selected are those which are economical at low levels of production. Casting, for instance, can be used with room temperature-cured and foamed resins and silicone molds to produce fine furniture pieces from wood carvings which merit a high retail price (up to $10 per item for 5-pound pieces). Other examples of low-run, high-price, high-margin items abound in the trade magazines.

Production runs of each of the five processes are shown below:

		Items per week at 40-hour week
Warm thermoforging	—Fast cycle machine at about 800 per hour (no cooling necessary)	
Stamping	—Regarded as an accessory process; fast cycle at 100 per hour	= 4,000
Casting	—2 banks of 10 molds on rotary table, ½ hour cure	= 800
Foamed plastics	—2 banks of 10 molds on rotary tables, with ½ hour curing time = 20 items per hour	= 800
Fabricating (thermoforming)	—2 machines, each producing 5 items per hour (cooling time is fairly long)	= 400

The average revenue per item sold is based on assumptions rather than calculations, since precise knowledge of the market is unattainable with such a wide product mix.

Warm thermoforging	.08	per item—(small simple parts)
Stamping	.10	per item—(a simple stamping process)
Casting	$2.00	per item—(complex, large items)
Foamed plastics	$3.00	per item—(complex construction)
Fabricating (Thermoforming)	$4.00	per item—(large size)

Utilizing the average 120 hours per week used by the Society of the Plastics Industry Survey of July 1970 as 65 percent of capacity, revenue calculations for the five processes are as follows:

Process	Capacity per week	Capacity per year	Revenue per item	Revenue per year at 65% capacity
Warm thermoforging	32,000	1,600,000	.08	$83,200
Stamping	4,000	200,000	.10	$13,000
Casting	800	40,000	$2.00	$52,000
Foamed plastics	800	40,000	$3.00	$78,000
Fabricating (thermoforming)	400	20,000	$4.00	$52,000

Projected Financial Statements for the Five Recommended Processes

INVESTMENT	Warm Thermoforging	Stamping	Casting	Foamed plastics	Fabricating (Thermoforming)
Machines—(number and cost)	(1) $15,000	(2) $ 4,000	(3) $15,000	(1) $10,000	(2) $10,000
Peripheral equipment—tables, forklift, pallets, conveyors, etc.	5,000	5,000	5,000	5,000	5,000
Stock materials for two months (one month for casting)	6,000	*	2,500	5,000	1,500
Total investment	$26,000	$ 9,000	$22,500	$20,000	$16,500
ANNUAL OPERATING STATEMENTS					
Revenue	$83,200	$13,000	$52,000	$78,000	$52,000
Expenses					
Indirect labor costs—					
Plant manager/toolman/designer	$13,000	$13,000	$13,000	$13,000	$13,000
Owner/manager/salesman	$ 8,000	$ 8,000	$ 8,000	$ 8,000	$ 8,000
Office girl	$ 5,000	$ 5,000	$ 5,000	$ 5,000	$ 5,000
Direct labor and other costs—					
Operators—(number and cost)	(1) $ 5,000	(1) $ 5,500	(2) $11,000	(1) $ 5,500	(2) $11,000
Power supplies	$ 1,000	$ 600	$ 200	$ 100	$ 500
Rent (at 10¢ per square foot per month)	$ 3,000	$ 3,000	$ 3,000	$ 3,000	$ 4,000
Depreciation, interest, and miscellaneous	$ 8,000	$ 2,000	$ 6,000	$ 7,300	$ 6,500
Materials cost as a percent of revenue †	$50,000	*	$15,500	$40,000	$12,000

* It is assumed that stamping uses stock already prepared in one of the processes.

† Warm thermoforging = 60 percent; Stamping = 0 percent; Casting = 30 percent; Foamed plastics = 51 percent; Fabricating (thermoforming) = 23 percent.

Many processors will want to invest in two of the processes and in addition, must invest in stamping in order to extend the range of operations and offer a comprehensive service in fabrication. The possible combinations of processes and the production ratio of each one are shown below:

1. Warm thermoforging/stamping/casting
2. Warm thermoforging/stamping/foamed plastics
3. Warm thermoforging/stamping/fabricating (thermoforming)
4. Stamping/casting/foamed plastics
5. Stamping/casting/fabricating (thermoforming)

A financial summary for the various possible combinations of processes is outlined below. The numbers refer to the combinations listed above.

	1	2	3	4	5
Revenue	$148,200	$174,200	$148,200	$143,000	$117,000
Expenses	141,000	160,900	138,600	129,800	107,500
Net income	7,200	13,300	9,600	13,200	9,500
Return on sales	4.9%	7.6%	6.4%	9.2%	8.1%
Investment	57,500	55,000	51,500	51,500	48,000

IV. STARTING THE NEW BUSINESS

The key to starting a new business in the plastics industries is to determine or create the product which can be produced and sold and to establish or acquire the technical ability to produce it. In some cases, the individual desiring to enter the plastics business may, through his knowledge of another industry or in some other way, have discovered how a new item can be produced in plastics and be able to establish the existence of a market for his proposed custom processing business. His next step is to make sure that he, himself, has, or that he can arrange to acquire, the necessary technical ability to produce efficiently and economically.

The individual proposing to start such a new business should have some ideas himself about what he wants to produce and where he can sell it. These ideas should stem from his own experience. It is unlikely that someone can enter the custom plastics processing business without previous background in the industry or in a related industry and establish a product line by trial and error afterwards. Moreover, no one would advance money on such a basis.

The starting point, therefore, would be an individual or a group of individuals who have some ideas, based on their own experience, about what they want to produce and to whom they propose to sell their production. The next step is to verify this market. A market survey should be undertaken.

If the product is a new line or a variation which is a new design of an existing line, samples will be required and visits made to prospective customers to determine their reaction to the line and the price at which it can be sold. Generally speaking, prospective customers can give the market surveyor an idea of how many of the items they might expect to purchase at a given price, how sales have been growing, what the competition is, and so on. This information can be used to determine the expected volume of sales for the new business and the revenue which can be expected.

If the proposed new business is to provide a variety of products to an existing industry, such as items for the furniture industry, the market surveyor should canvass proposed accounts within the industry to develop some estimates of the total volume of business, its growth pattern, the competition, pricing arrangements, and the like. Here again, the information can be used to develop estimates of volume and revenues.

If the individuals proposing to start the new business do not themselves have the technical ability, they should next arrange to acquire a production supervisor. An advertisement in the trade press might secure inquiries from someone who is presently a production supervisor or an assistant. It may be necessary and desirable to offer a partnership to such an individual, particularly if he is well-experienced, since he will be a key to success in the business.

Once the market and production capabilities are in hand, the next step is to arrange for machinery and production space. An automobile tour of industrial areas may establish the availability of appropriately sized and priced space. The production supervisor should advise on whether the space is adequate and of the right type. Industrial real estate brokers may also be able to determine what space is available.

Machinery suppliers will be listed in such trade press publications as Plastics Age. The production supervisor may also know about nearby dealers in used machinery. Machinery suppliers should be contacted to determine on what terms machinery can be leased or purchased on the installment plan. Some of the elementary machinery for thermoforming, spray-up, and casting may be homemade by a good tool and machine man. Used machinery can sometimes be purchased for about two-thirds of the new price.

With the market, production capability, location, and machinery in hand, it is time to establish the financial plan. This plan should establish how much capital will be put in by the owners, how much capital investment will be deferred through lease or installment purchase of machinery, how much capital will be needed to finance accounts receivable (until shipments are paid for) and how much will be needed to pay for materials and labor until the output can be sold. In starting a new business of this type, it is essential to provide an allowance for unforeseen startup costs. These are the costs of training new labor, wasted material until the machines are running right, returned shipments due to errors, and the like.

With a financial plan in hand, the potential new entrepreneurs should visit a local banker to determine the prospect of securing a loan. In most cases, banks will not normally provide unsecured money to a new business without previous experience. However, if there is a prospect that the Small Business Administration will guarantee the loan, there is more likelihood that the project can be financed.

If the prospective entrepreneurs are individuals considered to be members of a minority segment of the population, they should discuss their plans at an early stage with whatever local organization has been established to assist minority entrepreneurs. In many cases, these organizations are affiliates of the Office of Minority Business Enterprise, and they will have information on sources of financing locally. These financial sources may include, in addition to bank loans guaranteed by the Small Business Administration, loans from development corporations financed under the Special Impact Program of the Office of Economic Opportunity, and loans and equity investments from locally oriented Minority Enterprise Small Business Investment Corporations (MESBIC's).

APPENDIX A

TABLE 1

Custom Processors and Converters, USA, 1969-70

	Total Companies
Blow molders	95
Casting	117
Injection and extrusion	790
Molders of foamed plastics	200
Processors of F.R.P.	185
Formers of thermoplastic sheet	210
Powder molders	25
Total	1,622

TABLE 2

Injection Molders, Sample Survey Data

	Captive			Custom		
	A	B	C	A	B	C
Percent of firms	57%	28%	15%	57%	38%	5%
Average Number of employees	225	25-50	100-200	250	50-200	200+

Size groups: A—10 machines; B—10-24 machines; C—25+ machines.

Source: Modern Plastics, March 1969, p. 59.

TABLE 3

Growth of Plastics Markets
(million lbs.)

	1960	1965	1970	1975	1980
Building	1400	2900	4250	8370	14000
Transportation	229	610	1820	7500	15000
Packaging	1000	2200	4500	7000	13000
Electrical	830	1200	2000	3300	6000
Housewares	310	500	1150	1900	3000
Furniture	400	580	960	1750	2900
Appliances	180	300	530	1400	2100

APPENDIX B

Brief descriptions of several plastics processing techniques, not recommended for beginning small business, are outlined below.

a. *Blow Molding* (thermoplastics). This process is used in making bottles and other thin-walled containers. The base machine is an extruder which produces a tube in a downward direction. The tube is captured in a hollow mold. Air pressure is used to inflate the tube and form it against the sides of the mold. Ejection and cooling complete the cycle. P.P. (polypropylene) is the major material used in this process. Blow molding of bottles is now a vast industry producing billions of bottles per year on an automated basis. The low price of plastic bottles indicates that high capital investment, high labor productivity, and extremely long runs (in millions of parts per order) are a feature of this process. The average cost of a complete blow molding line is about $115,000, though a new system called "Aeropall" has recently been marketed at a machine cost of $25,000 (indicating a line cost of perhaps about $50,000). However, a blow molding operation to be feasible would need more than one line, and although minimum size is not known, an operation with at least two lines (some sources indicate four is essential) puts investment at about $100,000 to $250,000. The market for plastic bottles and containers is one of the fastest and healthiest plastics markets. Unfortunately the market is also well served at the moment by experienced producers working under contract to the large food producers, packers and retailers, and a wide variety of containers is also available out of the stocks held by suppliers.

b. *Extrusion* (thermoplastics). Extrusion machines operate on the same principal as injection machines, except that they have a continuous feed mechanism. The nozzle end is a shaped die, the cross section of which determines the final cross-sectional shape of the extrusion. The extrusion is then uniformly cooled by water or air and carried away on a continuous basis. The main extrusion materials are polyethylene (PE), A.B.S., P.V.C., polystyrene and cellulosics. Trims, sheets, house siding, molding, drinking straws, rods, pipes, hose, are all products made by this method. Extrusion is the second most frequently used method of processing plastics, and machinery with diameters up to 12 inches is available, making it possible to produce extrusion in very large lengths and in quantities of 2,000 to 3,000 pounds on a daily basis. Extrusion machinery is often complex (several screws and barrels are common) and expensive, while the die is the critical feature (similar to the mold in injection) and requires a high degree of skill and experience in its hand production. Diemaking is still considered an art, and a library of dies for extrusion is an expensive investment. Long production runs are obviously essential.

Variations on extrusion include coating of wire, encapsulating, and blown film extrusion (in which air pressure is used to continuously expand an extruded tube to produce very thin film).

Extrusion is the basic process for production of continuous output. Extrusion machines start at $70,000 (1½-inch capacity). At 4½-inch capacity, they cost about $150,000. Peripheral equipment for handling the extrusion is also expensive. A shop with two extrusion machines of 2½-inch and 4½-inch capacity with all equipment would represent an investment of $450,000. This process is highly capital intensive and requires a high degree of skill, particularly by the tool and diemaker who produces the dies which determine product shape. Long production runs are, therefore, essential, and the process is not recommended for beginning small businesses.

c. *Rotational molding.* One of the more recent of the processing techniques is rotational molding. A premeasured amount of plastic in powder form is placed inside a mold which is then rotated biaxially in a high temperature environment. The centrifugal forces distribute the material over the inside surface of the mold, cooling takes place, whole rotation continues. This method is used to produce large vessels with thick structural walls (e.g., garbage cans) as well as other large heavy parts. The machinery available has four or eight arms rotating around a central point. The molds are attached to the ends of the arms and also rotated. A heating and cooling environment is also essential. The capital costs are fairly high, even though the technology is simple, and the cycle time is long so that speed of output is not fast. Consequently roto molding has had only limited application to date, and the process involves large, complex machinery and various heating and cooling operations. It is not economical in small runs for the production of large vessels and parts. It requires very large runs to be economically feasible; above one million parts per run it is perhaps the cheapest of all processes. The cost of rotomolding equipment (4 oven, 160-ounce-capacity) means an investment of $100,000 to $120,000 and a large market to justify it.

d. *Other methods.* There are a variety of other methods in commercial use, mainly based on adaptations of the above processes, though some are totally different. Laminating involves the extrusion of various plastics layers onto wood, cloth, steel, alloys, or other plastics, producing items of great strength and toughness. Formica is one such product. Costs of equipment are high, however, and the market specialized. Calendering is the equivalent of the steel rolling mill in which plastic sheet is heated and by pressure applied through rollers is made thinner, or embossed and changed in shape. Radiation processing involves the impregnation of a base material, wood, brick, concrete, cloth with a resin, and its exposure to cobalt radiation which cures the resin imparting amazing qualities to the base material. Superhard, long-wearing, abrasion and corrosion resistant wood is produced this way. The technology is fairly simple, but the cobalt radiation machine is as yet an item of high investment. The process is suited to the production of modular building parts in high quantity.

Ultrasonic assembly, roll-leaf hot stamping, printing, high frequency sealing, electroplating, painting, vacuum metalizing, and decorative overlaying are some of the other commercially used techniques. However, new techniques, like materials and markets, are invented every week in the plastics processing industry as companies come across new low cost ways to produce plastic items. Most of the techniques now available were begun by small processors building their own machinery in garage-sized workshops. These techniques were subsequently developed by larger machinery companies.

BIBLIOGRAPHY

Concise Guide to Plastics. Herbert R. Simonds and J. M. Church, second edition. Reinhold Publishing Corporation, New York, 1963. $12.

Encyclopedia of Plastics Equipment. Herbert R. Simonds, editor. Reinhold Publishing Corporation, New York, 1964. $22.50.

General Plastics. Raymond Cherry. Revised edition. Taplinger Publishing Co., Inc., New York, New York, 1965. $6.

Machining Plastics. U.S. Small Business Administration, Washington, D.C. 20416. (In Technical Aids for Small Business, Annual No. 1) $1.

Modern Plastics. McGraw-Hill Publications, 1301 Avenue of Americas, New York, New York 10019. Monthly. $10.

Modern Plastics Encyclopedia. McGraw-Hill Publications, 1301 Avenue of Americas, New York, New York 10019. Annual. Included in subscription to Modern Plastics.

Plastics Design & Processing. Lake Publishing Corporation, Box 270, 311 E. Park Avenue, Libertyville, Illinois 60018. Monthly. Free.

Plastics Engineering Handbook. Society of the Plastics Industries. Third edition. Reinhold Publishing Corporation, New York, New York. 1960. $15.

Plastic Materials. J. A. Byrdson. D. Van Nostrand Co., Inc., Princeton, New Jersey 08540. 1966. $13.50

Plastics: Projects and Techniques Alvin R. Lappin. Taplinger Publishing Co., Inc., New York, New York. 1964. $4.

Plastics Technology. Bill Publications, Inc., 630 3rd Avenue, New York, New York 10017. Monthly. $10.

Plastics Technology, Basic Materials and Processes. Robert S. Swanson, Taplinger Publishing Co., Inc., New York, New York, 1965. $6.80.

The following are available from the Society of the Plastics Industry.

1. *Plastics Processing Companies,* Labor Survey No. 33, July 1970.
2. *Compression and Transfer Molding*
3. *Injection Molding*
4. *An Introduction to Extrusion*
5. *The Story of the Plastics Industry*

Stanford Research Institute, Menlo Park, California 94025. Long Range Planning Service:

1. *Reinforced Plastics,* Report No. 182, August 1963.
2. *Plastics in Construction,* Report No. 299, September 1966.
3. *World Plastics,* Report No. 381, August 1969.
4. *Specialty Plastics,* Report No. 428, December 1970.
5. *Foamed Plastics,* Report No. 358, October 1968.

U.S. Foamed Plastic Markets & Directory 1969-70, published by the Technomic Publishing Co., 750 Summer Street, Stamford, Connecticut 06902.

Preliminary Report on U.S. Production and Sales of Plastics and Resin Materials 1969, United States Tariff Commission, Washington, D.C. 20436.

Society of the Plastics Industry (SPI). Founded 1937. 250 Park Avenue, New York, New York 10017. Membership 1,350. Manufacturers and processors of molded, extruded, fabricated, laminated, calendered, and reinforced plastics; manufacturers of raw materials, machinery, tools, dies, and molds; research, development, and testing laboratories. PUBLICATIONS: 1) Proceedings of Conferences; 2) Membership Directory; 3) Accounting Manual; 4) Plastics Engineering Handbook; 5) Safety Handbook; 6) Handbook of Reinforced Plastics; 7) In-plant training booklets.

Plastic Container Manufacturers Institute (PCMI). Box 141, Rumson, New Jersey 07760. Founded 1962. Members, 50. Container manufacturers, raw material suppliers, machinery manufacturers, and others interested in the promotion of plastic bottles and closures.

National Association of Plastic Fabricators (NAPF). 1108 Standard Building, Cleveland, Ohio 44113. Founded 1956. Members 225. Manufacturers of decorative plastic laminate used for counters, furniture, horizontal and vertical surfacing, etc. Distributes information to members on production, sales, and management matters. Publishes periodic bulletins, technical reports, and specifications.

Plastic Products Manufacturers Association (PPMA), 1133 Broadway, New York, New York 10010. Founded 1937. Members, 115. Manufacturers of housewares, toys, handbag accessories and parts, costume jewelry, optical frames, etc.

DRY CLEANING

Section Contents

URBAN BUSINESS PROFILE

Dry Cleaning

(SIC 7216)

I. RECOMMENDATION

A sustained demand for dry cleaning services offers attractive opportunities for new business development in the field. Industry leaders expect that a growing population and rising incomes will enable the dry cleaner to expand his services, his sales levels, and his total profits throughout the coming decade.

The most important factors affecting profitability in the dry cleaning industry, assuming adequate capability in the plant, include the manager's ability to market the services of the establishment to his potential clientele and to train and manage his labor force effectively. Labor expenses can account for about 50 percent of total operating costs, and the manager who can obtain maximum performance from his employees is the one most likely to earn a profit from a given sales level.

Both the introduction of fabrics which require little or no dry cleaning and the establishment of coin-operated dry cleaning machines will affect the potential markets open to the professional dry cleaner in the years ahead. The prevailing opinion about this competition is that it will change the nature of the dry cleaner's work somewhat but will not cause a decline in business. The need for careful cleaning of the better or more prized garments in the wardrobe will certainly not diminish, and the effect of such technological changes is likely to be a focusing of the dry cleaning business on those garments and cleaning activities which return higher margins to the cleaner. A dry cleaning establishment that is well placed in its chosen market area, is marketed with flair and careful attention to the needs of its customers, and is diligently managed by a cost-conscious operator is likely to capitalize on the generally favorable trends in the industry.

II. DESCRIPTION OF THE INDUSTRY

A. Identification

Standard Industry Classification (SIC) 7216 includes businesses primarily engaged in dry cleaning and in the dyeing of apparel and household fabrics. Collecting and distributing units (branch outlets) that are owned and operated by cleaning and dyeing plants are considered part of the businesses owning them and are not treated as separate establishments.

B. Dimensions of the Industry

Dry cleaning industry statistics indicate that the industry is in a period of growth and concentration. Despite a decrease in the number of establishments from 1963 to 1967 (31,722 and 30,625 respectively), the value of total receipts has increased from $1.437 billion to $1.938 billion during the same period. The number of industry employees has similarly increased during the same period from 211,664 to 246,348.

The size distribution of dry cleaning establishments indicates the degree to which small businesses share in the total market. An industry survey conducted in 1966 revealed that the average dry cleaning establishment had an annual sales volume of $48,000 and that approximately 60 percent of all plants have sales volumes of under $50,000 per year.

Annual sales	Number of plants	Percentage of total
Less than $25,000	10,440	29
$25,000 to $50,000	11,160	31
$50,000 to $100,000	7,560	21
$100,000 to $200,000	3,610	10
More than $200,000	3,240	9

Though the averages have risen since that time, industry experts indicate that the composition of the dry cleaning industry has not changed considerably since 1966.

One of the factors explaining the growth in the total receipts of the dry cleaning industry is the diversification by the dry cleaner into other cleaning fields. The dry cleaner has increasingly branched out into the more profitable aspects of the traditional laundry business, and the expansion into such activities as shirt cleaning and laundering is likely to be continued. An important reason for this trend is the increasingly convenience-oriented customers' desire for one-stop cleaning/laundering service. The attraction of new labor-saving machinery and the consequent desire to increase business to support the use of such capital equipment is another trend explaining industry concentration at the higher volume end of the industry.

C. **Characteristics of the Industry**

1. *The Customer*

There are three basic markets for dry cleaning establishments. The first market is the luxury group. This group is more likely to require pickup and delivery service of the dry cleaner, although such service is becoming less and less important. This group will also require more hand processing and care with garments. Because the volume of a business that caters only to the luxury group would be relatively low, such establishments should locate only in large metropolitan areas where the luxury group is of sufficient size to support them.

A second market is the middle income group. The service required here must meet acceptable standards but can be considered as aiming at the mass market. Pickup and delivery service is not a requirement in this market, and a location convenient to a large number of convenience shoppers is important. This is a market most newer businesses aim to serve, and many older plants have had to adjust to it to survive.

The third market is the lower income market. This market is usually served by three kinds of service outlets: chainstore operations with highly efficient central plants and their own small stores; small neighborhood tailor shops with dry cleaning done by a wholesale plant, and "mom and pop" operations. Inevitably, this is a small margin field. Prices must be lower than standard, and profit must come through either high volume and maximum efficiency or a minimal cost structure. A heavy burden is placed on good management in this part of the dry cleaning industry.

2. *Types of Services*

The dry cleaners' recent interest in diversification has led to the offering of more types of service to the customer.

Approximately 70 percent of all dry cleaners now provide shirt service for their own customers. At least 50 percent of these do the work on their own premises, while others farm out the shirt service to a wholesale laundry. The advantages of providing shirt service usually outweigh the disadvantages. The typical dry cleaning customer, for example, is a monthly customer. But with shirt service available, the customer tends to bring in work on a weekly basis, and this usually means more dry cleaning as well. Also, shirt service is dependable in terms of volume, particularly among luxury and middle-income groups who usually use five shirts per week per male in the family.

To add in-house shirt service to a dry cleaning establishment does, of course, add to initial investment costs. Handling a weekly volume of $500 to $600 in shirt work would require additional space (at least 15 by 20 feet), additional equipment (a washer, an extractor, and a shirt finishing unit at a cost of approximately $7,500) and the employment of at least one full-time shirt operator. Low-income environments provide fewer shirt customers and smaller bundles, and are, therefore, not as likely to justify such an investment.

Other services that might be included by the expanding dry cleaner include alterations (paid repairs and reweaving), storage, and shoe repair. These usually involve minimal additional costs (for alterations, for example, the sewing machine is already installed), and may allow for more efficient use of existing assets and clientele.

3. *Pricing Policies*

The pricing policies of any particular dry cleaning establishment will necessarily reflect the market policies of the business. Those cleaning establishments catering to the upper income market normally charge up to 50 percent more than the standard charge for any given piece of work, while those serving the lower income market may reduce charges by as much as 20 percent. Within these broad ranges, the individual dry cleaning establishment will price its work so as to be competitive with others in its general class.

4. *Types of Business Organization*

Legal forms of organization within the dry cleaning industry have shown very little variation over the past 15 years. Approximately 62 percent of all plants operate as individual proprietorships. Of the remaining 38 percent, the number of partnerships has declined slightly to 16 percent, and the number of corporations has risen to almost 22 percent during this period.

Franchises have, however, begun to play an increasingly important role in the dry cleaning trade. These organizations offer the individual some of the advantages of the larger business (layout, equipment selection, advertising and promotion, training and financing) but allow him to retain a degree of independence. Several of the major franchises in the dry cleaning industry are listed on page 13.

5. *Space and Equipment Needs*

An individual expecting to achieve a sales volume of up to $50,000 a year would need a minimum of 800 square feet of space, including a cleaning plant and a possible call office or pickup and delivery store. No more than 10 percent of the total space should be allocated to the call office. The call office usually is located in a different location than the actual dry cleaning plant (this could be the optimal arrangement if the call office is located in a high-rent district). For dry cleaning establishments located on the main arteries that lead to shopping centers, parking space must be provided or available. This space could be for as few as four automobiles, although, on the average, a dry cleaning establishment provides space for six automobiles. If the call office is located in a downtown business area with a market composed mainly of transients and professionals who live and work in the immediate neighborhood, no parking space is required. For dry cleaning establishments located in shopping centers, there is, of course, no problem with parking. No outdoor workspace is required for a dry cleaning establishment.

The following is a list of minimum equipment requirements:

- Boiler
- Air compressor
- Spotting board
- Prespotting tank
- Dry cleaning unit, including integral or separate filter, still, extractor, tumbler, solvent reclaimer, and solvent storage tank
- Utility press
- Ironing board with steam electric iron
- Water spray gun per finisher
- Legger and topper press
- Puff irons
- Steam air forms
- Sewing machine
- Baskets, carts, and tables

Optional but desirable are the following:

- Wet cleaning washer and table
- Small extractor
- Compact dry cabinet
- Conveyor
- Mushroom press
- Silk offset press
- Bagger
- Tag holder
- Efficiency table
- Invoice holder
- Pants stand
- Pants holder

Equipment manufacturers, who may be located either through the local telephone director or through advertisements in trade journals such as Textile Services Management or the American Dry Cleaner, will provide free advice on equipment needs, plant planning, and layout. Two good sources for equipment manufacturers are *Coin-amatic Age Annual Buyers Guide: Purchasing Directory for the Laundry and Dry Cleaning Industry* and *McRae's Blue Book Annual*, an alphabetic directory of manufacturers and their local distributors.

6. *Manpower Requirements*

For establishments with $25,000 or less in annual sales, only two or three full-time workers can usually be supported. For full service establishments with annual sales in the $25,000 to $50,000 range, four or five people are usually required for effective operation.

About one-third of all dry cleaning establishments are unionized. In metropolitan areas, the number is higher and stood at 41 percent in 1967. The following job descriptions are indicative of the various types of employees needed in the dry cleaning trade:

a. *Assembler* (Matcher, Sorter, Assorter, Distributor). Sorts or assembles the various dry cleaned garments and other items of each customer's order; and matches the articles according to description and identifying number as shown by plant records.

b. *Clerk, Retail Receiving.* Receives work from routemen or from customers over the counter in the receiving office of a dry cleaning establishment. Work involves *most of the following:* maintaining a record of articles or bundles received; returning completed work to customers who call for it; collecting payment and maintaining simple records of money received; and, in establishments where dry cleaning is done in-plant, fastening an identifying marker to each article, examining an article for defects such as holes, stains, tears, and making a record of the identification symbol assigned to each article with a brief description of the article and of any defects noted. Store managers are excluded in this description.

c. *Finisher, Flatwork, Machine.* Performs flatwork finishing operations by machine. work involves *one or more of the following:* shaking out the creases in semidry washing to prepare it for the flatwork ironing machine; feeding clean, damp flatwork pieces into the flatwork ironing machine by placing the articles on the feeder rollers; and catching or receiving articles as they emerge from the machine and partially folding them.

d. *Presser, Hand.* Presses dry cleaned or wet cleaned garments with a hand iron, (usually dresses and other articles that cannot be satisfactorily or completely finished on a steam pressing machine) or pleats garments by hand.

e. *Presser, Machine.* Smooths the surfaces of garments, slipcovers, drapes and other shaped-fabric articles with a pressing machine to shape the articles, remove wrinkles, and flatten seams. May operate two presses, loading one while the other is closed.

Average earnings within the industry were $2.32 per hour in 1971, with the average employee receiving a weekly wage of $81.90.

7. *Capital Requirements—1971*

The initial investment for a small establishment with an annual sales volume of $25,000 would be approximately $14,000.

a. Downpayment on fixtures and equipment	— $ 4,000	(total cost of $20,000)
b. Supplies	— $ 1,000	
c. Rent deposit	— $ 1,400	(leased at $350 a month)
d. Utility deposit	— $ 500	
e. Initial promotion	— $ 1,000	
f. Operating capital	— $ 6,000	

8. *Profitability*

Available cost studies indicate that for good managers, the dry cleaning business is very profitable. Studies at the National Institute of Dry Cleaning indicate that net profit averages approximately 8 to 10 percent of sales. However, in recent past years, due, in part, to fluctuating economic conditions, average net profits were 6 to 7 percent.

III. BUSINESS FEASIBILITY

A. Major Factors

1. *Market Location*

Dry cleaning stores must be where the customers are. Like other services, there are three major areas that have proved successful for dry cleaning establishments: in shopping centers, on the right hand side of main arteries that lead to shopping centers, or, in some circumstances, downtown business areas. A general rule of thumb with regard to competition within the market area is to expect one establishment for every 1,500 families.

There are several reasons why a shopping center is a good location for a dry cleaning store:

a. The center will draw customers from a wide area—customers who might otherwise not be reached because of their proximity to other establishments.

b. In a study of consumer attitudes toward dry cleaning establishments conducted by the National Institute of Dry Cleaners, 74 percent of the consumers questioned said that they bring their dry cleaning to the cleaning establishment and pick it up. (These consumers represented a wide range of income levels.) In 62 percent of these families, the wife usually has the pickup and delivery job, and, more often than not, she combines it with other shopping. A shopping center with a supermarket is, therefore, a good location for a dry cleaning establishment. Arteries on the way to shopping centers are also convenient for the same reasons.

Downtown business areas of large cities are generally not good locations. Rents are extremely high, and unless the owner has an advertising gimmick of some sort, the establishment is not likely to be successful. Downtown markets are limited to transients and commuters, but the latter market is also served by lower priced establishments on commuter routes leading to and from residential areas. In small cities of under 100,000 population, where the downtown area is also the major shopping area, such locations are often feasible and profitable.

2. *Marketing and Promotion*

The dry cleaning industry is selling a service, and growth takes place by extending the range of service. This takes a great deal of skill and persuasiveness in advertising techniques, and competition is sometimes severe. The following promotional techniques have proved of value to many dry cleaning establishments:

a. *Newspaper Advertising*—Generally, newspapers reach more prospects than any other medium. Care should be taken to place ads in a newspaper that reaches the most women (women do most family shopping) on days when there are large numbers of supermarket sale ads. If the market to be served is only a segment of a large city, a community newspaper might be better than a large citywide daily.

b. *Direct-Mail Advertising*—If the mailing lists are carefully selected by income levels or geographic sections, direct-mail advertising can be most effective. It can also be lowest in cost because, theoretically, there is no waste circulation.

c. *Cut-Price Specials*—Specials are extremely good ways to attract new customers. But they should be varied and timed for promotional advantage. "Back to School" specials, "Spring Housecleaning" specials, or "Mother's Day" specials have proved particularly useful.

d. *The Yellow Pages*—Advertising in the classified section of the telephone directory is an unbeatable way to reach a prospect precisely when he is ready to buy. Advertisements in the Yellow Pages should be explicit regarding services offered and plant location.

Other useful promotional techniques include extending open hours to early morning and late evening times on weekdays and having radio and television specials. The specific advertising techniques to be used, of course, will depend on the location of the establishment and the market it will serve.

B. The Minority Entrepreneur

A recent study by the National Business League of black entrepreneurship in seven urban areas (Atlanta, Cleveland, Durham, Jackson, Los Angeles, Norfolk, and Richmond) reveals that laundries and dry cleaners account for 38.6 percent of the black public service businesses surveyed in those areas. These data coincide fairly well with national statistics on minority businesses. The location of minority dry cleaning establishments in shopping centers in minority neighborhoods is particularly feasible, although minority owned and operated establishments should not limit themselves to the minority markets. There appear to be no barriers to minority entrepreneurship that are *peculiar* to the dry cleaning trade.

C. Projection of Returns—Two Hypothetical Business Situations

The following hypothetical financial projections for two common sizes of dry cleaning businesses are based on industry averages for successful establishments. Projections for individual stores may vary widely from these.

Annual Operating Statement

Net receipts	$50,000	$100,000
Operating expenses		
Labor:		
Production	16,500	29,000
Sales and distribution	6,000	15,000
Administration	2,500	8,000
Total labor costs	$25,000	$ 52,000
Supplies and materials	4,500	8,500
Equipment maintenance	2,000	4,000
Total operating expenses	$31,500	$ 64,500
Overhead expenses		
Rent and utilities	$ 5,000	$ 8,000
Equipment depreciation	1,500	3,500
Indirect overhead	3,000	8,000
Total overhead	$ 9,500	$ 19,500
Total expenses	$41,000	$ 84,000
Net profit before tax, including owner's or manager's compensation	$ 9,000	$ 16,000

IV. ESTABLISHING THE NEW BUSINESS

A. Approaching the Market

The first step in starting a new dry cleaning business is to determine the market which the store is intended to serve. The prospective entrepreneur must identify the general type of consumer he proposes to cater to. For example, he may wish to cater to lower income inner-city residents or to the residents of a suburban fringe area with a particular income and ethnic character.

Whatever the decision, it will affect the location of the new store, how large it will be, and the services it will provide. In lower income areas, for example, a wide range of services is not needed, prices must be lower than standard, and profit must come through large volume and maximum efficiency.

The general procedure to be followed in selecting a store location begins with the identification of several potential locations where space is known to be available, the computation of the number of potential customers within the area of each location, and the determination of the amount of monthly expenditures each customer will make on dry cleaning. An analysis of competition in each area (by checking price structures, quality of service, packaging, types of advertising, etc.) will also suggest where underserved markets exist.

B. Securing Capital

A number of cities have organizations which specialize in assisting minority entrepreneurs to secure capital. A prospective entrepreneur should seek out these sources and go over his plans with them.

The local Small Business Administration (SBA) office or Office of Minority Business Enterprise (OMBE) affiliate may help put the prospective entrepreneur in touch with sources of capital and provide the names of banks which have made loans to minority individuals. Minority-owned banks may also be sources of debt financing.

The Small Business Administration can also help with a lease guarantee. Many landlords are unwilling to lease to a new and inexperienced businessman because they have no recourse in the event the business fails. The SBA has a program to reassure such landlords by insuring the lease of the small businessman.

C. Starting Operations

There are many legal details which must be attended to prior to starting a business. The prospective entrepreneur must get a license or permit to do business and will probably need to have a boiler permit as well. Some States (California, as an example) require that the cleaner, spotter, and finisher be certified as qualified technicians. The entrepreneur must investigate these and other requirements before starting operations.

Insurance is also a major factor to be considered. Basic insurance needs include fire, theft, and vandalism coverage. Because the dry cleaner is responsible for customers' costly garments while they are entrusted to his care, bailee insurance is a requirement. Also, since customers, salesmen, and visitors enter the store, public liability protection is important.

If the plant employees are inexperienced, careful time and attention should be paid to their training. If the entrepreneur himself has neither the time nor the ability to give this training, outside help should be secured. It is essential that all employees be adequately trained and productive.

BIBLIOGRAPHY

I. GOVERNMENT SOURCES

Small Business Administration, Washington, D.C. 20416. *Starting and Managing a Small Dry Cleaning Business*, 1966.

U.S. Department of Commerce, Bureau of the Census, Washington, D.C. 20233. *1967 Census of Business, Selected Services;* Series BC67-SA1.

U.S. Department of Commerce, Business and Defense Services Administration, Washington, D.C. 20230. *U.S. Industrial Outlook*, 1970.

U.S. Department of Commerce, Business and Defense Services Administration, Washington, D.C. 20230. *U.S. Industrial Outlook*, 1969.

U.S. Department of Commerce, Business and Defense Services Administration, Washington, D.C. 20230. *Marketing Information Guide*, 1970.

U.S. Department of Commerce, Business and Defense Services Administration, Washington, D.C. 20230. *Marketing Information Guide*, 1969.

U.S. Department of Commerce, Business and Defense Services Administration, Washington, D.C. 20230. *The Laundry and Dry Cleaning Industry*, 1964.

U.S. Department of Labor, Bureau of Labor Statistics, Washington, D.C. 20210. *Industry Wage Survey: Laundry and Cleaning Services*. April 1968 and April 1969.

II. NONGOVERNMENT SOURCES

Flourney Coles. *An Analysis of Black Entrepreneurship in Seven Urban Areas*. Washington, D.C., 1969.

Martin, Albert R., and Fulton, George P. *Dry Cleaning Technology and Theory*. New York, 1958.

"Turning a Big Shopping Center Plant Around." Textile Services Management, May 1969.

"Marketing Challenge: Conquering the New Downtown." Textile Services Management, September 1969.

"Market Research: You can do it." Textile Services Management, January 1970.

"Management's Methods Today." Textile Services Management, January 1970.

"Rebuild that Old-Time Professional Image." Textile Services Management, January 1970.

TRADE ASSOCIATIONS

Bureau of Laundry and Dry Cleaning Standards
914 20th Street, N.W., Washington, D.C. 20006

National Institute of Dry Cleaning
909 Burlington Avenue, Silver Spring, Md. 20910

REPRESENTATIVE DRY CLEANING FRANCHISES

Norgetown
Fednor Corporation
1200 Greenleaf Avenue
Elk Grove Village, Illinois 60007

One Hour Valet
1844 West Flagler Street
Miami, Florida 33135

One Hour Martinizing
20005 Ross Avenue
Cincinnati, Ohio 45212

Arnold Palmer Cleaning
5050 Section Avenue
Cincinnati, Ohio 45212

FURNITURE STORES

Section Contents

URBAN BUSINESS PROFILE

Furniture Stores

(SIC 5712)

I. RECOMMENDATION

Sustained market demand in the furniture industry offers attractive opportunities for new business development in the furniture retail field. With rising incomes, increasing population, and new housing predicted for the 1970's, furniture store sales are expected to rise throughout the decade.

Key determinants of profitability in the business include the ability to select styles and lines which appeal to customers, ample floor space to display merchandise, adequate storage for inventory, a good sales force, and access to a line of credit with which to finance purchases on relatively favorable terms. Managers must also give close attention to control of key elements of cost, such as inventory, advertising, wages and rent. Undercapitalization and shrinkage of working capital are major causes of failure.

There are many sources of information and help in furniture retailing. Organizations such as the National Home Furnishings Association provide members with assistance in store layout, advertising, sales training, and cost control. There are also many professional buying organizations which can help in the selection of proper merchandise. Thus, an individual who has a flare for retailing, management skills, and a fundamental knowledge of interior decoration should be able to establish and operate a furniture store successfully, provided he has picked his location carefully and is properly financed.

II. DESCRIPTION

A. Identification

Furniture stores Standard Industrial Classification (SIC) 5712 are described as establishments primarily engaged in the retail sale of household furniture. Many such stores also sell floor coverings, major appliances, and such home furnishings as lamps, draperies, decorative art objects, and mirrors. Types of furniture sold include upholstered furniture such as chairs and sofas, wood pieces, bedding, dining room pieces, dinettes, children's furniture, and the like.

B. Dimensions

There are presently about 27,000 furniture stores in the United States and, in addition, a great number of department and discount stores which handle furniture as part of their product line. The industry is a major factor in the economy, with 1967 retail sales amounting to about $6.5 billion and a 1967 payroll of $231 million for the 180,000 furniture retail employees.

Industry sales are expected to rise to $9 billion by 1975, reflecting growing income, increasing use of credit (making possible the financing of additional furniture purchases), and construction of new housing. The family formations which will occur as the members of the baby boom of the early 1950's reach adulthood are expected to bolster furniture demand for much of the decade.

The furniture retail industry is still characterized primarily by the small retailer. About three out of every four stores had fewer than eight employees in 1967, and 94 percent of the stores had fewer than 20 employees. The predominance of the small store is also reflected in sales figures; one out of every five stores does more than $100,000 of business annually and only one out of 20 stores has sales exceeding $500,000 per year.

The trend in the industry, nevertheless, is towards larger stores. Especially in urban areas with adequate markets, furniture stores are expanding product lines so as to better service the total furniture needs of the more affluent customers. This trend can be inferred from the fact that, though the total number of stores has not changed significantly in recent years, the total number of employees has grown considerably.

C. Characteristics

1. The Product and the Customer

A complete furniture store will display and sell living room furniture, including sofas, chairs, recliners, convertibles, credenzas and tables; bedroom furniture, including beds, mattresses, and springs, dressers, and night tables; dining room furniture, including tables, chairs, buffets, and serving tables; dinettes, floor coverings, children's furniture, major appliances, decorative art objects, mirrors, clocks, porch and outdoor furniture, odd chairs, hassocks, desks, card tables, bars, and lamps.

A furniture store sells a way of living and life style to its customers. Most homemakers have great aspirations for fixing up their homes to their hearts' desires. Their homes are not only to be used, but to be displayed. Women take pride in their homes and like to show them to others. To many families, a home symbolizes success and "the good life."

The homemaker usually has plans for a change or for improvement. Items to be purchased are seldom bought on impulse, but are thought about carefully and discussed in the home and with friends. Almost two-thirds of all purchases are made to replace items already owned. Convenience in shopping is a relatively minor factor. Families will make a furniture purchase in the store where they feel they will get the most value in appearance and style for the amount of money they have available.

Most purchases of furniture involve a relatively large commitment of the family funds, and two-thirds of all purchases are made by a husband and wife buying together. Credit is generally involved in the purchase. Many stores finance credit sales themselves and make an additional profit thereby. Others "sell" a portion of their installment "paper" to financial institutions.

The salesman is important to the furniture buyer. She asks his advice on color, texture, groupings. She is often unsure of how a particular piece will fit into her grouping, and she will seek confidence from the salesman that her choice is a good one. A furniture retailer who has sold customers quality merchandise in the past can often depend on his customers returning, particularly if the relationship is maintained on a satisfactory basis while the installment payments are being made.

Almost half of all families in the United States earning over $4,000 annually will make at least one purchase of an item of furniture (including mattresses/bedsprings and floor coverings) a year. About one out of every 10 customers is under 25 years of age, and about 15 percent of the customers are over 55. Well over half of the customers are in the prime 25 to 44 year age bracket. Forty percent of the customers will own their own homes. Eighty-six percent of the purchases will be for homes and the balance for apartment units, although with the rising number of apartment units being built, this ratio should change in the coming years. It should also be kept in mind that these percentages are on a national basis and could be expected to vary in specific areas.

Most customers learn about a store from discussions with family and friends, window shopping, or advertising. Many get specific ideas from furniture ads in magazines, from magazine articles, or from seeing furnishings in other homes.

Most customers do not buy by brand name, and many are unable to quote a brand name. The main reasons for selecting a particular store are store reputation, price, and assortment. Store reputation counts most heavily among shoppers in specialized furniture stores, while price is a more important factor among chain department store shoppers. The average sale in the furniture industry is about $160.

2. *Operations*

The successful furniture retailer should have these attributes:

a. *Taste and Skill in Selecting and Displaying Merchandise.* The ultimate determinant of whether or not a sale is made is whether the customer is attracted to the product. The owner/manager must see to it that his merchandise will appeal to his market and that it is displayed in a way which will induce his customers to want the merchandise for their homes.

b. *Good Salesmanship.* Retailing is basically selling. An order-taker will not do for a furniture store. The salesman must know his merchandise and how to sell.

c. *Ability To Learn and Keep Abreast of Changes.* The successful furniture retailer must be willing and able to learn from published material on the industry and successful practices in retailing, and he must be sensitive to changes in style and taste.

d. *Hard Work and Attention to Detail.* There are many things which can go wrong in retailing. Deliveries aren't made on time. Credit accounts are not handled properly. Merchandise is damaged. Inventory is shrinking without explanation. Displays need to be changed. Overstock needs to be reduced. Advertising decisions are required. Special promotions are needed. The owner of a retail store must be alert to all these matters. He must watch his cost ratios. He must pay his bills and collect his outstanding accounts. He will have to work long hours and at least 6 days a week.

e. *Ability To Understand and Make Decisions on the Basis of Figures.* A successful merchant must be sensitive to his books and accounts so that he can determine the actions which make money for him and those which are losing propositions. Basically, these decisions can be made on the basis of an analysis of his sales and costs. But the individual who does not easily understand accounts and numbers may find it difficult to understand what is happening to his business.

A good sales force is essential to successful operation of a furniture store. This requires continuous training. A good salesman will like to work with customers and will be appropriately patient while the homemaker ponders her decision. The salesman must know his products thoroughly; he must know the essentials of interior decoration, such as color, texture, form, arrangements, and space requirements; and he must know how to communicate this knowledge to the customer in a helpful and constructive manner which leads to a sale.

There are different arrangements for compensation. Some stores have a commission arrangement for salesmen; others have a straight salary; and others have a combination. Salaries vary considerably from place to place and depend a good deal upon the experience of the salesman. Thus an inexperienced salesperson in a relatively low-wage area might receive $80 to $90 per week, while a topflight experienced salesperson with interior decorating skills in a higher wage area might receive as much as $12,000 to $14,000 annually.

3. *Competition*

Furniture stores not only compete among themselves, but they also compete with appliance stores, stores specializing in floor coverings, department stores, chain department stores, discount chains, and specialty stores selling homefurnishings of various kinds.

Within inner cities, there is also competition from stores offering purported bargains at inflated prices and high credit rates. These stores may advertise special bargains as an inducement to bring shoppers into the store, but the salesman is generally skillful at steering the shoppers away from the so-called bargain. In many instances, stores of this type sell and resell repossessed merchandise, making their profit on a continuing series of downpayments. Fortunately, this type of operation is gradually being phased out with the increasing knowledge of the inner-city consumer and more stringent controls by authorities.

Highly effective and ethical price competition will be faced from the large chain department stores and mail-order houses. These establishments generally feature relatively high quality merchandise at economy prices. In recent years, they have improved their styling, as well. The furniture retailer must compete with these stores, as he would with department stores and with other furniture retailers, by offering value, style, and efficient service. Maintaining contact with present customers is important, and effective advertising can also be useful in bringing potential customers into a store.

The amount and variety of merchandise displayed by a furniture retailer is important in meeting competition. The opportunity to see a wide variety of furnishings will bring the shopper into the store, and the more choices that can be seen, the greater the possibility that the shopper will find something she likes. Thus, there is a trend toward greater and greater floor space on the part of the independent furniture retailer.

4. *Ease of Entry*

The individual who has the attributes and skills for success in furniture retailing must nevertheless find the right location and sufficient capital before he can enter the industry.

The right location is a place that will provide the retailer with ample floorspace at a reasonable price in a market which is growing and not overly saturated with competition. The location must also provide parking space if it is in a suburban area. If it is in the inner city, it must be reasonably accessible to the potential market. Before selecting a location, a careful market survey should be made to determine if there is sufficient business to justify the selection.

A new entrant, who is properly capitalized and who knows his business, should not be frightened away from establishing a furniture store simply because there is considerable competition already in the area. Unless he is prepared to hold his own in competition with other retailers and the chains, he should not enter the business. Even if competition is relatively scarce at a particular time, he can always expect newcomers or branch outlets of existing firms.

A major factor affecting ease of entry will be the ability to secure sufficient capital for inventory and to finance credit purchases.

5. *Capital Requirements*

Capital requirements are usually considerable for a furniture retailer. Capital is required for store inventory and supplies, warehouse backup inventory, fixtures and equipment, decorating and carpeting, and installment accounts. Inventory and leasehold improvements for the average independent full-stock furniture store require an investment of about $5 a square foot, or $50,000 for a 10,000-square-foot store doing an annual volume of about $250,000. A store doing this amount of business would need about $100,000 to $150,000 to finance installment sales, of which perhaps 20 percent would be required as an investment by the store itself, with the balance of the debt sold to a financing institution. This would require a total investment in the neighborhood of $75,000 for a store doing $250,000 worth of business annually.

There is very little trade credit available for this type of investment. Most suppliers require 30- to 60-day payment or faster, particularly for a new entrant in a field where failures are frequent. Some bank financing may be available, although the bank would require additional security, probably in the form of personal guarantees and assignment of personal property and/or a Small Business Administration guarantee.

6. *Profitability*

In 1966, at the height of an expansionary period, retail furniture stores ranked fourth in rate of failure among 23 types of retail establishments studied by Dun & Bradstreet. However, for those establishments which do succeed, profitability is generally good. In 1969, a relatively average year, profits before taxes averaged about 5 to 6 percent of sales for all sizes of stores.

Gross margin within the industry on sales runs to about 40 percent, with many firms earning an additional 4 to 6 percent on credit operations. However, those firms which sell their installment paper do not earn this extra amount.

7. *Dependence on Outside Factors*

Besides replacement sales and increases in consumer income, the retail furniture business is dependent upon growth in population, new family formations, and new housing. The long term trends in all these factors are up.

This business is affected by seasonality. Summer is generally slack as are the months of January and February. Most business is accounted for in the last 4 months of the year. Therefore, seasonal factors must be accounted for in normal planning.

Business cycles also affect furniture sales, but these cyclical factors are not as easily planned for. Home furnishing purchases are postponed when people are earning less and boom when pent-up demand is released. Thus it would be wise to postpone new entry into the industry at a time when consumers are worried and holding back on expenditures which can be postponed. Experienced store owners generally try to improve their financial strength during prosperous times in order to withstand recessionary periods.

III. FEASIBILITY ANALYSIS

A. Key Factors

The following are the principal factors which affect performance in retail furniture stores:

1. Management

Management must be alert to customer satisfaction and taste and must take care of all the details of a successful retailing operation, including sales training, credit management, advertising, stock control, display, control of pilferage, cost control, and so on.

2. Capital

Adequate capital is essential for investment in floor displays and ability to offer installment credit.

3. Market Location

The proposed establishment should be situated to serve a growing market, preferably one where consumer disposable income is growing and where new housing is being constructed. While specific location within such a market is not crucial, the store should be situated where it is convenient to and easily noticed by consumers.

4. Floorspace

The volume of business that can be done is closely related to the amount of floorspace available. Newer establishments try to operate from a single floor, but multifloor stores can be successful. A variety of tasteful displays will attract potential customers to the store and provide increased opportunities for salesmen to be successful.

5. Salesmanship

All aspects of salesmanship are important. This includes the possession of a well-trained, capable sales staff, the use of good advertising, and the preparation of good displays.

6. Customer Relations

Established customers are a source of repeat business, and installment payments provide a way to maintain relationships with these customers. Customers must have confidence in the store's integrity. The store must keep up to date on customers' style preferences.

7. Credit

The store must provide for installment credit for purchasers.

B. Problems and Potentials for Minority Ventures

1. Problems

New ventures into retail furniture are apt to run into problems from unethical competitors, legitimate price competition from the large department chains and discount houses, inadequate capital, and unsuitable locations.

Unethical competition can come from the unscrupulous ghetto retailer who preys on unsuspecting customers with overpriced shoddy merchandise, "bait" advertising, and quick repossessions. Fast-talking salesmen and apparent "easy credit" often dupe unsuspecting consumers into unwise purchases.

To the extent that a minority furniture retailer will be looking to the minority community for his prime market, he will be faced with serious competition from the department store chains and discount houses. Minority community shoppers usually have lower than average disposable incomes and are less able to afford more expensive furniture lines. Thus, they have a greater tendency to purchase the economical, budget-priced furniture of the department chains and discount stores.

Minority entrepreneurs have traditionally experienced difficulty securing adequate capital for their ventures, and without adequate financial resources, entry into the retail furniture business should be dismissed as a possibility for a minority entrepreneur. The average time it takes to receive goods from a supplier is 6 to 12 weeks. If a dealer has only a small credit line, his order will not be processed until the line is paid off or brought down to his credit limits. Small dealers without adequate capital are often forced to buy from suppliers whose furniture lines do not provide as much value as those who are more successful and more stringent on credit.

An undercapitalized furniture retailer will not be able to stock sufficient inventory to attract the more affluent customer. He will not be able to deliver merchandise to customers as rapidly as some of his competitors and will lose many sales for this reason. He will have difficulty securing financing for his installment sales, and he will lose customers to more securely financed operations. His equipment and fixtures will deteriorate more readily and detract from the overall appearance of his store. He may not be able to advertise competitively.

The entrepreneur who seeks to serve the inner-city minority market may find it difficult to secure adequate space in a suitable location. Many downtown shopping areas have become seedy and do not provide an appropriate atmosphere for the purchase of home furnishings. Moreover, problems of fire insurance and crime are magnified in a downtown location.

For all these reasons, minority entrepreneurs have not made a significant penetration into the retail furniture industry. In an industry which has over 27,000 establishments, there are less than 100 which are owned by minority entrepreneurs or less than one-half of 1 percent. Only one black-owned furniture store does an annual gross of over $1 million and most do under $200,000 of business annually.

2. Potentials

There is an awakening self-consciousness among minority consumers that could lead to consumer preference toward minority entrepreneurs. Thus, a furniture store offering good value and located within a minority community might be preferred by many minority homemakers over a chain department store, or a large suburban-oriented independent furniture retailer.

Recent improvements in financial packages available for minority entrepreneurs may also improve the potential for a minority business. Various civic groups have been organized in many cities to help minority entrepreneurs, and these may be able to assist the potential new businessman by helping him to do his advance planning and to secure necessary lines of credit. Special sources of capital and business planning assistance are available to businesses in many cities, and these may help an entrepreneur overcome the handicaps of inadequate capitalization. New minority-owned banks are becoming more capable of financing consumer installments and providing lines of credit for retailers.

C. Projections

The following figures represent financial projections which are typical for many furniture retailers. Individual stores may vary widely from these percentages, and each individual situation should be studied carefully on the basis of its own conditions. Two potential situations are projected: one, a smaller store with a volume approximating $200,000 annually; and the other, a moderate-sized store with a volume of about $600,000.

	Situation 1		Situation 2	
	Amount	Percent	Amount	Percent
Gross sales	$208,000	104	$636,000	106
Returns and allowances	8,000	4	36,000	6
Annual volume	200,000	100	600,000	100
Cost of merchandise	120,000	60	348,000	58
Gross margin	80,000	40	252,000	42
Income from credit operations	6,000	3	24,000	4
Operating expenses (total)	70,000	35	240,000	40
Net profit from operations	16,000	8	36,000	6
Deductions from income (interest, bad debts, etc.)	6,000	3	12,000	2
Net profit before taxes	10,000	5	24,000	4
Typical investment	75,000		200,000	
Return on investment		13.3		12

Profits and return on investment from furniture stores vary much more among stores within a certain size range than they do among the averages of different size ranges. This suggests that size, itself, is not a dominant factor in profitability. Other factors such as management, reputation, and location are much more important.

The following are some key indicators for the two sizes of stores:

	Situation 1	Situation 2
Installment sales as a percentage of total sales	84%	80%
Installment accounts receivable as a percentage of installment sales	63%	58%
Bad debts charged off on installment accounts as a percentage of installment sales	1%	1%
Amount of average sale	$140	$180
Dollar sales per square foot of selling space	$ 28	$ 32
Sales per employee	$34,000	$35,000
Sales per salesman	$100,000	$128,000
Sales per handling and delivery employee	$105,000	$107,000
Ratio of assets to liabilities	2.6X	3.0X
Net sales per $ of net worth	$ 1.90	$ 2.00

IV. ESTABLISHING THE NEW BUSINESS

A. Establishing the Market

The first step in starting a new furniture store is to determine the market which the store is intended to serve. The prospective entrepreneur must identify the general type of consumer he proposes to cater to. For example, he may wish to locate in the inner city and make his appeal largely to inner-city minority residents; or he may wish to take a location which is on the fringes so that he can cater not only to the inner-city population, but to some suburban population or inner-city residents moving to the fringes of the city. He may wish to cater to young marrieds starting out in small apartments or he may desire to sell more to established homemakers and residents of single family homes.

Whatever the decision, it will affect where the new store is to be located, how large it should be, what its total market is, and what kind of furniture lines it should carry from the standpoint of both styles and price. For example, young marrieds may want the more modern styles with vivid colors and economical prices; more mature families may prefer Early American and may be willing to pay higher prices for more substantial furniture.

When the character of the market is determined, the entrepreneur should determine its potential size. There are various local statistics available which can be used to clarify how many people with certain characteristics live within shopping range of various potential locations, how much they spend annually on furniture, how their incomes are changing, and the like. Market data may be available from local chambers of commerce, planning commissions, or councils of government. The feasibility of a new store may be glimpsed in the following way. Visit the furniture stores in the same shopping area, as well as the department stores. Determine what types of customers they try to serve. Make a list of each one and estimate how much floorspace each has. Using estimates of sales per square foot, either locally used or industrywide (about $30 of sales per square foot), estimates can be made of total sales volume for each competitor. These can be compared to the estimated total furniture purchases for the market, providing insights into the volume which might be achievable in the store being planned. For example, if the estimated sales volume of all stores based upon square footage is considerably more than the total estimated purchases in the market area, it is likely that the market is oversaturated with furniture stores.

The general procedure to be followed in selecting a store location begins with the identification of several potential locations where space is known to be available, the computation of the number of potential customers within the shopping area of each location, and the determination of the amount of annual expenditures on furniture that each will make. An analysis of competition in each area will suggest where underserved markets exist.

B. Determining Size of Operation

The size of the proposed business will be determined by the size of the market, the amount of competition which can be expected, the available capital resources, and the amount of experience of the proposed management. These should be carefully weighed against each other. For instance, even though a large market is anticipated, the proposed store should not be larger than the capital resources which the individual has available to support it. Moreover, if the proposed entrepreneur is somewhat inexperienced, he may be wiser to make his mistakes learning the business in a smaller operation that is more securely financed, than in a larger operation in a precarious financial position.

C. Getting All the Facts

The prospective new entrepreneur should collect all necessary information supporting his business plan prior to his presentation to potential sources of capital. Here are some of the items which should be contained in this analysis:

- Address of proposed location or possible locations
- Landlord's name
- Total building area
- Amount of sales space on each floor
- Amount of office space
- Amount of warehouse space needed
- Parking spaces
- Term of lease required and options to renew
- Annual rent
  - Minimum
  - Percentage of sales
- Amount of rent in advance
- Estimated sales
  - First year
  - Third year
- Cost of occupancy—first year and third year
  - Annual minimum rent
  - Other costs of insurance, taxes, maintenance payable by tenant
  - Other costs of occupancy—water, heat, power, etc.
  - Total occupancy costs
  - Percentage of sales
- Investment required
  - Store inventory and supplies
  - Warehouse inventory
  - Fixtures and equipment
  - Decorating and carpeting
  - Installment accounts less amount to be financed
  - Other receivables
- Operating data
  - Estimated sales
  - Credit service charges
  - Gross profit
  - Selling payroll
  - Other payroll
  - Fringe benefits
  - Store occupancy costs
  - Advertising
  - Delivery expense
  - Warehouse costs
  - Accounting, credit, and administrative costs
  - Operating profit
  - Interest costs
  - Net profit
  - Return on investment (percentage of profit to investment)

D. Securing Capital

A number of cities have organizations which specialize in assisting minority entrepreneurs to secure capital. A prospective entrepreneur should seek out these sources and go over his plans with them.

The local Small Business Administration office or OMBE affiliate may help to put the prospective entrepreneur in touch with sources of capital and to provide the names of banks which have made minority loans. Minority-owned banks may also provide capital.

The Small Business Administration can also be helpful with a lease guarantee. Many landlords are unwilling to lease to an inexperienced and new businessman, because they have no recourse in the event the business fails. The SBA has a program to reassure such landlords by insuring the lease of the small businessman.

E. Starting Operations

The new businessman should seek experienced help in completing negotiations with the landlord. There are a number of variables to the standard lease which many real estate organizations are willing to grant but which are not offered if the tenant does not ask for them. An experienced businessman or lease negotiator can be useful during these negotiations. Help should be requested from a local organization specializing in assisting minority entrepreneurs.

Unless the prospective entrepreneur is very experienced in the trade, he should investigate affiliation with an established buying office. Such an office is worth its cost in advising the businessman on lines to carry and in taking the time to visit the various furniture markets to be on the lookout for good buys. A buying office cannot substitute for the businessman's own knowledge of his customers and their taste, but it can be a valuable and profitable supplementary service, particularly to the small furniture retailer who cannot take the time and expense to visit all the markets.

Every effort should be made to have attractive displays of furniture ready for the opening. There are many articles and books on display and layout, and these should be studied carefully and the recommendations should be adapted to the particular store. It is more important to spend original capital on display inventory, fixtures, and proper displays than on warehouse inventory. In most cases, customers are willing to wait several weeks for merchandise, and shipments from the factory can generally be secured in ample time. Warehouse inventory should be used for special purchases and fast sellers.

If the sales force is inexperienced, careful time and attention should be paid to their training. If the entrepreneur himself has neither the time nor the ability to give this training, outside help should be secured. It is essential that the sales staff be first rate.

The businessman should spend considerable time and money planning for the opening. Special values should be featured. Even special gifts or prizes should be purchased and given to persons coming into the store during the opening days. Advertising which is appropriate to the size of the store and the investment available should be prepared and used. Advertising is extremely important in bringing customers to the store.

V. SUMMARY

Although it is a difficult business, demanding long hours and constant supervision, furniture retailing does offer the individual with an interest in furniture and a talent for selling an opportunity to enter a business which has growth and profit potential. Moreover, to the extent that minority homemakers can be persuaded to give shopping preference to stores which are owned by members of the same minority and located in the same community, such stores would have a competitive advantage to offset traditional disadvantages associated with inadequate capital resources and limited experience in business management.

In summary, sound management, a trained sales force, and adequate financial resources are keys to success in furniture retailing.

APPENDIX

BIBLIOGRAPHY

References

A HOME FURNISHINGS CONSUMER STUDY AMONG BUYERS AND INTENDING BUYERS. A research report prepared for the Home Furnishings Marketing and Research Council, Inc., National Family Opinion, Inc., July 1967.

THE HOMEMAKER AND HOME FURNISHINGS. A research report prepared for the Home Furnishings Marketing and Research Council, Inc., Social Research, Inc., July 1967.

THE IMPACT OF INDUSTRY ACTIVITIES ON CONSUMER PURCHASING OF HOME FURNISHINGS. A research report prepared for the Home Furnishings Marketing and Research Council, Inc., Arthur D. Little, Inc., July 1967.

HOW TO PLAN THE "IDEAL" HOME FURNISHINGS STORE. A reprint from *NRFA Reports to the Home Furnishings Industry,* June 1968.

STORE EXPANSION: KEY TO PROFIT GROWTH. A reprint from *NRFA Reports to the Home Furnishings Industry,* January 1968.

THE HOME FURNISHINGS INDUSTRY: TRENDS TO 1975. Stanford Research Institute, July 1965.

Government Publications

FURNITURE RETAILING, Small Business Bibliography No. 48, Small Business Administration, Washington, D.C. 20416, April 1967, 8 pp., free.

SELECTED INDUSTRY PROFILES, PART V, FURNITURE STORES, prepared for the Small Business Administration by Business and Defense Services Administration, U.S. Department of Commerce Washington, D.C. 20230, April 1969.

Note: Small Business Bibliography No. 48, referred to above, contains a list of additional bibliographies of government and nongovernment publications which would be of use to a prospective furniture retailer. A list of trade journals and trade associations is also furnished.

TRADE ASSOCIATION

The principal trade association for the retail furniture owner is the National Home Furnishings Association (NHFA) (formerly the National Retail Furniture Association), 1150 Merchandise Mart, Chicago, Illinois 60654. The NHFA provides detailed confidential services to members on trends in the industry, promotion and advertising, store planning, operating experiences, and other special subjects of interest to the retailer.

The association offers management services, including an inventory control system, a recruitment and selection service, successful techniques for selling, and successful operating techniques. The association also holds continuing sales education and management workshops, represents the industry in Washington, and offers members low-cost group life insurance.

INDUSTRIAL LAUNDERERS AND LINEN SUPPLY

Section Contents

URBAN BUSINESS PROFILE

Industrial Launderers and Linen Supply

(SIC 7218 and 7213)

I. RECOMMENDATION

The industrial launderers and linen supply industries are both growing sectors of the U.S. service industry. Since the technology and markets are basically similar, these industries are often combined in one business. A new business can be started at any level of capitalization between about $20,000 and $200,000. The technology is simple, and the skills needed are primarily related to managerial capacity.

The ability to "sell" is an important one. The industries are highly competitive, and selling is vital. The enterpreneur must have the confidence to respond to closed bid competition, the main method by which clients select a laundry or linen supply firm. This confidence will come from experience, good management, and cost control. The industries have had a fairly high failure rate, due largely to poor cost accounting which results in the submission of bids on which the firm can only make a loss (for a contract period as long as 2 to 3 years).

Since the labor productivity has traditionally been low in the industries, and labor costs often represent 50 to 75 percent of total costs, the ability to manage labor is also important. Indeed, every effort must be made to accumulate capital quickly so that the expensive labor saving machinery available can be used.

There is a critical size in the growth of firms in these industries of about $500,000 to $1 million annual revenue, at which labor productivity is often too low to compete with larger firms, while overheads are so much higher than those of small firms that underbidding is frequent. The small entrepreneur should be able to outbid all but the cheapest of the larger companies—but only if he is capable of controlling his overhead costs carefully, while being constantly aware of the need to increase labor productivity at a rate faster than the growth of his total revenues.

This is a critical management problem, and it requires considerable managerial aptitude. With this aptitude the entrepreneur can succeed; without it he will probably fail very quickly as his firm begins to grow beyond a small-size operation.

II. DESCRIPTION OF THE INDUSTRIES

A. Definition

This report treats two industries in parallel. They are:

SIC 7218 Industrial launderers providing cleaning and reconditioning service for uniforms, towels, safety equipment, work clothes, dust control items. Items are owned either by company or customer, and establishments may or may not operate their own laundries.

SIC 7213 Linen supply (or services) supplying uniforms, gowns, bed and table linens (on a rental basis) to commercial and service establishments may or may not operate their own laundry.

B. Dimensions of the Industries

1. *General*

Both of these industries are part of the Nation's $600 billion "services" sector, and because of this orientation, are growing fast. There are, of course, many features contributing to the growth and to the differences in the growth rates of the two industries.

TABLE 1

Growth of Output and Establishments

	Linen supply			Industrial launderers		
	Number of establishments	$ Millions	Output Percent of growth	Number of establishments	$ Millions	Output Percent of growth
1958		433				
1959		463	6.9			
1960		491	6.0			
1961		498	1.4			
1962		540	8.4			
1963	1,469	571	5.9	768	272	10% average annual growth (1963–1967)
1964		611	7.0			
1965		664	8.6			
1966		734	10.6			
1967	1,435	804	9.5	918	408	
1968		885	10.1			

The Standard Industrial Classification (SIC) definitions suggest more of a distinction between the two industries than actually exists; the industries are in most respects very similar. Almost all industrial laundries (IL) do some "flat work" (sheets, tablecloths) and many linen supply establishments (LS) supply industrial-type goods such as mats and dust mops. Both industries devote much of their output to garment supply, but it is within this latter activity that they are somewhat distinct.

Both industries are fairly small. Linen supply has an output now of about $970 million per year, and industrial laundries about $700 million, while in terms of numbers of establishments, 1,435 were classified as linen supply and 918 as industrial launderers in 1967.

2. *Size Distribution*

Size distribution is important since it indicates the degree to which small businesses share in the market. Both industries have many small companies with low revenues and few employees serving a small segment of the market. At the other extreme there are a few large companies with fairly large revenues occupying an increasingly large part of the market as they grow by amalgamation and through the purchase of smaller companies. Data presented in Table 2 reveal the preponderance of small reporting units in the industries in both 1965 and 1970, with possible indication of increasing size in the latter year. Nevertheless, the heavy concentration of facilities in the lower employment group categories (46 percent of total employment in 1970 was in reporting units employing less than 20 employees) indicates continuing opportunities for small businessmen.

TABLE 2

Distribution of Reporting Units With Employees, by Employment Size (1965, 1970)

Employment size	Number [1] 1965	Number [1] 1970	Linen supply [2]	Industrial launderers [3]
1–7	693	530	374	156
8–19	371	445	322	123
20–49	442	475	324	151
50–99	339	348	213	135
100–249	220	262	188	74
250–499	36	44	31	13
500 and more	3	4	4	—
Total	2,104	2,108	1,456	652

[1] Reporting units—linen supply and industrial launderers combined
[2] Reporting units—linen supply, 1970
[3] Reporting units—industrial launderers, 1970

Bureau of the Census, County Business Patterns, 1965 and 1970.

3. *Location*

Firm location is a function of population and population density, and all major metropolitan areas have industrial launderers and linen service representatives. National chains try to place at least one establishment in each metropolitan area. Exceptions to this occur where there is a component of demand greater than the population would seem to indicate. Hospital centers, State capitals, university towns, and cities near large military establishments are particularly attractive locations to the industry.

C. **The Market**

1. *General*

An idea of the general orientation of the market is available in Table 3, estimated from the 1963 market structure. In an industrial laundry, over 60 percent of the business comes from renting garments owned by the industrial laundry itself. Only 5 percent of business is done with articles owned by the client. Other categories of the market are wiping cloth rental (12 percent) and dust control rentals (8 percent). In the linen supply industry 80 percent of total revenues are derived from renting to businesses, but most of this is in "flatwork" (sheets, towels, tablecloths) rental which is the linen service's main business. However, 28 percent is now garment rental to businesses—a growing proportion, up from perhaps 20 percent in 1963, and bringing the two industries closer in the types of business they do and the markets they serve. This major distinction (in degree to which the two industries are specializing in garment rental) is perhaps the single most important factor in their growth differences. Garment rental is not only the fastest growing market sector, but also the most profitable. Originating in a "uniform" rental business, garment rental has now expanded to "career apparel" including clothes for all types of service workers—in hospitals, banks, restaurants, retail shops, garages, academic institutions, car rental agencies, transportation companies, public utilities, and so on.

TABLE 3

Market Structure

A. Industrial launderers

	Percent
Garment rental	63.2
Wiping cloth rental	11.6
Dust control	7.6
Garments and wiping cloths owned by customer	5.3
Linen supply rental	4.1
Other sources	8.2
Total	100.0

B. Linen supply

	Percent
To homes (linen supply)	1.0
Garment rental (to business)	28.0
Flatwork (to business)	52.0
Drycleaning work	1.3
Family work	1.7
Commercial work	3.5
Industrial laundry work	11.8
Other	0.7
Total	100.0

Details of the linen service market are available in Table 4, showing that restuarants, motels, and hotels are the major customers. Receipts from these customers are growing primarily as a function of the garment rental rather than "flatwork" rental; the latter is also less profitable except in very large quantities for major clients.

TABLE 4

Sales, linen supply, industry — 1968

Customer category	Percent of annual volume *
1. Restaurants (includes country clubs)	25.9
2. Food stores (grocery stores, supermarkets)	8.0
3. Industrial (other than food processors: includes gasoline service stations and new/used car dealers)	7.6
4. Hotels and motels	11.6
5. Medical (doctors, dentists, clinics, nursing homes, hospitals)	10.9
6. Other	36.0

* Results of a 1968 membership study conducted by the Linen Supply Association of America.

In both industries, growth is taking place by:

a. Expansion of rental service into homes—particularly for towels, and
b. Expansion of services to existing clients by introducing the idea of prestige, image-producing "career apparel," mainly in the customer contact industries.

2. *The Supply Chain*

The service provided by industrial laundries/linen service companies varies in at least two ways. First, the articles can be owned by the client, or the industrial laundries/linen service, or (increasingly) by the manufacturer of the articles in a licensing or franchising agreement with the industrial laundries/linen service. Second, the service can be initiated by the client, as a request; from the industrial laundries/linen service, in a sales bid; or from the clothing manufacturers, some of whom are realizing that the rental clothing market is a very fast growing one indeed.

3. *Economic Threshold for Entry into Market*

Several factors have a bearing on the scale of operations which must be obtained before market entry is feasible.

Both industries are highly labor intensive. This characteristic is changing due to more activity by unions and expanded research into more capital intensive methods designed to cut labor costs and increase labor productivity. The large firms (with access to capital) are in the forefront in this trend, and are able to hold down prices as a result, while smaller operations are being forced to close if lack of capital prevents them from investing in the "new" machinery. "Minimum threshold size" is, therefore, growing.

Another major component of cost (over 25 percent in most cases) is attributable to the distribution of clean articles and collection of soiled items. These costs are increasing due to road taxes, trucking industry wages, fuel bills, and the costs of vehicle servicing. This means that there is an advantage in securing large clients who have large orders, and a disadvantage (even a loss) in serving a small client. Interviews in the industries suggest that the current cost of making one service call may be about $5 to $7. The advantage of a large client is obvious:

100 customers, 10 pieces each = 100 calls per week = $500-$700

10 customers, 100 pieces each = 10 calls per week = $50-$70

4. *Ease of Entry*

The "minimum threshold," therefore, tends to be a function of both contract size and total business, and this makes it difficult for the small firm, since entry with small capacity prevents access to the most profitable large order market.

Initially, at the "mom and pop" size, the firm might be quite competitive in bidding for contracts as labor and overhead costs would be low. Despite low labor productivity due to low capitalization, survival would be feasible even serving small clients with small orders where distribution costs are high per item. Capital investment totaling $10,000 would be sufficient for this type of operation, with the following items of equipment probably required:

1	100 lb. washer	$2,000	Employment: 4-5 persons
1	press	2,000	
1	tumble dryer	2,000	Plant size: 2-4,000 sq. ft.
2	delivery vehicles	3,000	
	stock (setup costs)	1,000	
		$10,000	

However, expansion beyond this stage is difficult. As soon as the firm is able to secure larger contracts (inherently more profitable), then a change of scale is needed, entailing new machinery, a larger, and possibly unionized, work force, a sales effort to keep the new machines fully occupied, and administration costs, all of which tend to raise the operating costs despite higher labor productivity. Prices in bidding will then be higher than both "mom and pop" size stores with low overhead and large companies with high productivity.

In effect, the cost per item processed is higher in the size range $50,000 to $100,000 than it is for companies of smaller and larger size.

5. *Market Potential*

Future growth of linen supply and industrial launderers will no doubt be considerable, but there are many complicated factors to be taken into account.

The two industries have grown because of the great convenience which their services offers—it relieves the client of an unpleasant, costly, time-consuming, job, and the market for rental garments and other items will grow because of this. An even more convenient method, however, is now available to solve this problem and is on the market—the use of disposable items in flatwork (wiping cloth, sheets, towels, napkins, tablecloths) and in the garment areas (coveralls, surgical aprons, patient coveralls, and so on). The economics of disposables are making them more attractive as the price of labor (and therefore of linen supply and industrial launderers services) grows.

The Linen Supply Association of America (LSAA) is aware of this trend and is encouraging its members to expand into the disposable market by adding disposables to their services to be used where most economical. Given this possibility, the industrial laundries/linen service might grow even faster. The linen supply industry expects the market for career apparel to grow to $70 billion by 1980.

This optimistic LSAA estimate of the market for "career apparel" based on the penetration of the "career clothing" idea to some very large markets, such as banks, utilities, and university communities, where uniforms are not as yet fully accepted. Recently, for example, Minnegasco (Minneapolis Gas Co.) outfitted all its employees from president to janitor with several alternate types of clothing, including various lines of dresses (evening wear included) and pant suits for women employees, all imaginatively styled and updated on a fashion conscious basis. This "image" building activity may well provide a very important market for linen supply/industrial launderers.

D. **Competition**

1. *General*

Competition within the industries is severe in most metropolitan areas, and survival depends largely on two factors:

a. The success of the firm's marketing effort.
b. The degree to which the firm can reduce labor costs.

Most large companies, institutions, hospitals, restaurant chains, and the like take care of their laundry needs by asking for bids from the industry. The ability to assess one's own costs in relation to the types of items needed, the frequency of service, and the quality required is a critical feature. Bidding tends to be highly competitive, and in some areas a price-cutting "war" develops in which firms "steal" contracts from each other by bidding below cost.

Great variation in local labor rates, due to the differing bargaining power of local unions, causes significant differences in the competitive stance of firms. Currently, wage rates in Oakland, California, are 60 cents per hour higher than those in Los Angeles, allowing Los Angeles companies to compete successfully for Bay Area business despite the 400-mile distance. As a result, all but two of the existing Oakland firms are now for sale.

Recent expansions by the national chains have also increased competition, since the large companies have greater resources in marketing and bidding. By mid-1970, 50 percent of the industrial laundries market was controlled by the top eight companies and 60 percent of the linen service market by only five companies. The swing toward higher capitalization in response to rising labor costs favors the large companies.

2. *Form of Organization of Competition*

Tables 5a and 5b feature the industry structures from the point of view of organizational form. It is clear that the dominant organizations are corporations (70 percent of all ownership), which control 90 percent of the market. Small businesses, individually owned and in partnerships, represent over 20 percent of the firms, sharing 3 to 5 percent of the market. Despite this, however, in 1963 the industries were still composed primarily of single establishment firms, with only 20 percent of industrial laundries having more than 11 branches (21 percent of market). Today the leading chains control perhaps 50 percent of the market. This growth in chains has steadily lessened the available opportunities for small businessmen during the last decade, particularly in the linen supply industry.

TABLE 5a

Legal Form of Organization — 1963

	Industrial launderers				Linen supply			
	Establishments		Receipts		Establishments		Receipts	
	Number	Percent	$ Millions	Percent	Number	Percent	$ Millions	Percent
Individual owner	201	23.2	$ 12.4	3.8	366	22.5	$ 25.8	4.7
Partnership	76	8.9	31.0	8.3	143	9.0	33.1	7.0
Corporation	587	67.9	326.9	87.9	1,079	67.5	505.4	88.3
Other legal forms	4	—	2.1	—	3	—	2.3	—
Total	868	100.0	$372.4	100.0	1,591	100.0	$571.6	100.0

Source: 1963 Census of Business

TABLE 5b

Single and Multibranch Firms

	Industrial launderers					Linen supply				
	Firms	Establishments		Receipts		Firms	Establishments		Receipts	
	Number	Number	Percent	$ Millions	Percent	Number	Number	Percent	$ Millions	Percent
Single	567	567	65.3	$182.2	49.8	1,010	1,010	63.5	$257.6	45.2
2-10	74	163	18.8	113.0	29.5	96	194	12.7	106.9	18.7
11+	11	138	15.9	77.2	20.7	17	387	23.8	207.1	36.1
Total	652	868	100.0	$372.4	100.0	1,123	1,591	100.0	$571.6	100.0

E. **Technology**

Recent attempts to increase productivity in response to rising labor costs have resulted in many new processes and machines being introduced. Yet the technology used by both industries remains basically simple.

Standard equipment includes the following *:

Washers 25-400 lb. capacity	$20,000
Washer/extractors	17,000
Tumble dryer, up to 400 lbs.	3,000
Flatwork ironers	55,000
Steam presses (hand)	5,000
Steam presses (machine operated)	10,000
Tunnel steamer	10,000
Solvent drycleaning, up to 400 lbs.	30,000

* Prices are averages for one item of the largest capacity.

Additional necessary equipment includes conveyor (overhead and ground), loading and unloading equipment, parcelling machines, a hot water system of large capacity, and perhaps dye vats. Trucks for delivery are also needed. All of this equipment is simple and can be maintained "in-house"; it is also fairly reliable and downtime is normally not excessive.

Major technological changes include the recent introduction of the "hot box" by LSAA—a heating and steaming box operating at high temperatures (300° to 400° F) for cleaning garments. This major innovation performs some of the functions of washers, driers and presses, and labor saving possibilities are large. Some hot boxes are now in use, permitting increases in productivity of 80 to 200 percent and cutting down on the labor force proportionately.

Another major technological change without which the hot box cannot be used is the development of increasingly long-lasting, man-made fiber mixes and manmade/natural fiber mixes. In uniforms the 65-percent dacron 35-percent cotton garments can last up to 2 years (four times their cotton equivalents) at an extra initial cost of only 30 to 80 percent. They are essential if a firm is to take advantage of such methods as the hot box. Item replacement is an important component of cost in the industry.

Finally, new continuous process machinery developed in Europe is now being brought into the U. S. market, permitting even lower labor handling costs. The LSAA is increasing productivity at the distributor end of the business by providing advice to the salesmen's problem of least-cost delivery with optimum service to customers.

All of these improvements require high volumes to justify themselves economically. Capitalization in the industry is growing rapidly, raising the economic threshold for entry into the market.

F. **Cost Structure**

The extent of labor productivity has been the major factor in the structuring of costs in the industry. During the past decade there has been a gradual substitution of capital for labor as labor costs have risen. Nevertheless, the recent technological breakthroughs have been associated with increasing union pressure for better wages and working conditions.

Annual replacement ratios for items in the linen supply industry vary considerably. Industry statistics show the ratio for continuous towels to be 1.623 per 100 whereas that for pants is 5.316 per 100. The use of "new" fiber in garments is expected to close this gap, and ratios may change considerably as the need for hot processing methods (to raise labor productivity) forces companies to use the long-lasting product mixes.

G. **Productivity**

Productivity is a different concept to deal with in a service industry. Clearly it is important to raise output per man-hour but such efforts could conceivably lower the quality of service to the customer, which is ultimately the only measure of success that is relevant. The very low labor productivity figures which have until recently been common in the industry (Table 6) are more an indicator of the degree to which the industry has been dependent on labor (instead of capital) than in indicator of "inefficiency" per se.

During the period 1963 to 1967, output per man-hour grew at a rate of 4½ percent per year in industrial launderers and 6 percent per year in linen supply. However, in both cases, output per dollar of labor cost declined.

TABLE 6

Productivity of Labor
(Estimates only)

	Industrial launderers		Linen supply	
	1963	1967	1963	1967
Output per $1 of labor cost	$2.65	$2.63	$2.68	$2.60
Total receipts per man-hour	$5.55	$5.95	$4.01	$4.90

This low productivity feature is related to low capital investment figures, which even after the relatively heavy investment of the 1965-1970 period range only between $1,500 and $6,000 per employee, with an average of about $3,000, depending on the size of the company.

Data on productivity in relation to revenue and to weight of goods processed are in Table 7, which distinguishes between firm sizes. The table shows that productivity per pound increases as firms increase annual volume to $1 million of revenue while revenue per employee increases up to companies doing $2 million worth of business. Beyond these points average productivity begins to decline.

TABLE 7

Productivity Measures
Linen Supply Industry — 1968

Company size	Productivity Revenue per lb. (cents)	Revenue per employee
Under $200,000	—	—
$200,000 to $500,000	20.1	$ 8,178
$500,001 to $1,000,000	21.5	$10,934
$1,000,001 to $2,000,000	20.0	$12,017
Over $2,000,000	18.8	$11,426

Source: LSAA survey 1968

These data indicate that the smaller firms with low productivity of labor receive a fair revenue per pound of work processed. Above $1 million in sales, revenues per pound start to fall due to increasing overheads (such as sales, administration, and equipment amortization costs) despite increasing labor productivity.

Economies of scale do not emerge in these figures, but they certainly are available in many forms. The advantages of having large clients and large volume in lowering distribution costs have already been discussed. Almost all capital expenditures in these industries cut down labor costs and produce economies since the larger and faster machines use so much less labor per pound of output. One problem associated with capital intensity, however, is the need to generate quantum increases in business in order to run new machinery at full capacity, involving much greater expenditures on sales and the marketing function. Lowering production-labor costs, therefore, involves an increase in administration and sales-labor costs. There is no evidence that these types of overhead eventually make further expansion less profitable. The available economies of scale do not seem to have a cutoff point as long as advances in technology take place.

H. Pricing Policy

Pricing is one of the critical skills affecting success in industrial launderers, linen supply industries. Most sales made to large- and medium-sized organizations take place by the bid method in which 20 or more firms are requested to submit bids from which the client makes his selection. Bid prices are based on the cost of processing individual types of items and vary considerably from such simple items as towels to the complex "career apparel" items. Competition is severe, and accurate knowledge of costs is, therefore, a requisite for survival in the industries.

TABLE 8

Average Price Received for Selected Clean Items Delivered

	Percent of total sales	Price per item	Price per lb.
Office towels	5.4	9¢	55¢
Pants	5.8	45	34
Shirts	4.7	39	20
Wiping cloths	1.2	3	15
Sheets	9.1	13	17
Tablecloths	3.7	13	18
Dresses	5.4	35	33

Source: LSAA Handbook 1970

These data show great variation in the price per pound received. These prices must cover labor costs, the machine-hour rate (MHR) and replacement costs for the items due to wear and tear and loss. Obviously, bidding on a contract which might include many different items is a difficult process and requires great skill and good cost accounting. It is common for many firms to bid at "below-cost" prices, not only because of their desire to get the contract, but because of ignorance over certain aspects of the costs of one or two items in the total contract. The price per pound to process shirts and pants (which need to be pressed) is obviously greater than that of towels. Sheets and tablecloths require a special item of equipment—a flatwork ironer—which represents a $50,000 investment, and large volumes of business are needed to fill the capacity of even the smallest flatwork ironer. Margins are slim and small slips cost money.

I. Profitability

Profitability per item is difficult to generalize about because of all the variables involved, but industry sources stress the profit potential of garment rental (given adequate new machinery) and the difficulty of making money in flatwork. Indeed, firms will often offer flatwork as a "loss-leader" in order to gain associated garment contracts.

The LSAA Survey of 1968 (44 firms) indicated the following average operating ratios:

Gross profit (margin)	42.2%
Operating expenses	34.4
Operating profit	7.8
Income taxes	2.8
Net profit	5.0%

The average after-tax return on investment was about 19.5 percent. These margins are fairly wide by service industry standards, exceeding much of the retailing industry in operating and net profit. Return on investment is handsome.

Variation in profitability varies considerably by size of company.

TABLE 9

Linen Supply Industry — 1968
Operating Ratio Percentages by Annual Receipts Categories

	Under $500,000	$500,000 to $1 million	$1 million to $2 million	$2 million +	$30 million +
Gross margin	42.9%	39.1%	41.8%	40.5%	31.7%
Expenses	35.2	34.2	32.3	30.7	21.1
Operating profit	7.7	4.9	9.5	9.8	10.6
Taxes	2.2	1.1	3.7	4.4	5.2
Net profit	5.5%	3.8%	5.8%	5.4%	5.4%

Expenses decline systematically with size—a function of the economies of scale discussed earlier. This means that operating profit tends to increase with size, apart from the "dip" in the medium-size company which experiences low-profit levels.

III. ANALYSIS OF BUSINESS FEASIBILITY

A. Major Factors Determining Industry Success

1. *Marketing and Sales*

The industry is selling a service, and growth takes place by extending the range of those services. This takes a great deal of skill and persuasiveness by the firm. Bidding is at the heart of the company-client relationship and competition is severe. A good sales staff, adequately paid, is an essential. Subscription to lists of "contacts" is invaluable.

2. *Cost Control*

The pressure placed on margins by the increasing cost of labor in this industry means that efficiency in all other areas is essential. This applies particularly in distribution where good management can reduce costs effectively.

3. *The Critical Growth Gap*

Entry can be achieved with a very small amount of capital, but growth beyond the $500,000 per annum level is difficult as overhead becomes larger. At this point, access to larger amounts of capital is essential in order to reduce labor requirements and raise productivity. Failure to do this reduces net profit to critically small margins, and it becomes difficult to win any contract at "above cost" prices.

4. *Size of Client*

Of all the critical features this is the most difficult to deal with. It is clear that very small clients cannot be served profitably once the firm grows beyond the "mom and pop" stage, and many firms have a minimum contract value ($5 to $10 per week) below which they will not service a client. This feature is a difficult one from the point of view of a new small business.

5. *Product Mix*

Garments are the most profitable end of the business but require larger sums of investment both on behalf of the firm (in processing machinery) and the client (in his stock of garments). Unless entry is made at a fairly large size, this valuable market may not be open to the new firm with little experience.

B. Problems of Minority Enterprise

A new minority enterprise in these industries must face all of the problems discussed above and probably several others. But, there may be opportunities not open to nonminority competitors.

In Detroit, Cleveland, and Oakland, California, and some other large cities, the minority community clientele may be sufficient to support a fair-sized industrial laundry, given guarantees of support from minority company trade associations. Most of these companies are relatively new, however, and are unlikely to be very receptive to attempts at selling "career clothing" or other industrial launderers/linen supply services.

C. Projection of Returns—Two Hypothetical Situations

Two situations likely to characterize minority enterprise are discussed next. The difference between them is mainly one of scale, a function of the capital investment made by the entrepreneur at the outset. In both cases, emphasis has been placed on the high profit side of the industry (garments) and less on the flatwork side.

TABLE 10

Financial Projections
for Representative Businesses of Two Sizes

	Case 1			Case 2		
	Small proprietorship ($50,000 annual gross)			Medium-sized proprietorship ($200,000 annual gross)		
Capacity—lbs. per yr.	250,000 lbs.			1,000,000 lbs.		
lbs. per day	1,000 lbs.			4,000 lbs.		
Equipment Costs:						
Washer extractor	1 (200 lb.)		$ 4,000	1 (400 lb.)		$ 20,000
Spare	1 (50 lb.)		1,000	1 (100 lb.)		3,000
Dryer	1 (100 lb.)		2,000	1 (400 lb.)		4,000
Press	2 (manual)		1,000	1 (automatic)		5,000
Drycleaning machine	1 (small)		5,000	1 (large)		30,000
Heating plant	1		2,000	1		12,000
Installation			1,500			8,000
Other			500			2,000
Vehicles	1		2,000	3		6,000
Total			$19,000			$ 90,000
	Annual operating statement					
Gross receipts			$50,000			$200,000
Operating expenses						
Labor:						
Production	(3)	$16,500		(6)	$42,000	
Distribution	(1)	7,500		(3)	26,750	
Sales and administration				(2)	17,500	
Nonwage benefits	(nonunion)	3,500		(union)	22,000	
Total labor costs		$27,500			$108,250	
Supplies		1,000			4,000	
Equipment maintenance		1,000			5,000	
Materials replacement		5,000			35,000	
Total operating expense			$34,500			$152,250
Overhead expenses:						
Rent and Utilities	(3,000 sq. ft.)	4,000		(10,000 sq. ft.)	12,000	
Equipment depreciation	(10 yr.)	1,900		(10 yr.)	9,000	
Total overhead			5,900			21,000
Total expenses			$40,400			$173,250
Net profit before taxes and owner's compensation			$ 9,600			$ 26,750

Certain Assumptions are Made

1. All buildings and real estate are rented, not purchased.
2. Input capacity is determined by the capacity of the washer/extractor machine. All other equipment capacity is geared to this. This is not unreasonable, but in practice other measures of capacity would be necessary also.

3. An assumed revenue of 20 cents per pound of goods processed is used as base (the average of the linen supply industry).

4. Labor needs are calculated as follows:
   a. production—from manufacturers' literature
   b. distribution—it is assumed that the average client has a contract worth $30 and is serviced once a week. From projected net receipts, it can be estimated that Case 1 firm has weekly revenues of about $1,000 and Case 2, of $4,000. The number of contracts this revenue represents is:
      Case 1—$1,000/$30 = 33
      Case 2—$4,000/$30 = 133

   Each vehicle can make 10 calls per day, or 50 to 60 per week; Case 1 needs one vehicle and driver, and Case 2 needs three.

IV. GUIDANCE FOR ESTABLISHING THE BUSINESS

A. Approaching the Market

The most opportune situation for both Case 1 and Case 2 might be to purchase an existing business with an established clientele. This may not be possible, however. Marketing is a very important part of the industrial launderers/linen supply industry and can be thought of as two activities:

1. Direct selling to potential customers.
2. Being placed on bidders' lists (for institutional and other larger customers).

Both these activities can be started by subscribing to "contact leads" published by specialist organizations covering the industrial laundries/linen service market locally. A blanket mailing coverage of all establishments in the "customer types" list (LSAA) derived from the local yellow pages of the phone book is another basic approach. The "customer types" list as shown in Table 4 is large and can yield much valuable business.

Minority businessmen will, of course, attempt to contact local minority-owned businesses in the customer-types listing. Direct person-to-person contact with the potential client is more effective than any other means of selling. Initially, it may be that only small clients, who are difficult to service without making a loss, are recruited; however, in the beginning "all business is good business" and small contracts will help. The aim should be to bid effectively on the larger contracts let periodically by larger companies, chains, restaurants, and so on. Public institutions and military agencies welcome potential bidders; other larger organizations must be "sold" more heavily.

Specialization in a particular market that is also a particular product group is an additional possibility. Specialization in servicing gas stations, for instance, might yield high profits as experience grows and knowledge of the "gas station" industry is accumulated. Another profitable area of specialization might be dentists' and doctors' offices, particularly where the latter are grouped together in "medical centers" and have minority representation. Indeed, this latter factor can be a criterion used to search out markets, since minority businesses are most frequently found among gas stations, automotive repairs, food franchise outlets, some areas of retail trade, beauty shops, and bars.

Attempts at getting "guarantees" of business from minority operations have sometimes been successful in other industries and can be applied here, too. Certainly this would be an effective method in larger cities which have a large minority community.

B. Obtaining Financing

Established firms in industrial launderers/linen supply industries make use of bulk credit and of equipment-secured debt to finance operations and expansion. For the newcomer to the industries, financing can be difficult to obtain, and for minority newcomers, even more so.

There are, however, opportunities for minimizing startup capital needs. The use of used machinery and vehicles is an obvious one, as is the purchase of stock and other materials from other companies which are going out of business, or being amalgamated, or spinning off some operations. The trade journals "personals" are an effective market source for this. Leasing premises rather than buying or constructing them is an obvious capital-saver, but less obvious is the possibility of lease/lending machinery from some of the major manufacturers. In times of slow business and poor credit, manufacturers tend to be more open to the possibilities of lease/lend in order to move their stocks of machinery.

The new business will, of course, need some new capital to start and to continue operations. In order to obtain this as cheaply as possible, a sound "financial plan" is essential. Elements of this include knowledge of the Federal, State, and local loans and guarantees programs available for small business. Another listing of nonprofit "help" agencies for minority business, some of which have financial resources, is the publication *Private Programs Assisting Minority Business,* issued in 1970 by the Office of Minority Business Enterprise, U.S. Department of Commerce, Washington, D.C. 20230.

APPENDIX

Data on labor requirements, capital needs, and plant size have all been discussed in Section II of this report. Further information specific to the industry in these areas can be obtained from the industries' trade associations and their local branches.

1. Linen Supply Association of America
   925 Arthur Godfrey Road
   Miami Beach, Florida 33140
   Phone: 305/532-6371
   Publication: Linen Supply News (monthly)
2. Institute of Industrial Launderers
   1726 M Street, N.W.
   Washington, D.C. 20036

MACHINE SHOP JOB WORK

Section Contents

URBAN BUSINESS PROFILE
Machine Shop Job Work
(SIC 35993)

I. Recommendation

Successful operation of a machine shop which specializes in job work requires technical experience and strong managerial talents. Individuals wishing to enter the industry as shopowners should have considerable experience and very high motivation.

If a new machine shop is located in a metropolitan area where manufacturing activities are growing, it should have good prospects for success—if management is technically competent, resourceful, willing to work long hours, and dedicated to controlling costs. Risk can be minimized if the market for the proposed new job shop is clearly defined and substantiated by information received from prospective customers.

Investment requirements are minimal provided that the owner shows ingenuity in finding inexpensive space, securing second-hand machinery, and/or arranging for leasing more expensive equipment. Careful attention should be paid to the availability of a technically competent work force, particularly when there is a high demand for machine shop services. At such times, it is often difficult to secure the skilled labor which is required.

II. Description of the Machine Shop Industry

A. Identification

A machine job shop, Standard Industrial Classification (SIC) 35993, is a service-oriented activity providing custom service to repair, make, or otherwise improve an existing manufactured product or a new product of the same kind. All items are custom made. There is some overlapping between the operation of a machine job shop and a tool-and-die shop, since many machine job shops manufacture tools and dies, and some tool-and-die shops machine parts to order, as well as design and build special machinery. Many machine job shops specialize in the repair and reconditioning of machinery, and a typical aspect of their work is the availability of repair service on a 24-hour basis.

Many of the technical, financial, and operational aspects of machine job shops and tool-and-die makers are similar. However, tool-and-die makers tend to have more complicated and expensive machinery, often using numerical controls, and they are somewhat larger. The average tool and die shop employs about twice as many persons as the average job shop.

The essential operation of a machine job shop is to take a piece of metal and alter it to the customer's specifications. This may include plating, assembly welding, fabricating, diecasting, stamping, or grinding, or any combination of these operations. In most cases the metal is supplied by the customer. Various types of metal forming machinery, such as lathes, presses, planers, millers, and drills are used for this purpose. The most important shop costs are labor and investments in machines. An operation which can be accomplished quickly on a small and inexpensive machine will be less costly than a complicated and time-consuming operation on an elaborate machine. However, labor is more costly than machinery, and it is usually more profitable to use a more expensive faster machine than one which is slow but inexpensive.

B. **Dimensions**

There were some 3,000 machine shops employing 66,500 workers doing jobwork, according to the 1967 Census of Business. Their total sales were reported to be above $1.2 billion. The National Tool, Die, and Precision Machining Association, which includes tool-and-die manufacturers as well as job machine shops in its definition of the industry, reports that there are about 7,000 firms in the industry doing $3 billion of business annually. There are many other operations which are captive operations of other firms, and these latter do machine work only for the company by which they are owned.

Growth in the industry is directly related to growth in manufacturing and particularly the growth in the use of machinery. Thus, it can be expected that, with the continuing increase in population and standard of living, there will be corresponding increases in the value of manufactured output and the need for contract machining. Continuing introduction of laborsaving devices and other machinery are also bound to increase the output of machine shops.

There are significant factors affecting the independent contract firm. These include:

Cyclical factors,
Single-industry ties,
Captive operations.

Cyclical factors. Machine job shops generally tend to be hurt by the ups and downs of business. When industrial output is not expanding, machines are used less intensively, and there is less need for repairs and special machine work. The machine shop industry generally has considerable excess capacity when industrial production is lagging and has insufficient capacity when production is booming.

Single-Industry Ties. Unless a machine job shop is large and located in an area where industry is diversified, its output tends to be specialized to serve one or two customers or a single industry. This leaves the machine shop operation overly dependent on customers over whom it has no control. This can result in seasonality of work, abrupt loss of work when a customer closes his plant or moves, loss of work if a particular industry is declining, and so on.

Captive Operations. Captive operations, which are shops owned by the companies which purchase their output, are always a threat to the independent. In recessions, captive operations get the work before a company provides any orders to outside suppliers.

Machine job shops tend to be located in the industrial concentrations of the Nation. They are particularly concentrated in and around the automotive industry and in places like Chicago. However, agriculture centers have machine shops serving agricultural machinery, and there are other concentrations serving the mining industry, the petroleum industry, and the logging industry. While urban centers are good locations because of their proximity to diversified manufacturing operations and the availability of used machinery and skilled labor, there are often opportunities to be found in other areas near industries which are expanding or which are introducing new machinery into their operations. For example, the rapid mechanization of coal mining and the surge in the demand for coal has resulted in a very rapid upsurge in machine shops in West Virginia and Kentucky.

There has been very little penetration into the machine shop industry by black or Spanish-speaking entrepreneurs. Ownership in the industry is concentrated among a group of persons, many of European extraction, who have established close working relationships with each other over a period of years. The National Tool, Die and Precision Machining Association does, however, report that at least one of its members is a black owner of a machine shop.

C. **Characteristics**

1. *Nature of the Product*

The contract machine shop serves other industries. It provides machine time, technical skills, and know-how. It uses its customers' materials and works them to repair or produce new parts for existing machines, and turns out relatively small quantities of parts and other metal items needed in the manufacturing process.

2. *Nature of the Customer*

The customer of a machine shop is anyone who uses machinery, whether he be manufacturer, farmer, miner, logger, transporter, etc. The basis for choosing a particular machine shop can be any one or combination of the following:

a. *Convenience*. The machine shop is handy and can quickly provide and deliver the required service.

b. *Quality*. The machine shop can be relied upon to provide accurate machining to very close tolerances, or to repair machines.

c. *Price*. The machine shop can perform work at an economical cost. (Much business is secured through competitive bidding.)

d. *Ingenuity*. The machine shop can figure out a way of doing something more quickly or more economically, or can modify a machine to make it work more effectively.

A machine shop may have a number of different types of customers. If the shop makes tools, dies, molds, and other forms, its customers will be the manufacturers who produce other products (such as automobiles, appliances, aerospace products, etc.).

Other types of machine shops specialize in one-of-a-kind jobs, machining or welding a particular part needed for the operation of another machine. Many shops also specialize in repairing and maintaining machinery particular to a specific industry such as textile manufacturing, mining, agriculture, and the like.

In most cases, the machine shop must be located close to its customers. There are some exceptions, particularly in imports from Canada and Europe in tool-and-die production, but the imports have a cost advantage in labor rates which would not be applicable to operations in the United States located at a distance from customers.

3. *Technology*

The machine job shop is an outgrowth of the Industrial Revolution. It had its first development in the early 19th century when Eli Whitney invented interchangeable parts for guns. Most of the early equipment was used on wood, and much of the basic machinery performs the same operations today which were performed by the early woodworking machinery of the 19th century. Technological changes have come from size of machines, speed of operation, ability to work with more complicated metals, closeness of tolerances, and capability of using more highly automated controlling devices.

The technology involved in operating a modern machine shop is quite complex. The manager must know mathematics, mechanics, metal engineering, the theory of metal cutting, the properties of various metals and alloys, and the workings of machines.

In addition, a manager must know cost estimating, plant layout, and wage and salary administration. Quality control is an essential ingredient of successful machine shop management, as are careful estimating and rigid control of costs.

Machine shops may be classified by the size of job orders and the degree of precision to which they work. For example, a shop may specialize in light jobs weighing less than 10 pounds when completed, medium work, weighing between 10 and 50 pounds, and heavy work, which may weigh up to several tons when completed.

Rough work is that in which finishes are seldom smoother than 125 micro-inches and tolerances seldom better than 0.007 inches. Medium work finishes are seldom smoother than 63 micro-inches and tolerances down to 0.002. In fine work, finishes may be as smooth as 8 micro-inches and tolerances as close as 0.0002.

Machine shops may specialize in different types of metal, such as steel, aluminum, or bronze, or in the case of the aerospace industry such exotic alloys as titanium, beryllium, and the like.

The machines to be purchased for a machine shop will depend upon the nature of the market the owner wishes to serve and the technical requirements for machinery to produce for that market. The prospective owner must have a clear idea of how large his work will be, what precision will be expected, the type of metals with which he will be working, whether numerical tapes will be available for automatic operation, and so on.

There are some one-machine shops where the total output is performed on one machine having unique properties such as the ability to perform very heavy work, or the ability to work at very high speeds with consequent savings in costs. Such machines are usually automatically controlled and expensive.

A machine shop is generally labor-intensive with a moderate investment of $7,000 to $10,000 per worker required. Total wages for the industry as a whole represent about 44½ percent of the total value of the work performed in the industry.

The basic skill utilized in the labor force is that of the skilled machining worker. The various occupational titles for this skill are listed in D.O.T. 600 through 607.886, 609.280 through .782 and 609.885, in the *Dictionary of Occupational Titles,* U.S. Department of Labor, third edition (1966).

Most training authorities believe that apprenticeship is the preferred way to learn the machinist trade. While a typical apprentice program lasts 4 years, many companies have training programs that qualify their employees as machinists in less time. Training includes the operation of various types of machine tools and such skills as chipping, filing, handtapping, dowel fitting, riveting, and other hand operations. A machinist must also know blueprint reading, mechanical drawing, shop mathematics, and shop practices. The National Tool, Die and Precision Machining Association conducts an apprenticeship program in cooperation with those of its members who wish to participate.

Depending on the type of work done, the average machine shop might have about half the work force skilled, a third semiskilled, and the balance in unskilled or learner category. About 75 percent of the workers in the industry are nonunion, although in some areas union membership is the practice. Wages are generally high, ranging in 1970 from about $3.50 an hour in low-wage areas to about $6 an hour in the areas where higher wages are more common.

4. *Competition*

As in most industries where there are generally a large number of small suppliers and it is relatively easy to enter, competition can be intensive. When work is scarce, competitors tend to shave prices and forget about overhead. However, during rush seasons, work can be found very easily, particularly if delivery schedules can be maintained.

The machine shop also faces competition from the captive operation that is owned by a manufacturer or by the in-plant toolroom. Many manufacturing operations which reach a certain size will install a toolroom of their own to do many machining operations and to maintain and repair machinery. This can often result in the machine shop's losing an important customer. However, a job shop offers a manufacturer many advantages over an in-house operation, including lower cost in some instances, greater flexibility, and higher skills. These can be marketed aggressively.

The introduction of new machinery can often make business difficult for a machine shop that is attempting to compete on a relatively large scale for the production of tools and dies or molds. Financing must often be found for new machinery or else the business must be given up.

As noted above, there is a certain amount of clannishness within the industry, and competitors may help each other by making machine time available on certain types of machines. While this has advantages for those who are already in business, it may pose problems for a newcomer not known by or friendly with existing shopowners.

5. *Ease of Entry*

Machine job shops still offer opportunities for small entrepreneurs because customers are always looking for reliable suppliers who can be depended upon to deliver orders quickly and according to exact specifications. This places a premium on geographical proximity to customers, flexibility of operations, and careful craftsmanship, all of which become more difficult characteristics to maintain as the size of operation increases. Given the qualifications for operation of a machine shop and a market for his services, an individual can become a machine shop operator with relative ease. There are no special licensing requirements or unusual capital needs.

Many owners of job shops got their start by picking up one second-hand machine for less than $1,000, reconditioning it themselves, and operating it at nights and weekends in their basements or garages. As business increased, they secured more machines, hired some friends or relatives, and eventually moved into a small garage-type building.

On the other hand, the industry would be impossible to enter successfully if one did not have solid experience in the field and a broad range of acquaintanceship with potential customers. Moreover, the industry would be particularly difficult to enter during one of its many periods of excess capacity. Entry is most easily accomplished when work is easy to find and customers are desperately searching for places to get their contract machining accomplished.

6. *Financing*

An experienced operator with some connections with potential customers and a good personal credit record should experience relatively little difficulty securing the necessary financing. Little or no investment is required for materials. Used machines can be purchased relatively cheaply or new machinery can be leased. Firm orders can usually be used as collateral to obtain bank loans for wages and supplies; the loans are expected to be retired by order payments.

The actual amount of money needed for investment will vary greatly. An individual wanting to purchase all new machinery for cash in a building all his own would need perhaps $125,000 in capital for a relatively small operation with sales of about $250,000 annually. However, as noted above, it is possible to use someone else's machine and start with nothing. Somewhere in between, an experienced individual who has enough work for two or three others, in addition to himself, and who can secure some leased space without putting up a lot of money for a lease, ought to be able to get started with about $2,500 of his own capital and about $7,500 of borrowed funds.

7. *Profitability*

Although the potential for profitability in a job shop operating at 100 percent of capacity over a long period of time is high, the actual profitmaking potential for the average shop is relative low and is often achieved only at the expense of long hours of work and overtime by the owner-manager. Profit-reducing factors include:

a. Keeping workers on the payroll when there is no work. Many owners will keep workers on the payroll when there is no work out of consideration for the worker's welfare or because work is expected and the owner does not want a valuable employee to go elsewhere. If the expected work is delayed or does not materialize, the drain on profits can be significant.

b. Investment in new machinery and equipment. While an individual starting on a small scale may be content with secondhand machinery, there is always a temptation, once a business is established, to invest in more elaborate machinery on the assumption that the addition will make it possible to bid on a greater variety of potential contracts. If the assumption proves overoptimistic, the payments on the idle machine can drain away profits. However, it is better to have idle machines than idle men.

c. Seasonal and cyclical factors. Shops generally tend to have too much work or not enough. During rush seasons or a booming economy, extra help must be found, productivity goes down, overtime goes up, and profits are not as great as might be expected. During slack time, machines and men are idle, and profits are affected correspondingly.

d. Quality control. As business grows, it becomes more and more difficult to control quality. This means that material is sometimes wasted and must be replaced at a cost. It may also mean taking longer to perform an operation than estimated, a factor which would reduce profits on individual contracts and may even result in losses.

e. Competition. Competition is often intense, not only from captive shops and in-house toolrooms, but from new entrants into the business whenever times are good and work is plentiful.

There are no specific figures on actual profitability, but the range of profits for firms in the miscellaneous machinery field (SIC 3599) and metalworking machinery and equipment, which includes tool-and-die, suggests an average rate of net profit somewhat under 4 percent of sales. Thus, a firm employing about 15 persons and doing an annual business of approximately $250,000 might generate annual profits of somewhat less than $10,000, not including the owner's direct labor.

8. *Dependence on Outside Factors*

As pointed out above, there are many factors outside the control of the owner of a machine job shop which would affect his profitability. These would include the following:

a. Decision by major customers to install or expand their in-house machining capabilities.

b. National business cycle. Machine shops would be affected more than most businesses by the ups and downs of the national economy.

c. Long-range or short-range trends in the industries served. The prosperity of machine job shops is affected by what happens in the major industries they serve. Those catering to the automotive industry tend to do well or poorly on the basis of how well the auto industry is doing. Others are affected by mining, aerospace industry, etc.

III. Feasibility Analysis

A. Review of Key Factors

These factors are essential to feasibility of a machine job shop:

1. *Management*

The proposed management must be technically competent, experienced, and highly motivated toward making profits. In the absence of other factors suggesting unusual competence, at least 10 years of experience in the industry, 3 of which have been spent in supervisory capacities, are the very minimum which should be required of the management. In addition, there must be something in the proposed management's background which indicates a profit orientation, such as skill in handling his personal finances, or previous successful experience. The extent to which a prospective manager knows his precise market, where he is going to get his machinery, and has shown cost consciousness in his initial projections would also be indicative of the likelihood of success.

2. *Market*

A very specific market should be identified to assure feasibility. Such a market may be identified by the following:

a. A nearby booming industry which is unable to get all the contract machining it needs. Interviews with purchasing agents can establish the existence and size of such a market. Some judgment should be made as to the prospects for continuation of the boom.

b. Acquaintanceship by the proposed management with sources of business and reasonable assurances by such sources of an adequate volume. There may be special factors here, such as a willingness to help minority entrepreneurs, but reliance on such a special factor should be approached cautiously.

c. Knowledge of a need for a new technical procedure or introduction of a new machine which can be offered by the proposed new shop at a competitive advantage. This, too, can be documented by interviews.

d. A special factor such as location or technique that offers an opportunity to prospective customers to get work more conveniently or more inexpensively. The requirement for such convenience or economy should also be documented by interviews.

3. *Location*

The proposed location should be such that the proposed market can be served inexpensively and conveniently and rental is minimal.

4. *Machinery*

The machinery required must be available at a cost commensurate with the sales and cost projections for the proposed shop.

5. *Work Force*

Depending upon the size needed, there should be assurance that the required work force is available. It is often true that the available work force, more than any other factor, limits capacity. Thus, if there is an unfilled demand for contract machining in a particular area or region, the problem is more apt to be related to the inability to secure a work force than to any other. If there were existing manpower competent to perform the required work, the existing shops could put them to work by putting on second and third shifts or adding machines. Thus, a newcomer to the business within a specific area cannot expect to succeed because there is an unfilled demand for contract machining unless he has a solution to the manpower shortage.

B. Special Factors for New Minority Ventures

A minority entrepreneur seeking to establish a new machine shop would have one potential advantage and one potential disadvantage with regard to existing shops. All other factors would be potentially neutral.

1. *Advantage*

As indicated above, many large manufacturing and other concerns are under somewhat extensive pressures to exhibit concern for minority economic development. Thus, a minority-owned machine job shop might receive special considerations from purchasing agents.

It should be stressed, however, that such special considerations would not extend to paying a premium for the work or accepting work that is not up to standard. Thus, a minority business would be expected to produce quality work at competitive cost.

There would be limitations on the amount of preference which might be exhibited toward minority machine job shops. With many small existing jobs already in the business, a small shift in work might well have a disastrous effect on one or two existing shops, and such an eventuality would have to be taken into account by all concerned.

2. *Disadvantage*

As also indicated above, existing owners of machine job shops tend to have ethnic and family relationships and might tend to view entrance of a minority entrepreneur with more hostility than that normally felt with the advent of a business competitor: This might lead to excessively competitive practices, such as heavy price-cutting, to the detriment of the new business. At the very least, it would make it difficult to secure the cooperation that now exists among many firms in the industry.

C. Projections of Attainable Returns in Industry

Projections are furnished below for two different types of operations. The first is for a small three-man operation on two or three basic machines. The second is for a larger operation employing about 15 persons.

1. *Small, three-man operation*

a. Revenues (includes small amount of income from sale of waste materials such as metal cuttings)	$40,000	
b. Operating expenses (all materials supplied by customers)		
1) Direct labor (including proprietor's direct labor)	25,000	
2) Other (includes power, selling expense, cost of transportation, consumable supplies, rent, etc.)	8,000	
Total operating expenses	33,000	
Percent of sales		82.6%
c. Gross operating profit	7,000	
Margin		17.4%
d. Other expenses (interest, depreciation, taxes)	4,000	
e. Net profit	3,000	
Percent of sales		7.6%
f. Investment	5,000	
g. Return on investment		60.0%

A high return on investment is shown for an operation of this type, because it is assumed that relatively little investment is required and that the entrepreneur has been able to find a facility (such as his garage or comparable) which does not require heavy preparation for machines. It is also assumed that the machines can be secured on lease or secondhand with relatively small downpayment. Very little depreciation is assumed. It is also assumed that there is relatively steady work for the three persons and that they are able to work on billable contracts for about 80 percent of the time. This may require some unpaid overtime on the part of the owner.

There are three major risks involved in setting up an operation of this type: (1) the work may not come in; (2) the machinery will break down; (3) the workers will not be available. However, an experienced man who knows the machinery and who has lined up reliable workmen and sufficient contracts may reasonably expect profitable operations from the very beginning. Due to the cyclical nature of this business, however, the prospects of maintaining profitability at this level will probably diminish as the volume of available work fluctuates over time. It is unlikely that an operation of this size can last long since it will either go out of business as soon as there is no work, unless the new firm is unusually well capitalized, or else it will attract enough business to grow and expand, secure more machinery, and hire a larger work force.

2. *Medium-sized 15-man operation*

a. Annual revenues	$250,000	
b. Operating expenses		
1) Direct labor (includes overtime and owner's direct labor)	112,500	
Percent of Revenue		45.0%
2) Manufacturing expense (incudes indirect labor, fringe benefits, depreciation, tools and supplies, power, light, heat, etc.)	61,875	
Percent of direct labor		55.0%
3) Selling expense (includes delivery)	39,375	
Percent of direct labor		35.0%
4) Administrative expense	16,875	
Percent of direct labor		15.0%
Total operating expenses	230,625	
Percent of sales		92.2%
c. Gross operating profit	19,375	
Gross margin		7.8%
d. Other expenses (interest on capital of about $100,000)	10,000	
e. Net profit	9,375	
Percent of sales		3.7%
f. Investment	25,000	
g. Return on investment		37.5%

NOTE: The above figures exclude materials. These are most often supplied by the customer, but even when they are supplied by the vendor, they are generally furnished at cost.

Given good management and a carefully chosen location with respect to markets, the chances are better than even that the above profit can be earned on the average over a number of years. However, the risk would be slightly higher in any given year depending on the business cycle and the current conditions in the principal industry being served.

IV. Establishing the Business

A. Approaching the Market

Whether he is contemplating a small operation or a medium sized operation, the prospective entrepreneur for a machine job shop should have a very clear idea of his market, backed up by interviews with prospective customers, and commitments, if possible.

This should be the first step in establishing a machine job shop, and if it has not been accomplished, there is no point in going any further in planning to establish a business.

The approaches to the prospective market may be based upon convenience, technical competence, price, friendship, or good will, or any combination of these. The prospective entrepreneur should establish the basis on which he expects to solicit the business and then visit potential customers to determine whether such a basis is valid.

The new entrepreneur should be careful not to depend upon promised opportunities to bid on contracts in formulating his own business plans, unless the potential customer's assurance appears based on a realization of cost advantages (by virtue of location, skill, machines used) in the proposed business relationship.

B. Plant Requirements

The small operation should seek minimum space, either in a garage or some similar structure. An existing business (not a competitor) may be willing to rent out a small amount of space. Room will be needed for a workbench and for whatever machines are considered essential to the type of work which is available and which the operator plans to get.

For the medium-sized operation, the operator should seek ground level space of about 1,200 to 1,500 square feet in a cement floor building, with enough room for a small office, a storeroom, a toolcrib, a space for finished parts, three workbenches, milling machine, two turret lathes, engine lathe, hacksaw, three drills, and three grinding machines. A furnace may also be required for heat treating tools, and electric welding equipment may also be desirable.

Most metropolitan areas have a number of suppliers of machine tools and a prospective job shop operator should make the rounds of these suppliers to ascertain the availability of secondhand machinery. Assuming the purchase of good secondhand machinery, and the acquisition of one or two real "bargains" at an auction, it is estimated that the necessary equipment can be secured for about $100,000. This would include special costs of installation.

C. Financing

The basic investment involved in machine job shops is the purchase of machinery. Since machinery has considerable value in secondhand condition, most machines can be financed with relatively little difficulty. Often, the seller will arrange for financing, or arrangements can be made for leasing machines from the seller or from an equipment leasing firm with an option to buy. Some cash outlay would be required for installation of machines and for expendable supplies such as office supplies, transportation equipment, cutting bits, hand tools, and the like. About 1 month's working capital would be required to cover rent, operating expenses, and wages.

Some typical financial arrangements might include the following:

Small Operation

Capital required:	
Machinery installed	$ 5,000
Working capital	3,000
Supplies, etc.	2,000
	$10,000
Source:	
Own funds	$ 2,500
Bank loan	7,500
	$10,000

Given the requisites for successful operation, it should be relatively easy for a bank officer to approve a small loan for such an operation. If the requisite conditions are not present, the business is not viable and should not qualify for a loan.

In most cases, the bank loan could be secured through a guarantee by the Small Business Administration, which has a special program to promote minority enterprises, and which might be expected to cooperate.

Medium-Sized Operation

Capital required:	
Machinery installed	$ 90,000
Working capital	25,000
Supplies, etc.	10,000
	$125,000
Source:	
Equipment loan	$ 75,000
Own funds	25,000
Bank loan	25,000
	$125,000

It is likely that most of the machinery can be financed and that the bank loan can be secured through a Small Business Administration guarantee. In the event the proposed operator does not have the required $25,000, it would be well to consider a small operation, perhaps employing one to three men. However, in exceptional circumstances, where an unusual individual with the necessary experience and business management ability has an opportunity to enter a market and make a success of contract machining on a somewhat larger scale, and he cannot secure $25,000 from his own funds, he may be able to secure funds from a local source specializing in providing equity for minority businesses.

D. Labor Force

As indicated above, a skilled work force is essential to the successful operation of a machine job shop. For a small operation, the work force should be nearly all skilled. (For a three-man operation, two skilled machinists and an apprentice might be appropriate.)

A labor force breakdown for a 15-man operation might include:

Manager	1
Foreman	1
Skilled	6
Semiskilled	4
Unskilled	2
Office	1
	15

The foreman or shop supervisor is a key to successful operation. He can see to it that the work force is kept busy, that the machines are scheduled for maximum productivity, that work commitments are met, and that quality control standards are maintained.

It is often possible to start a shop of this size with two principals, one serving as the foreman-supervisor, and the other as the business manager-salesman.

Prospective operators of a new business should have a very clear idea of where they will get their key employees. In boom times, skilled machinists are exceptionally hard to recruit, and unless a new entrepreneur knows of some men who are capable and willing to come with him, it would be wise to give up the idea until such men are found.

Wage scales and union affiliation are influenced heavily by local conditions and cannot be generalized on a national basis. While most machine job shops are nonunion, it is important in certain areas that they be unionized. Wage scales can vary extensively from one section of the country to another. A prospective operator of a job shop should know the going level in the area in which he intends to locate and adjust his figures accordingly.

V. Summary

For an individual who knows the machine shop technique, who is experienced in the trade, and who is a good businessman, there are opportunities to establish and to make money in the ownership and operation of a machine job shop. Such an individual will know in advance what his market is and how he intends to capture it and keep it. He will know who his customers are going to be and why they will purchase from him rather than from others. He will know what machines he wants and how he can get them at a bargain and for relatively little investment. He will know where he will get a reliable labor force. If he does not know these things, then he is not ready to establish a machine job shop.

BIBLIOGRAPHY

SMALL BUSINESS BIBLIOGRAPHY NO. 69, MACHINE SHOPS-JOB TYPE, June 1968, free. Ten-page pamphlet giving brief description of operations along with applicable bibliographic listings of selected references. *Small Business Administration,* Washington, D. C. 20416.

Books

Armstrong, William H. *Machine Tools for Metal Cutting,* $5. Technical information on the materials, tools, and manufacturing processes used in machine shop.

Black, Paul H. *Theory of Metal Cutting,* 1961. $8.95. Discusses the "metal-cutting mechanism" and the mechanics of what happens near the cutting edge of a mechanical cutting tool during the machining process.

Doyle, Lawrence E. *Metal Machining.* $11. Gives elementary description of metal machining equipment, methods, and techniques, including the engineering significance and application of metal machining through a study of process planning.

Fundamentals of Tool Design. American Society of Tool and Manufacturing Engineers, 1962. Paperback, $2.50. Presents the principles of tool design for four basic manufacturing processes—material removal, joining, casting, and pressworking processes.

Hall, Herbert D., and Horace E. Linsley. *Machine Tools—What They Are and How They Work.* 1957. $5.50. Introduction to fundamentals of mass production—the tools, machines, gauges, and methods that make up modern metalworking industries and automated production lines.

Hine, C. R. *Machine Tools for Engineers,* second edition. 1959. $10.50. Treats the fundamentals of machine tools.

Immer, John R. *Layout Planning Techniques.* 1950. $7.95. Discusses basic principles of production flow and layout and methods for solving layout problems.

Jones, Franklin D. *Machine Shop Training Course,* 2 volumes, $6 each, $10 per set. Standard treatise on machine shop practice.

LeGrande, Rupert. *New American Machinist's Handbook.* Metcut Research Associates, Inc., 3890 Rosslyn Drive, Cincinnati, Ohio 45209. $13.

Machining Data Handbook. 1966. $12.50. Lists by trade designations more than 850 alloys; categorizes each as to hardness, condition, and response to heat treatment, and makes machining recommendations.

Metals Engineering—Processes. American Society of Mechanical Engineers. 1958. $13.50. Treats designing for processes, such as casting, forging, stamping, metallizing, milling, turning, spinning, welding, and gives their scope, advantages, and limitations.

Nordhoss, W. A. *Machine-Shop Estimating,* second edition (1960). $12.50. Explains methods for determining the time required to do machining operations; an aid to quick, reliable estimating.

Oberg, Eric and Franklin K. Jones. *Machinery's Handbook.* 1964. $14. Mathematical and mechanical tables, standards, rules, formulas and general data useful in machine shop operations.

Pappas, F., and R. A. Dimberg. *Practical Work Standards.* 1962. $8.50. Shows how to establish specific labor costs, to determine plant schedules, to justify spending for capital investment, to determine plant and production-line layouts, to set up incentive pay programs, and to make other practical work decisions.

Parsons, C. W. S. *Estimating Machining Costs.* 1957. $9. A guide to estimating the costs of machine-tool operations.

Also published is a series of booklets from data extracted from the *U. S. Air Force Machinability Reports,* Air Force Materials Laboratory, Wright-Patterson Air Force Base, Ohio 45433. Examples are: *Machining Data for Numerical Control.* $1.50. *Matching Data for Titanium Alloys.* $1.50. *Grinding Ratios for Aerospace Alloys.* $1. *Machining Data for Beryllium Metal.* $1.

Machine Tools for Sale

Industrial Machinery News. Monthly. $5 a year; 50¢ a copy. (16239 Meyers Road, Detroit, Michigan 48235). Concerned with the buying and selling of metalworking machinery and equipment.

Industrial Market Place. Every 3 weeks. (2725 W. Howard St., Chicago, Illinois 60645). Advertising on used industrial equipment.

Machine Shop Magazine. Monthly. $6 a year; 50¢ a copy. Thomas Skinner & Co., Ltd., 111 Broadway, New York, New York. 10006.

NTDPMA Journal. Monthly. Free to members. National Tool, Die and Precision Machining Association, 1411 K Street, N. W., Washington, D. C. 20050. Also publishes a *Buyers Guide* for the tool-and-die industry. Write direct for information.

Surplus Record. Monthly. $4 a year; 50¢ a copy. (20 N. Wacker Drive, Chicago, Illinois 60606). Classified index of industrial machinery advertised by dealers and rebuilders. Free to buyers of machinery and equipment for industrial firms.

Used Equipment Directory. Monthly. $1 a copy. (30 Vesey Street, New York, New York 10007). Lists available used machine tools and heavy industrial machinery, with dealers' names and addresses.

American Machinist/Metal Working Manufacturing. Biweekly. $3 a year; 75¢ a copy. McGraw-Hill Publishing Co., 330 West 42nd St., New York, New York 10036.

Cutting Tool Engineering. Monthly. $6 a year; 50¢ a copy. Technifax Publications, 704 East Willow Ave., Wheaton, Illinois 60187.

Grinding and Finishing. Monthly. $6 a year; 50¢ a copy. Hitchcock Publishing Co., Hitchcock Building, Wheaton, Illinois 60187.

Grits and Grinds. Monthly. Free. Norton Co., 3 New Bond St., Worcester, Massachusetts 01606.

Iron Age. Weekly, $2 a year; 50¢ a copy. Chilton Co., Chestnut and 50th Streets, Philadelphia, Pennsylvania 19139.

Iron and Steel Engineer. Monthly. $7.50 a year; $1.50 a copy. Association of Iron & Steel Engineers, 1010 Empire Building, Pittsburgh, Pennsylvania 15222.

Machinery. Monthly. $10 a year; $1 a copy. Industrial Press, 93 Worth Street, New York, New York 10013.

Machine and Tool Blue Book. Monthly. $7.50 a year. Hitchcock Publishing Co., Hitchcock Building, Wheaton, Illinois 60187.

Metal Finishing. Monthly. $5 a year; 65¢ a copy. Metals and Plastics Publications, Inc., 99 Kinderkamack Road, Westwood, New Jersey 07675.

Mill and Factory. Monthly. $10 a year; $1 a copy. Conover-Nast Publications, Inc., 205 East 42nd Street, New York, New York 10017.

Modern Machine Shop. Monthly. Free, controlled circulation. Gardner Publications, Inc., 431 Main Street, Cincinnati, Ohio 45202.

Plant Engineering. Monthly. $10 a year; $1 a copy. Technical Publishing Co., 308 East James Street, Barrington, Illinois 60010.

Production Equipment. Monthly. Wilson-Carr, Inc., 407 South Dearborn Street, Chicago, Illinois 60605.

Steel Weekly. $25 a year. Penton Publishing Co., Cleveland, Ohio 44113.

Tool and Manufacturing Engineer. Monthly. $6 a year; 50¢ a copy. American Society of Tool and Manufacturing Engineers, 10700 Puritan Avenue, Detroit, Michigan 48238.

The Machinist. Weekly. $3 a year; 10¢ a copy. International Association of Machinists and Aerospace Workers, 1300 Connecticut Avenue, N. W., Washington, D. C. 20036.

Technology

ASM Review of Metal Literature. Monthly. $20 a year. American Society for Metals, Metals Park, Ohio 44073. Abstracts about 12,000 reports yearly from world literature; classifies subjects with code symbols for each abstract (ASM-SLA Classification of Metallurgical Literature).

Applied Science and Technology Index. Monthly. H. W. Wilson Co., 950 University Ave., New York, New York 10016. Publishes about 77,000 references a year to articles in 200 English language journals on science and technology in aeronautics, communications engineering, construction, electrical engineering, instrumentation and control, mechanics, metallurgy, and transport engineering.

The Engineering Index. Monthly. For price, write to: The Engineering Index, Inc., 345 East 47th Street, New York, New York 10017. Price includes weekly card service in 249 subject divisions. Carries over 34,000 abstracts yearly from world literature on subjects such as aerospace sciences, civil engineering, computers, electrical engineering, engineering materials, industrial economics, instrumentation, marine and naval engineering, mechanical engineering, and other technology.

TRADE ASSOCIATION

The principal trade association serving machine job shops is the National Tool, Die and Precision Machining Association. This association has over 1,000 members, many of whom produce tools, dies, and molds, in addition to performing contract machining and machinery repair.

NTDPMA is located at 1411 K Street, N. W., Washington, D. C. 20005. It was established in 1943. In addition to representing the industry in Washington, NTDPMA conducts, through its membership, an apprenticeship program; conducts management workshops; publishes a newsletter and management aids; carries on a public relations campaign on behalf of the industry; and provides management counseling.

MOBILE CATERING

Section Contents

URBAN BUSINESS PROFILE

Mobile Catering

(SIC 5812)

I. RECOMMENDATION

Success in the mobile catering industry requires both managerial ability and a technical knowledge of food service operation. While entry may be attempted on a very small scale with little prior experience, at least 1 year of experience is necessary for an operation of moderate to large scale, especially where food product purchasing and preparation is involved. The prospective entrepreneur must have a personality readily adaptable to selling and public relations activities, since he is meeting customers on a recurring basis. Establishing firm agreements with customers and following through with provision of good service is the best insurance for maintaining a route and against loss of sales to competitors.

An awareness of growth patterns in major market segments as well as of current developments in associated food manufacturing industries is an essential part of the mobile catering field. A metropolitan area with high concentrations of industrial locations and with a high construction rate should offer an excellent opportunity for a mobile catering operation. Since labor is significant to the mobile catering industry, careful attention should be paid to determining the availability and proximity of an adequate labor supply.

Investment requirements may be minimal if the operation is begun on a small scale and if a perceptive selection of routes, equipment, and supply location is made. Each year, however, the food service industry accounts for 20 percent of all retail failures, reflecting the necessity for careful planning and some understanding of the industry prior to committing capital and beginning operations.

II. INDUSTRY DESCRIPTION

A. Identification

Mobile catering is one type of fast food operation within the broad field of the food service industry. Food service applies to all types of facilities or operations serving food to people while they are away from home. The food service industry may be broken into three major categories. The largest of these provides meal service to the general public. The second category includes organizations in which meals are prepared and served by employees who are part of the organization, such as a day-care center. The third category covers employee, student, and hospital patient feeding, which has increasingly relied on outside contractors for food service.

Fast food services comprise the major part of the first category and make up the largest portion of the away-from-home food services. Included in fast food operations are coffee shops, cafeterias, snack bars, carryouts, drive-ins, and vending machines. Mobile catering has become an increasingly important form of this fast food service, fulfilling the needs of a particular segment of the food service market.

Mobile catering, Standard Industrial Classification (SIC) 5812, provides food service at locations where, because of the number of employees or the geographical location, vending machines or contract food services are either infeasible or uneconomical. Mobile catering operators today use specially built truck bodies, generally with swing-out doors that cover display trays for food products, urns for liquids, and soft drink storage dispensers.

Mobile catering trucks follow routes that consist of a series of sales stops during the business day. Routes are established for the most part through informal agreements with customers, usually construction companies, businesses, and industrial locations in a given area. The nature of these agreements is such that the particular mobile catering operator will have access to the premises at specified times during the day and on specified days of the week. The operator establishes these contracts by directly contacting the organization and, in effect, selling his services. Once agreements are made, the operator "owns" the route and may lease or sell it to other operators.

The mobile catering truck driver may operate under several conditions. He may be independent, owning his truck and developing his own route. Or he may be semi-independent, owning his truck and leasing a route from a commissary company. Also he may be a contractor, leasing both truck and route from a commissary company. Mobile catering companies are organized to operate a number of routes that they lease to independents, or for which they purchase their own trucks and hire drivers to utilize some combination of both leasing and working their routes.

Nearly all companies operate out of commissaries, whether trucks are owned by independent routemen or by the catering companies. Most established companies began operating their own commissaries at about the same time they began mobile catering. Those commissary facilities purchase, prepare, package, and dispense food products to route trucks. Commissaries may take one of several forms: (1) total food preparation facilities on the premises; (2) purchase of food from other suppliers and operation as a distributor or wholesaler; and (3) a combination of these two forms, both buying and preparing food for resale.

B. Industry Dimensions

The retail value of all food served through food service outlets—restaurants, snackbars, drive-ins, caterers—is currently greater than $27 billion annually, a 56 percent increase in total retail value of meals served away from home since 1960. American families spend an average of $400 to $500 per year on food-away-from-home, an amount equal to approximately 5 percent to 6 percent of the household budget.

Currently, fast food services account for approximately 80 percent of the total $27 billion food-away-from-home dollar value. These fast food operations, of which mobile catering is a part, concentrate on food products served quickly and conveniently, with a relatively low emphasis on such esthetic factors as decor, space, and personal service.

The mobile catering business is a fast-growing component of this fast food industry. Nearly 1,100 operators sold $1.1 billion worth of food products and merchandise in 1970, representing an $80-million increase over 1969 industry sales with a nearly equal number of operators and a $290 million increase over 1968 sales. The number of catering routes similarly expanded from 21,830 in 1969 to 23,271 in 1970. Route sales, however, averaged $171 per day in 1970, as compared with the $181 per day average of 1969. Industry size is growing in terms of employees as well; some 30,000 people were directly employed in the industry in 1970 as compared with 28,400 in 1969.

C. Industry Characteristics

1. *Product*

Fast food products are selected and prepared for the customer who is "necessity or convenience food" oriented. Mobile catering food products are primarily frozen and convenience foods, prewrapped and prepackaged prior to being served to the customer. The following is a breakdown of sales share by product in 1970:

Sandwiches	29.0%
Hot drinks	12.9
Dairy products	12.0
Cold drinks	11.5
Pastries	10.6
Canned entrees	6.4
Commissary prepared foods	5.3
Miscellaneous	12.3
	100.0%

Commissaries purchase the majority of food products sold on trucks directly from the manufacturer or processor; of secondary importance are local suppliers for fresh produce, meat, and similar items. Prepackaged items and convenience products are generally obtained from the manufacturer on a direct basis, and local distributors are of only minor importance.

Mobile caterers' menus are frequently cycled on a weekly, monthly, or quarterly basis. Cycling prevents the serving of identical foods on the same day of consecutive weeks or months or quarters, and cycle menus may be planned and scheduled by commissary managers in the larger operations and by the owner-manager in smaller companies. Several considerations with reference to customers are taken into account when making a selection of foods: (1) average customer age (younger customers tend to buy more dairy products); (2) sex of customers (men tend to prefer heavier foods in larger proportions than women); (3) ethnic composition of customers (menus tend to be reflective of neighborhoods); (4) income levels of customers (high-priced platters tend to sell well only in higher income areas).

Industry sources indicate that usually the only food prepared on the truck is coffee and, in a few cases, sandwiches. Time, health laws, and weather conditions are factors that greatly limit preparation of food on the trucks. The driver salesmen, however, in most cases select the food products they stock in their trucks, since they are in the best position to evaluate the varying tastes and requirements of the customers on each route.

2. *Customer*

Customers of mobile catering services may be considered captive markets in the sense that they require food service not immediately available at their particular locations. That is, they may not be able to leave the worksite and have no internal food service facility or access to eating places close by. Since there are limitations on the types of foods and the manner in which they may be prepared and served in this type of situation, interesting, varied menus and good service are essential to maintaining a route. It is for this reason that cycle menus have become a more important marketing approach in addition to the advantages of eliminating monotony, time and expense in planning, and buying and preparation of food.

Customers are found at the following types of locations:

	1969
Construction sites	15.20%
Industrial locations (less than 100 persons)	50.30
Industrial locations (more than 100 persons)	27.30
Office	6.40
Parks and recreational areas	0.43
Special events	0.37
	100.00%

As indicated by the chart, industrial locations employing fewer than 100 persons make 50 percent of total industry sales and have retained the lead in sales in the industry through the 1960's.

On the average, a good customer requires about four stops a day—before work, lunch meal, and two coffee breaks.

When determining the market size necessary for operating a route, three factors are usually taken into consideration: the mileage length of the route, the types of location stops available (i.e., construction sites), and the number of stops. These factors determine the sales revenues that may be expected of a potential route.

3. *Technology*

The entrepreneur who begins on a small scale with one truck and one route may require few specific skills to start. However, several abilities are immediately essential. The most important function fulfilled by the independent truckdriver is the selling function, which involves making a selection of food products that have the highest salability value, handling routine cash transactions, and performing public relations type activities on a regular basis. The operator with more than one route and at least one commissary must employ labor and must manage truckdrivers in the performance of all the functions indicated for an independent; he must supervise commissary operations (involving food purchasing, cooking and preparation, packaging, and dispensing to trucks), menu planning, fleet traffic management, and general management functions. The management of a company with fewer than 20 routes will generally find it necessary to perform sales duties as well, including locating, establishing, and maintaining routes. Companies with more than 20 routes employ on the average:

1 management or supervisory employee for every 3 routes;
1 salesman for every 30 routes;
1 maintenance employee for every 5 routes;
1 commissary employee for every 2 routes.

There is a high degree of labor required in nearly all the activities of the mobile catering industry. This feature reflects the importance of labor to the industry and the additional personnel problems and costs that may result. Food preparation facilities may be made more capital intensive as new equipment and methods become available, reducing the need for labor intensity in the commissary operation.

The mobile catering industry, and the fast food industry in general, are relying more and more heavily on prepared foods. Prepared foods are processed products that have undergone all preparation except heating or cooking. Frozen prepared meals is one of the fastest growing categories of prepared foods. This trend is particularly noted in the case of mobile catering, where almost all food products are selected for ease and speed of preparation.

There has been a recent industry trend toward leasing operations. This leads to greater diversity in wage rates within the industry, since commissions on sales constitute a major form of income, and commission rates vary as do the revenues yielded by routes. However, according to U. S. Department of Labor statistics, the 1968 average hourly earnings for employees in eating and drinking places was $1.57. Federal minimum wage laws require operators grossing $500,000 annually to pay $1.60 per hour. This affected fewer than 2 percent of all public eating places in 1968 and, when in 1969 the gross ceiling was lowered to $250,000, still only about 5 percent of eating places were affected. Some States do have their own minimum wage laws, however, that might also affect the entrepreneur's labor costs.

4. *Competition*

The mobile catering industry has a real competitive advantage over other forms of fast food facilities, since by definition it fulfills a food service need, the response to which has already proven uneconomical for other types of food services. To this extent other types of food service do not pose a competitive threat since they may not be easily substituted for the mobile catering service. Mobile caterers are competing in a market that again is relatively captive and where the demand is for low-priced, fast foods, or where the slant is toward necessity and convenience in away-from-home food service. However, competition within the industry is often quite severe, especially for establishing ownership and control of new routes. Getting control of a route as an independent may be quite difficult, since existing operators are constantly on the lookout for new market areas and may be well informed far enough in advance to lock out prospective newcomers.

Good service and quality and variety of prepared food products remain the most essential competitive factors within the industry. The most essential and recent form of change or development in the industry is menu cycling and innovative, prepared food products. The operator of either an independent or multiroute company with its own commissary operation, who is perceptive enough to successfully introduce new products marketed by prepared food manufacturers and the frozen-food industry, will be ahead in providing better quality and variety to customers. An awareness of developments in associated industries is a basic facet of competition.

However, other fast food businesses are increasingly interested in diversifying into the mobile catering service. Industry sources indicate that vending companies may be the most immediate competitive threat; many have already expanded to include mobile catering in their total operations. The vending companies apparently recognize advantages in having both internal and external sales locations, for when a potential market need cannot be satisfied by installing vending machines, it can be served by mobile catering, which offers both mobility and low capital investment. On the other hand, mobile catering companies have shown distinct disinterest in diversifying into vending operations. In fact, in 1969 several mobile caterers with vending machine operations completely divested themselves of their vending operations. Most mobile caterers involved in other food service activities are in party and special function catering.

Almost all of the medium and large companies are corporations. Small independents are for the most part proprietorships (and to a lesser extent corporations). Franchising plays a continually more important role in the fast foods field, but it has not lent itself to mobile catering as well. This may be attributed to the fact that the increasingly important leasing arrangements prevailing in the industry reduce the appeal of the franchise form of business organization somewhat.

5. *Ease of Entry*

Entry into the mobile catering industry depends on several factors:

1. Licensing requirements: As a rule, each State has its own set of minimum health and sanitation laws and the associated licenses and permits required to begin and maintain operations. Permit fees in the food industry generally range from $1 to $60 per unit.

2. Capital requirements: Initial capital requirements may be quite low if a prospective entrepreneur is willing to begin at a very modest scale. The cost of catering truck, route, and beginning inventory are the major expense factors.

3. Locational requirements: The mobile catering industry's greatest advantage is the mobility factor. Easy access to a commissary location is extremely important both in the case of the operator with one or more commissaries and in the case of the one-truck independent. Usually a commissary should be located in as central a position as possible relative to the total number of routes.

The development of a route is an essential prerequisite to the establishment of a mobile catering business. The new entrepreneur in many cases does not even purchase capital equipment until he has had the opportunity to cover a route for several days, assuring himself of expected revenues. Existing operators are sure to have a strong market position in established market areas. While established routes are available for lease or purchase in most cases, the best, least-cost opportunity for newcomers may be in the development of new routes as new construction sites and industrial complex locations spring up. However, intense competition may be expected when new markets of this nature become available.

6. *Capital Requirements*

The four major items included in the initial capital investment for a mobile catering operation include:

1. Cost of route(s) (buy, lease, etc.),
2. Cost of truck(s),
3. Cost of commissary facilities,
4. Warehousing and office space.

In addition, whether independent or franchised, the operator's cash investment will typically require:

- Lease deposit (usually 2 to 4 months' rent);
- Operating capital sufficient to cover operating expenses for 3 to 6 months;
- Initial food inventory;
- Equipment financing for the commissary—a minimum downpayment of 25 percent and 3 to 5 years to pay off.

Route values are assessed on the basis of daily sales. Currently, for every $1 of daily sales revenue a route draws a market value of from $40 to $50. A good route area ideally should be 20 to 30 miles one way from point of supply pickup. A good 8-hour working route will require a 10- to 12-hour day and have 40 to 50 stops along a 15- to 20-mile run.

The complete unit for a mobile catering truck costs between $6,000 and $8,000. These trucks are generally financed over a 3-year period, but some security is often required by financiers due to the single purpose nature of the vehicle. On the average, truck chassis are retired after 4 years, the bodies every 6 years; tire replacement varies from 20,000 to 25,000 miles.

In addition to trucks, warehousing, and office space, companies intending to own and operate one or more commissaries to supply their routes will require a minimum of 1,000 square feet for kitchen, preparation, and packaging. Costs approximate those of a regular food service kitchen facility, which runs between $15 and $25 per square foot. Kitchen equipment costs average $25 per square foot of kitchen area. The following types of equipment were most frequently included in equipment buying plans for 1969:

- Slicers
- Mixers
- Ovens
- Grills
- Coolers
- Compressors
- Sandwich wrapping units
- Walk-in boxes
- Filling machines
- Coffee makers
- Walk-in freezers

This equipment is considered basic to the operation of a commissary. Analysis of the failure of food service ventures indicates that one of the major factors is undercapitalization. In many cases lenders require that the prospective businessman have 35 percent to 50 percent of the total cost of the initial investment in cash before the balance of the capital requirement is made available. This is often the minimum extent of participation—equity or risk capital—expected for the operator to obtain financing.

7. *Profitability*

The mobile catering company has three main sources of revenue:

1. Commissary sales of drivers (food and supplies)	60% to 70%
2. Truck lease to drivers (typically $12 to $30 per day including gas, insurance, and maintenance)	20% to 25%
3. Route lease to drivers (route rental frequently based on 5 percent to 10 percent of truck's daily gross, or on percentage of food purchased from commissary)	15% to 20%

Industry sources determine that a fairly typical annual return on investment figure is 10 percent. The following industry operating ratios are based on a survey made by Vend magazine and reflect the experience of many mobile catering companies:

	Average for Responding Companies	Range for Responding Companies
Gross sales	100.0%	
Operating expenses		
Cost of goods sold (including commissary overhead)	52.7	23% to 77%
Gross profit	47.3%	
Other expenses		
Driver salaries and commissions (2)	17.3%	5% to 24%
Office and general overhead (including salaries)	10.2	2% to 31%
Truck depreciation	3.6	1.8% to 4.0%
Truck maintenance (including downtime)	3.9	0.1% to 5.0%
License fees	1.0	0.01% to 2.1%
Other depreciation (equipment and buildings)	2.9	1% to 10.4%
Building rental	2.9	1% to 10%
Sales taxes	2.8	0.2% to 4.75%
Total	44.6%	
Projected net profit (before State and local income taxes)	2.7%	

Operators leasing all routes to independent contractors are primarily involved in the preparation and sale of merchandise to truck drivers. This type of operator shows considerably higher product costs than a company that employs its own drivers and sells its own products at retail. Generally, the larger the company the higher the product cost among those companies that do employ their own drivers. Companies with less than 10 routes tend to have lower product costs of from 24 percent to 48 percent, while companies with more than 10 routes tend to experience product cost from 52 percent to 54 percent. The median for salaries and commissions is 18 percent; this cost figure shows rather wide variations within the industry.

Average industry gross profit per year is $42,500, with an average net profit of from $7,000 to $9,000 including owner's compensation. For the independently owned, one-truck, one-route operation, the following are ranges for average operating ratios:

Gross sales	100%
Food and supplies	55% to 60%
Maintenance (including downtime), repairs, and insurance	10% to 15%
Depreciation, interest, taxes and licenses	1% to 3%
Net profit, including owner's compensation	27% to 32%

Trucks are usually depreciated over 5 years.

8. *Effects of Outside Factors*

There are several factors external to the industry which greatly affect sales revenue. The mobile catering industry is greatly influenced by weather hazards, which can limit and even prevent sales. Also since construction sites account for over 15 percent of the market, construction slow-downs in the shortrun can have a serious effect on the fortunes of a company. From a long-range point of view, economic and industrial slow-downs may directly affect the mobile catering industry, in that new industrial locations and complexes potentially yielding new routes and greater sales are to some extent diminished.

Another factor greatly influencing mobile catering is the product research and development in the food manufacturing industry, particularly in frozen and instant foods, which have contributed toward improved quality foods with lower preparation times.

III. FEASIBILITY ANALYSIS

A. Key Factors

The factors of major importance in terms of contribution to successful performance in the mobile catering industry are the following:

1. *Management*

An independent one-truck type operation in which food products are purchased from an existing commissary requires less knowledge and experience than would be necessary in a company with one or more commissaries, multiroutes and a truck fleet to operate. The one-truck independent with sufficient risk capital to invest in a route and truck, however, should at least be informed as to what constitutes a good route, what the relative operating costs are likely to be, and what types of food products are most likely to be successfully sold. In addition, basic salesmanship and public relations abilities are equally important when this type of direct sales contact is made repeatedly each day. While these same requirements apply to larger operations, a much higher technical competence is needed for commissary operations and fleet management. Knowledge of commercial kitchen equipment and layout, menu planning, food product purchasing and processing, as well as the managerial functions, including traffic management, is needed. In all scales of operation a willingness and ability to cope with the intense competition frequently characteristic of the industry is also a basic ingredient of success. A prospective newcomer to the industry should be certain of a high degree of motivation well in advance of actual investment.

2. *Service*

Once routes have been established through promotion efforts, a high level of quality food products and service is absolutely essential to the maintenance of customers. This, of course, is due to the fact that most agreements with customers are merely verbal. This has the effect of making ownership of routes vulnerable to "pirating" by other operators, especially when service begins to drop off. For the most part, foods served by mobile caterers are convenience items, and, if the operator does not make his products available at the times customers want them, another operator will. Another aspect of service is menu variety. The operator who relies on cycling is capable of marketing much more interesting food products to his customers.

3. *Location*

Location is important especially where growth patterns for construction and industrial sites are concerned. The operator interested in expansion must be well informed about such development if he expects to arrive there first and secure new markets.

B. Minority Ventures

Mobile catering can be a particularly suitable business opportunity for a minority entrepreneur. It lends itself well to low capital investment and requires little experience. An associated advantage in this instance may be the better market acceptance of a minority entrepreneur in a community area where the majority of residents are members of the minority group to which the entrepreneur belongs. The entrepreneur in this case would also have some awareness of the types of food products that would be likely to have the greatest market acceptance and highest demand.

The bulk of the markets, however, will be places of employment such as corporations and construction sites. The minority entrepreneur must usually sell to the general market, therefore, and he is likely to have little comparative advantage in lining up routes. The beginning entrepreneur may find it useful, then, to obtain an existing route (that may feature a fairly high portion of minority workers) and to obtain experience in serving this market before attempting to establish a new route. Service and food quality will in any case be the basis of competition.

C. Projection of Attainable Returns

A description of the business and projection of attainable returns are furnished for a one-man independent operation and a small company operation. These examples are meant to be representative of each of two common forms of businesses in the industry and may be particularly illustrative of returns attainable by minority ventures.

1. *One-Man Independent Operation*

This type of operation would generally involve a single truck purchased at a cost of about $6,000. The average route, which would itself have a marketable value of approximately $6,800, would be developed and owned by the operator. The workweek would generally entail 5¾ working days of 8 to 10 hours each day during which 43 stops are made. The route is expected to yield approximately $170 in sales revenue each day. Total initial capital requirement would be about $10,000. Startup capital is obtained from both equity and debt sources; the entrepreneur obtains a $5,000 bank loan on his personal guarantee and finances the purchase of his truck over 3 years. Capital requirements are broken into the following categories: Downpayment on truck, $1,800; food, supplies, equipment, $4,000; operating capital and licenses, $4,200. First year projections are as follows:

Gross sales	$44,200	100%
Food and supplies	25,600	58
Butane, oil, and gas	1,800	4
Repairs, maintenance, and insurance	3,500	8
Depreciation, interest, taxes, and licenses	1,300	3
Net profit before tax (including owner's compensation)	$12,000	27%

The profit earned in this operation is representative of only one hypothetical situation and may vary widely, depending on a variety of factors both internally and externally related. While prior experience in the field is not essential on this level, day-to-day observation of commissary operation will contribute toward accumulating technical knowledge if and when expansion should be considered. This does not, however, eliminate the need for careful planning and good management from the beginning. A high level of service will have to be maintained to assure sales and to retain the route.

2. *Small Company Operation*

This type of operation would own and operate six routes and a commissary. The company would have the option of either leasing its routes or hiring its own drivers, and in this case the company hires its own drivers. The total labor requirement would generally be at least two managerial level employees (presumably at least one would be an owner), one maintenance employee, and three commissary employees. The use of one commissary for six routes requires a fairly central location, which means being situated in an area highly competitive with other mobile catering companies. An emphasis on service and menu cycling becomes increasingly important in this type of situation. Leasing of a building with sufficient parking area for the six trucks and at least 1,000 square feet of food preparation area, plus an additional 400 square feet for warehousing and a small office area, would be required.

Capital requirements for this operation would be approximately the following:

Downpayment on 6 trucks	$ 18,000
Initial food inventory	10,000
Lease deposit	1,800
Licenses, etc.	2,000
Building preparation and adaptation, office equipment	20,000
Operating capital	30,000
Food preparation equipment financed over 5 years	25,000
	$106,800

The capital structure of such a business might be as follows:

Owner's equity	$ 43,000
Bank loan with 90 percent SBA guarantee	63,800
	$106,800

Trucks would generally be in use 6 days a week, 8 to 10 hours per day, with 45 stops per day per truck. Estimated daily sales revenue per truck ranges from $170 to $175.

Projected sales revenues and operating costs for the 1st year are as follows:

Gross sales	$324,500	100%
Cost of goods sold (including commissary overhead)	172,000	53
Gross margin	$152,500	47%
Operating expenses	$139,500	
Driver salaries and commissions		18%
Office and general overhead (including salaries)		10
Truck depreciation		3
Truck maintenance		4
License fees		1
Depreciation—equipment and building		3
Building rental		2
Interest—trucks		2
Net profit, before taxes (including owner's compensation)	$ 13,000	4%

This net profit is only a single, though representative, example of what might be earned in the 1st year for an operation of this nature and size.

BIBLIOGRAPHY

Bertel, Herb, "Vend's First Mobile Catering Survey," Vend, November 1, 1969.

McKenna, Maureen S., "Writing Vending Menus for the 70's," Menu Planning, March 1, 1970.

Vend Staff Report, "Vend's Second Annual Mobile Catering Survey," Vend, September 1, 1970.

"The Food Service Business," Small Business Reporter, Vol. 8, No. 2, Bank of America, 1968.

"The Changing Institutional Food Market," Stanford Research Institute, 1963. Stanford Research Institute, Menlo Park, California 94025.

TRADE ASSOCIATIONS

Mobile Industrial Caterers' Association, 20 E Street, N.W., Washington, D.C. 20001.

Industrial Caterers' Association, 1140 Crenshaw Boulevard, Los Angeles, California, Suite 100, 90019.

Industrial Food Manufacturing Association, 1 East Wacker Drive, Chicago, Illinois 60601.

BIBLIOGRAPHY

[illegible]

TRADE ASSOCIATIONS

[illegible]

PET SHOPS

Section Contents

URBAN BUSINESS PROFILE
Pet Shops
(SIC 5999)

I. Recommendation

The successful operation of a pet shop that satisfies the needs of pet owners and animals alike requires a strong liking for animals, a knowledge of their characteristics, and managerial competence. Individuals wishing to enter the pet shop industry in an entrepreneurial capacity should also bring considerable experience in the industry to their new business.

There are good prospects for success in the industry if it is located in the suburbs of a metropolitan area where pet ownership is the greatest. The new entrepreneur must be technically competent, willing to perform occasionally undesirable maintenance tasks, and able to keep abreast of the new trends in the industry, particularly as related to his trading area's demands. The risks in the industry can be minimized if the pet shop owner clearly defines and analyzes his market, keeps good inventory records to establish a pattern for stock turnover, and utilizes the many resources of advice available to him.

II. Description

A. Identification

Retail pet shops are classified under Standard Industrial Classification (SIC) 5999 which encompasses miscellaneous retail stores not elsewhere classified. Retail pet shops are involved in the sale of pets and pet products including food and accessories. They may also offer grooming services. Other segments of the pet industry which are not described in this profile include pet breeders, wholesalers and distributors, manufacturers of pet products, veterinarians, and trainers. Pets and pet products are sold at retail by independent pet shops including franchise operators, department stores, chainstores, discount stores, and variety stores. This profile will be specifically concerned with the operation of a retail pet business by an independent entrepreneur operating either under his own name or under a franchise.

B. Dimensions

There are now an estimated 12.5 million American households with one or more dogs and 5.3 million with at least one cat. The estimated dog population is 25 to 28 million, the cat population about 33 million, and the fish population about 300 million, with each type of pet having particular needs that may be met by the pet store. It is estimated that eight million households have birds—75 percent of which are parakeets. The industry has shown continued growth, especially in the area of pet supplies. In 1970, owners spent about $3 billion on their pets—almost three times as much as they spent in 1960.

A most important part of business is an analysis of future trends in the area of interest. Currently there is a strong demand for pets, pet foods, and accessories, with a high probability of bringing good profits to the owners of pet shops.

The demand for particular pets, such as dogs, cats, birds, and fish, always has existed, but the rate of demand is increasing rapidly. Tropical fish are a good example of people's desire to own pets. One of the largest tropical fish farmers in the world shipped over 20 million tropical fish throughout the United States last year, and his records reflect that his output doubled in the span of 3 years. Industry experts report that tropical fish have become America's second largest hobby, behind photography. There are about 15 percent more hobbyists yearly, with the number now exceeding 20 million.

Other factors reflect the growth potential for the pet industry. Research and development departments of pet shop supply manufacturers and supermarkets are placing heavy emphasis on pets in their projections for the next 15 years. Supermarket studies have led to conclusions indicative of the anticipated pet population growth. Grocery industry statistics indicate that retail sales of cat and dog foods have climbed from $600 million in 1965 to $1 billion in 1969. Pet products as a category of goods stocked by grocery stores has been one of the standout performers in the past 5 years. Projections show that in the next 5 years pet products will be among the top four grocery categories in terms of annual tonnage sales gains.

What are the external influences affecting growth? One of the primary causes may be found outside the pet industry itself—in the continuous growth and expansion of the American economy. Population is expected to rise to 213 million in the United States by 1975 and 225.5 million by 1980. Demographic data indicate that urbanization (settlement in areas with populations of 50,000 and over) will be the trend. The A. C. Nielsen Company estimates that, of the 26 million additional consumers expected by 1980, 20 million new residents will settle in metropolitan areas including city suburbs. Since the pet ownership tendency is greatest in these areas (with 50 percent of pet owners living there), this growth means a sales market with great potential.

Disposable income, too, is expected to grow rapidly, reaching over $1 trillion in the United States by 1980, nearly double the 1968 figure of $588 billion. This trend has led Progressive Grocer to say that "more people plus more people moving to cities and suburbs plus more money to spend equals more pets."

Market data such as the above indicate that the pet industry is well established, yet has plenty of growth potential. The business establishments that service this market demand reflect these characteristics. In 1967 the Census of Manufactures indicated that there were between 4,500 and 6,000 pet shops in the country, with about 300 new shops being added to the industry annually. More recently, a trade publication entitled Pets/Supplies/Marketing Magazine indicated that there were over 8,500 retail pet supply outlets in operation with an even higher outlet growth rate. The exact value of annual industry receipts is not known to the Census of Manufactures. The approximate value of industry receipts can be gauged, however, by the fact that the annual sales volume of the retail pet store usually ranges from $40,000 to $175,000, with some stores reaching $1.5 million.

The retail pet shop has become a more specialized operation in the past decade. There are still a great many stores that carry a wide variety of pets and accessories, but large numbers of pet shops specializing in dogs and fish have sprung up to fill the demand for these types of pets. Some shops also emphasize grooming services as well. The growth of specialty shops is closely related to increasing customer interest in knowledgeable advice and a wide range of products and services for their favorite pets.

C. Characteristics

1. *Nature of the Product*

What do pet stores offer? The product as described consists of pets, nonprescription medications, accessory items, recommendations as to the purchasing and care of pets, and possibly grooming. The stock of the store will obviously depend upon whether the store is of the all-inclusive type or is a specialty store. The average all-inclusive store will have the following breakdown of pets on the basis of average volume of sales:

Dogs	30%	Fish	25%
Cats	15%	Miscellaneous	10%
Birds	20%		

Pets tend to satisfy human needs for companionship, love, education (especially on the part of children), and protection. Pet shop owners address themselves, consequently, to a combination of the needs of the pets and the needs of the owners or prospective buyers. Through the understanding of the needs of both a pet and its owner, a pet shop owner develops the essential expertise to allow him to recommend suitable animals for his customers and suitable products for the pets' needs.

The animal's need for the food and nonprescription medicines dispensed by a pet shop are obvious. The fact that the so-called pet toys are a necessary part of an animal's life is perhaps less evident. Toys fulfill the absolute necessity of providing the animals with a form of recreation and exercise, particularly essential to those city animals kept indoors for so many hours every day. Most owners of pets buy their products on impulse, through seeing a particularly appealing item in the display window or on the shelves in the sales area. (Hence the need for good advertising, a well-organized store, and knowledgeable personnel.)

Although many items are necessary to the health of a pet, they are actually not regularly purchased items, primarily because of the durability of the equipment (cages, aquariums, animal houses, and beds) and because of the irregular and often seasonal occurrence of many of the diseases. Food is perhaps the most regular sales article, although it constitutes only about 12 percent of the receipts of the average pet store. Most larger stores carry a complete variety of pet foods for dogs, cats, birds, fish, and other small pets. Dry foods and pet "treats" are usually the particular specialty of the pet shop, however, and the vast bulk of retail pet foods is sold in volume through grocery stores and other food outlets.

The pet business, despite recent progress in stabilizing sales levels through the addition of products and the emphasis on pet care, is still a seasonal one. The two slowest months are July and August, and sales usually peak around the Christmas season.

The services rendered by pet shops obviously depend upon whether the shop is of the all-inclusive type or is a specialty store. In all of them, however, most of the business is conducted when customers come into browse, although those businesses that have branched into grooming do business by appointment. The technique most often used in promotion is the placing of stock in the display windows. Cleverly arranged windows will attract the attention of passersby. Customers will continue to patronize a store only if they see that the animals are well cared for and healthy and if they receive sound advice from the personnel on first aid products, foods, accessories, and pet care in general. Only through this personalized service can pet shops compete with the grocery stores and chainstores, which offer similar products at a lower price but on an impersonal basis.

2. *Nature of the Customer*

The wide distribution of pets among our population and the strong growth rate in the industry suggest a fairly broad base of market demand to support the business of new pet shops. The key influences on consumer purchases of pets and pet supplies, however, include place of residence, household size, income, and emotional factors.

a. *Place of Residence*

Over 50 percent of all pet owners live in suburban areas, and these owners spend the largest amount of money per family on their pets, according to a 1965 Stanford Research Institute study of the pet industry. Within Standard Metropolitan Statistical Areas, a steadily increasing percentage of families spend money on pets as the distance from the center of the SMSA increases.

The types of dwellings that characterize an area are another important influence on the area's market demand for pets and pet products. Families living in single-family detached dwellings are almost twice as likely to own dogs as persons living in apartments, for instance. The following figures illustrate dog ownership by type of dwelling and by population size of city in which the owner lives:

	500,000 or more	50,000-500,000	under 50,000
Multiple-type	16%	24%	26%
Single-family	34%	40%	49%

The spread between the types of dwellings is not so noticeable for cats and most other animals, since apartment living lends itself better to the smaller and quieter pets.

There are also variations in pet ownership among the several regions of the country. The South has the highest number of dogs per capita and has correspondingly high numbers of other animals. The north-central and northeast regions follow closely behind the South in the extent of pet ownership.

b. *Income and Households*

According to a 1965 Stanford Research Institute study on pet products, the proportion of households owning pets tends to rise fairly rapidly as incomes rise to the lower middle income level, when it appears to flatten out. Average expenditures of pet owners, however, continue to climb with income, thus indicating a greater expenditure per animal in the middle and upper income levels.

Consumer units with after-tax incomes under $6,000 account for only approximately 25 percent of total expenditures on pets, though accounting for over 50 percent of total consumer spending units.

Consumer units with after-tax incomes of $10,000 and over account for over 35 percent of total pet spending, but less than 20 percent of all consumer spending units.

Studies regarding the unmarried consumer reveal that aggregate spending is lowest for this group, being only about 6 percent of the total.

Per capita ownership of pets is highest in families of over two persons, while average expenditures on pets are highest in families of only two persons. Aggregate spending by families of two persons accounts for about 29 percent of the total and by families of more than two persons, 65 percent. The over-65 families account for less than 10 percent of total expenditures.

The rising affluence of the consumer, the need for apartment-adaptable pets, and a certain quest for status among many pet owners have created a trend toward exotic pets. Monkeys, ocelots, snakes, margays, and other such animals are gaining popularity, and other small animals are being added to the stock of the larger pet stores and specialty shops every year. These animals are particularly useful as an attraction for the street-side display windows of the shop.

The minimum population required to sustain an average pet shop or a full-line pet shop is 20,000. All other factors being equal, profit will rise with increase in population. (Exceptions to the rule have been found, of course. Those pet shops supplying exotic pets have been known to attract customers from many miles away.)

Several factors must usually be considered in establishing a retail pet outlet. Since over 50 percent of all pet owners live in suburban areas, it is usually best to establish in areas with this high population concentration or in areas with a potential for population expansion. The urban-oriented pet shop may best be located in a business area bordering on the residential sector. Residential areas of apartment buildings are not good site selections in general, however, because most apartment buildings do not allow pets. In small communities, the main street is desirable; in large cities shopping center pet shops are most popular. In fact, a clean, odor-free pet shop is an asset to a shopping center, largely because it attracts additional pedestrian traffic and generates impulse buying. Also, because of new techniques for creating odor-free, soundproof shops, it is sometimes possible to lease space from a department store and create a pet shop as a department within the store. (Pet shops selling both pets and accessories are usually placed in the back of the department store because they will generate interest on their own behalf and will attract customers through other parts of the store. Those offering only accessory items are placed in the front because their drawing power is not nearly as great.) In any event, it is a prerequisite to check with State and local licensing and zoning regulations to make certain pet shops and the related services are allowed.

Loyalty is usually based on services rendered, congeniality and knowledgeability of staff, location convenience, and atmosphere of store. Customers patronize pet shops where they get good professional service and advice. Therefore, pet shops with a strong, reliable reputation can survive in an out-of-the-way location. A new shop, however, in an out-of-the-way place will take longer to develop.

Understanding the market, the types of customers, their needs and reactions, and the factors surrounding location are all important. Also important is the need for comprehension of the necessary "technological" skills.

3. *TECHNOLOGY*

The manpower requirements of a pet shop will to some extent be dictated by the size and orientation of the establishment and its services. The owner of a pet shop must be extremely knowledgeable about all the animals he sells, for not only will he be responsible for the business management, but he will also be providing advice and consultation to his customers. The owner will be considered the expert on all matters of health care. Thus, it is necessary that the owner have some background or experience. A 1969 survey showed that the average pet shop dealer had 9 years of experience in the trade and 8 years as an owner of a shop. The pet shop owner should have a working arrangement with a local veterinarian, and obedience school, and a boarding kennel, the former to care for the health of the pets, and the latter two to recommend to customers.

The pet store manager may be able to obtain needed information about pets or operating practices by contacting pet journals for reprints on specialized topics. These reprint services often can provide useful knowledge to the manager on a wide variety of pet subjects.

Most pet shops are open Monday through Saturday including evenings (approximately 51-55 hours per week). Some shops are open on Sundays, but surveys in the trade show that Sundays are not as desirable as evening hours. Part-time employees are needed in staggered shifts to feed animals and clean cages and maintain the sales area. Knowledgeable employees are important to the store, since there must always be one employee available to answer questions and to give advice and service. The part-time employees must like animals and should have over-the-counter sales experience.

If grooming services are offered, a trained groomer must be affiliated with the shop. Grooming services consist of brushing to remove snarls and matting, clipping to obtain a pattern, shampooing and drying, reclipping to smooth off the animal, and a general scissor cut. In addition, many groomers will clean ears and clip toenails. The art of grooming has long been in existence. It was practiced in kennels and by local veterinarians, and in rural areas it is still these industries that are almost exclusively responsible for grooming. The vast majority of grooming establishments or pet shops with grooming facilities are located in the city or nearby suburbs. Many established groomers received their background as dog show exhibitors or by grooming neighborhood dogs.

The rise of the poodle in popularity precipitated the trend towards grooming salons or facilities within pet shops. As the demand rose for groomers, a demand for training facilities was created. Today, there are at least 10 groomers' schools in the country. Licensing for groomers is at this time an almost meaningless term. In many areas licensing is not required, and in those areas where it is, there are few standards. An emphasis on professionalism within the industry is increasing, however, and licensing of only proficient groomers appears to be the standard being sought by trade associations and pet owners.

The locational determinants for grooming shops are the same as for pet shops in general—population and, to a lesser extent, income. Grooming can be a factor to induce buying of other merchandise in a pet store. Its attraction is not as strong a factor as window displays and other forms of promotion, however.

Competition in grooming takes place on the basis of quality and proficiency in work. It is the opinion of one grooming establishment that there are never enough groomers for the demand and that the internal competition only reinforces quality.

Charges for services vary from area to area. They are based on the breed of dog, size of dog, type of cut needed, labor (time required to do the job), and markup to cover overhead.

There are ample opportunities for ownership of pet shops among men and women of all educational levels. A husband and wife combination is very popular and common in the ownership of pet shops.

4. *COMPETITION*

The rapid growth in market demand for pets and pet products has created a large number of retail outlets and a wide variety among them. In addition to the approximately 8,500 retail stores (either independent or franchised) in the industry, there are at least 4,000 "pet departments" in variety, discount, and department stores. About 90 percent of discount-type stores have pet departments. Variety and discount stores are expected to handle an increasing share of nonfood pet products. Grocery stores also play an important role in the pet industry. Between 75 percent and 85 percent of all dog and cat foods are now marketed through grocery stores. Over 10 different varieties of foods are currently offered to the consumer, and research and development departments are constantly finding new ways to improve what is offered and enlarge upon the scope of prepared pet foods.

The retail pet industry is dominated by the independent proprietorship. Franchises are available from any of the 12 pet store franchises listed in appendix B, but franchises have not made the inroads in the pet industry that they have in certain other lines of business. The pet industry includes several strong wholesalers, and the Pet Industry Distributors Association includes wholesaler members from around the country. Both wholesalers and franchisers are likely to be a valuable source of information to the prospective pet store owner.

The franchise is a fairly popular new vehicle for entry into the pet industry. The better franchises offer assistance to the new entrepreneur in planning, display, and inventory purchase and control. Some franchisers provide brief training courses to new franchisees and place franchiser staff members in the new store to assist the franchisee in hiring and training staff, ordering inventory, and coordinating the events leading up to and immediately following the store's opening. Another common form of franchise assistance is the assumption by the franchiser of the advertising responsibilities of the local franchisee.

The possible disadvantage of a franchise, however, may reduce its appeal to some entrepreneurs. Franchise fees may range as high as $60,000 (for those franchises which provide plant, equipment, and retail inventory), and the relatively limited line product of most franchisers that their franchisees are obligated to market occasionally prevents the store manager from appealing to the particular needs of his local market.

Competition among these outlets is based on price, service, quality, and types of products offered and developed. The independent pet store, which handles over 60 percent of the total volume in nonfood pet products, has encountered competition from other retail outlets, particularly the variety stores. The smaller stores are the ones hardest hit, and penetration of their share of the market is likely to continue. The well-run, well-stocked, and innovative pet stores will continue to benefit from the interest in the pet industry. Tropical fish shops and dog specialty stores, above all, will continue to reflect buoyant growth.

5. *EASE OF ENTRY*

The retail pet industry has few barriers to entry for the prospective entrepreneur. There are, however, several special factors, in addition to a thorough review of the pet market in the several areas of potential location, that the new pet entrepreneur must consider before opening for business. One of the most important hurdles for the new entrepreneur to clear is the establishment of a satisfactory working relationship with the regional pet supply wholesaler. These wholesalers can often be helpful to the person interested in owning a pet shop by suggesting good locations for a store, and they usually offer valuable advice to the new manager on inventory matters. The wholesaler can thus be a valuable resource of information to the retailer as well as the source of appealing and attractive pets and supplies.

Licensing and locational requirements vary from area to area, but the State requirements are similar. One must obtain the usual vendor's license, consult the local health department about its requirements, and inquire as to the zoning ordinances of the area.

Currently, however, some States are considering the enactment of laws in the sphere of the pet industry for the protection of public health. California is perhaps a forerunner in this cause, having imposed quarantines on the South American monkey (raising their cost to the consumer by 200 percent), outlawed the sale and display of piranhas, and required all cats sold in pet stores to be altered. At the present time, the State legislature is considering placing temporary quarantine restrictions on any animal brought from outside the United States. The longrun ramifications of such restrictions will definitely be seen in the cost of ordering, maintaining, and selling these animals.

Another potential drawback to entry might stem from qualified personnel. Part-time staff is essential to the small pet shops, and the costs of training people can be great if turnover is high.

6. *FINANCING*

There are three types of capital requirements for establishing a pet shop of any description:

- a. equipment and fixtures,
- b. basic inventory,
- c. working capital.

Total shop investment typically runs $15,000, $22,000, and $30,000 for small (22 by 60 feet), medium (50 by 60 feet), and large (60 by 90 feet) shops, respectively.

The average dealer in 1969 spent $20,000 for livestock. The average markup for livestock is 50 to 55 percent. This covers care and feeding of the animals and the high risk of animals becoming ill. The average small pet dealer spends about $250 per month in rent. A breakdown of earnings conducted by the trade in 1968 indicates that, for every dollar of sales, 65 percent goes into new inventory and 35 percent into operating expenses and profit.

To finance such a business one may utilize such sources of funds as personal acquaintances, banks, lending establishments, and the Small Business Administration. There are no special sources of financing for those interested in pet shops. When dealing with a franchise, the franchise company may arrange for financing part of the business.

7. PROFITABILITY

There are many factors that affect pet industry profitability—location, population, size of shop, whether it is all-inclusive or a specialty shop, managerial expertise, types of stock will all affect the profit potential. Estimates have been projected by the Small Business Administration (SBA), however, that may provide a general picture of the annual sales over a 15-year period (assuming continuance of the growth rate prevalent in the late 1960's):

	Small	Medium	Large
First year	$30,000	$45,000	$ 55,000
Second year	36,000	55,000	65,000
Third year	48,000	65,000	80,000
Fourth year	55,000	75,000	95,000
Fifth year	60,000	85,000	110,000

Factors other than annual sales projections suggest the high profit potential associated with the pet shop industry. The average gross margin for the industry is 66.66 percent, a relatively high figure for retail businesses. The fact that the average inventory turnover in the industry is five to seven times yearly is indicative of the fact that there is a frequent return of cash to the business.

III. Feasibility Analysis

A. Review of Key Factors

The following factors are essential to the successful operation of a pet shop:

1. Management

The owner/manager of a pet shop should possess both technical competence and experience. Experience is recommended in both an apprenticeship role and a managerial role, with a 9-year background experience being the average in the industry. Extensive knowledge of the products with which he is dealing, precise identification of his market, a good rapport with the wholesaler and breeders with whom he deals are all prerequisites to success. Some of the most successful new pet shops are managed by younger pet fanciers with a business background.

2. Market

A very specific market should be identified to assure feasibility. A sound pet shop market is the following:

a. An area with a population of at least 50,000 is considered to be the best location for a pet shop. Interviews with wholesalers can help identify the existence and magnitude of the market. Predictions should be made regarding the future of the area.

b. Competition in the area must be carefully judged, remembering that a minimum population of 20,000 is essential to support a pet shop and an aquarium store. Competition for this market will come from department stores and discount shops as well as pet shops.

3. Location

Single-family dwelling units as the norm, as opposed to apartments or multiple-family units, are preferred since the highest pet ownership concentration and tendency are found in this category. Some of the most successful pet shops are located in shopping centers or malls with considerable customer traffic, since the pet shop depends heavily on "impulse" sales.

4. Service

The pet shop must offer sound advice to the customer on the care of pets. It must offer a high level of personal service by both the owner and the employees. The atmosphere must be one of cleanliness and orderliness, the latter so that the customer, who often buys on impulse, may see the full range of products offered.

B. Special Factors for New Minority Business

There are no particular advantages or disadvantages to minority entrepreneurs seeking to establish a pet shop. Opportunities are equally open to anyone interested in this industry. (A clean store, with personable and knowledgeable attendants that is built around the universal appeal of animals is a good base for business success to any entrepreneur.)

C. Projections of Attainable Returns in the Pet Industry

Two common forms of participation in the pet industry have been portrayed below to represent the financial returns available to a pet shop owner. A scenario and financial projections are provided for both types of operations.

Franchise Store

The hypothetical franchisee is required to have a minimum capital investment of $60,000, which includes leasehold improvements, fixtures, equipment, and $25,000 of retail inventory. Of this $60,000, the owner's cash requirement is $30,000, the balance to be financed through a Small Business Administration loan or an SBA guaranteed bank loan. The franchiser requires a training program and provides technical advice continually through each step in setting up the operation. The location selected is a suburban shopping center where the target market is a middle to upper income level area with the population residing primarily in single-family dwellings. An "exclusivity clause" is included in the lease to prevent another pet shop from leasing store space in the shopping center. The shop has 2,000 square feet of selling space and a frontage display window running the length of the shop, which faces the main walking concourse for maximum exposure. The store stocks a variety of livestock including puppies, kittens, birds, tropical fish, and exotic animals. The inventory includes a variety of pet supplies. Livestock and supplies are purchased from the franchise company, which offers higher discounts off list price than can be obtained through local wholesalers.

Projections for the 1st year are made on the basis of facts known about the industry.

First-year operating projections are as follows:

Net sales		$250,000		100.0%
Cost of goods sold		112,500		45.0
Gross margin		137,500		55.0
Operating expenses		125,000		50.0
Rent	$10,000		4.0%	
Payroll	65,000		26.0	
Advertising	15,000		6.0	
Maintenance	10,000		4.0	
Supplies	3,750		1.5	
Telephone and utilities	3,750		1.5	
Other	11,250		4.5	
Loan interest and amortization	6,250		2.5	
Net profit before taxes		$ 12,500		5.0%

Small, Independent Store

An investment of $20,000 is made in a small pet store operation. Financing is accomplished through $10,000 in owner's equity and $10,000 from an SBA guaranteed commercial bank loan. The store selected has 1,000 square feet of selling space and is located among a group of five other small businesses on the fringe of a downtown business district and the edge of a middle to upper income residential area. The store's front display windows are located on either side of the entrance and have been fixtured for displaying exotic animals rather than the more conventional livestock. The store's inventory includes puppies, kittens, birds, and tropical fish. It emphasizes its collection of exotic animals, however, as well as a variety of pet supplies.

Good trade relations have been established with two local wholesalers for pet supplies and livestock. The livestock wholesaler was selected and contacted particularly because of the rare types of animals he is able to obtain. Both have extended trade credit. Other livestock and supply wholesalers are used as needed to fill occasional inventory needs.

Some additional problems in fixtures have to be dealt with because of the unusual types of animals stocked. Four additional employees are required, three to help with sales and the handling of the animals and a fourth to care for the animals. Finding trainable staff experienced in handling a variety of animals poses a problem and is expected to entail a slightly higher wage expense. A fairly large amount of advertising in local newspapers, radio, and the regional shopping advertiser is planned, especially in the 1st year, to inform the public about the store and its interesting collection of unusual animals.

First-year operating projections are as follows:

Net sales		$100,000		100.0%
Cost of goods sold		47,000		47.0
Gross margin		53,000		53.0
Operating expenses		48,000		48.0
Rent	$ 6,000		6.0%	
Payroll	23,000		23.0	
Advertising	8,000		8.0	
Maintenance	2,000		2.0	
Supplies	1,500		1.5	
Telephone and utilities	2,000		2.0	
Other	4,000		4.0	
Loan interest and amortization	2,000		2.0	
Net profit before taxes		$ 4,500		4.5%

IV. Establishing the Business

A. Approaching the Market

Whether the potential entrepreneur is contemplating a franchise or a small, independent pet shop, he should have a precise definition of his market, substantiated by interviews with wholesalers and a "drive-through" tour of the potential site in order to pinpoint potential competition.

The approaches to the prospective market must be based on local customer needs, both real and potential. Inventory based on demands of the chosen trading area must be readily available and logically displayed. Most wholesalers will be glad to assist the new store in the selection of initial inventory. The selection of a local prime wholesaler, therefore, may provide valuable marketing information to the new dealer.

Advertising, as well as personal service, will contribute to the success of the stores. It has been estimated that pet shops have spent 3 to 8 percent of their annual sales volume for advertising Costs obviously will vary, depending upon the dealer's selection of media.

Newspaper ads are the most widely used form of advertising. Some pet shops take advantage of dealer ad mats and co-op advertising from the manufacturers. Other devices suggested are the tailoring of ads to seasons and holidays and the reutilization of particularly successful ads. Many pet shops advertise in the classified section in the "Pet" column. They may also run large ads for promotional events, i.e., pets for special holiday gifts or announcements of new animals.

Advertising in the Yellow Pages has proven to be an effective means of making all pet services known to the customer when he is ready to buy. The Yellow Pages have the advantage of reaching outlying communities to achieve full coverage of the trading area.

Radio and limited television spots are becoming more and more popular with businesses of all forms and have proved particularly beneficial to pet shops located in a tourist area during the vacation season (since more and more people are traveling with their pets). Time contracts provide a dealer with an easy, effective way to save money on spot radio advertising and guarantee special times for the broadcasts (which helps build up the recall value of the business with listeners).

A unique form of promotion is available to pet shop owners because they have access to unusual animals. An exotic animal or a group of puppies in the window is the best method of attracting customers into the store.

Some pet shops have built promotional strategies around the offering of community services—having school children, scout troops, and similar groups visit the pet shop to learn about various kinds of animals and their care.

An obvious promotional device and an extremely important way to introduce the presence of a shop is the Grand Opening. This will bring a shop to the attention of great number of people. Such promotional aids as free gifts (goldfish) and speeches by a member of the humane society (whose approval is important to the success of the venture) will draw large groups. The newspapers and radio should be used to announce the opening; it is news and may be treated as such by the media. It is also a good idea to have a guest book from which you may later be able to procure names for a mailing list. Another promotional tool is the direct mail circular mailed throughout the local market area.

B. Requirements

1. Space—Interior

The minimum square footage requirement for a small pet shop is 1,320; 5,000 to 6,000 for a large one. The store must provide for window display space facing onto a street or concourse. Most pet shops are arranged with one main display and sales area visible from the street through the window. Some of the new and larger stores have separate rooms for various groups of animals, but room dividers are usually glass.

If grooming services are offered, a small room to the side or in the back must be available. There must also be a storage space for stock and cleaning equipment, as well as for food for the animals in the shop. A new pet shop, in order to compete successfully, must be well-lit, extremely clean, and odor free. Excellent ventilation is essential; in most locations, central air-conditioning is a must.

2. Space—Exterior

A carefully planned window display with frontage on a heavily traveled pedestrian way is the most important requirement for exterior space. Parking facilities are desirable but do not necessarily have to be adjacent to or in front of the store. Municipal parking provisions will be satisfactory. Access to pedestrian traffic is most important for pet shops, as it is for any business catering to impulse buying.

Outdoor space is not required for an urban retail store. Zoning ordinances in most cities and suburbs prohibit commercial kennels, thus automatically eliminating the need for outdoor space.

3. Equipment

Minimum capital equipment needs for the sales and display area would include the following:

Animals: Dogs, cats, birds, tropical fish and aquatic animals, small pets such as hamsters, gerbils, and any of the more exotic animals desired.

Food, clothing, and grooming accessories for these pets.
Cleaning equipment.
Refrigerator for perishables.
Tropical fish tanks with aeration pumps.
Goldfish tanks with running water.
Heating and lighting equipment for fish tanks.
Cages for animals and birds.
Display gondolas.
Tables, stands, and display shelves.
Office supplies.

Supplies for a grooming area would include:

Bathtub with adjustable water flow and spray hose.
Grooming table.
Galvanized iron or stainless steel cages.
Electric clippers, scissors, combs, brushes, etc.
Shampoo, towels, electric dryers, etc.

Advice on equipment and display may often be obtained from the wholesaler or distributor. He should be able to arrange for the prospective entrepreneur to visit some other retail shops he supplies to see how they stock merchandise or arrange displays. The trade journals give advice about equipment and provide directories of wholesalers of both animals and stock items. Information on associations, franchisers, and trade shows is contained in the appendices.

4. Transportation

There are no major transportation requirements for a pet shop. Incoming stock is usually shipped air freight for long distances or trucked for short distances to create the least possible disturbance to the animals. Nonlivestock items are delivered by parcel post or truck, but special loading facilities or warehouse space is not required. Customer delivery service is not required of a pet shop because customers pick up their own pets. It is advisable, however, to use local distributors if at all possible, even in lieu of saving money, to prevent damage to the animals from long distance travel. The health of the animal is most important in establishing a good reputation.

Many pet shops receive their pets through local kennels or owners who breed animals for the specific purpose of selling through pet shops. The larger stores often have their own fish farms or else deal with fish farms throughout the country, particularly in Florida or other southern areas.

C. Obtaining Requisite Financing

The best sources for start-up capital for the new pet shop are personal savings, funds supplied by acquaintances, loans through banks, the Small Business Administration, or the franchises. There is also credit available to the entrepreneur through his wholesaler. Trade credit is a good way to finance open inventory. There are no known special sources of capital for new minority pet shop owners.

D. Employing a Labor Force

Employing a labor force specifically equipped to deal with the animals is sometimes difficult. Since most of the pet shops need part-time help; it is perhaps advisable to locate in an area where there will be students (who constitute the majority of part-time employees in pet shops). This will insure a fairly reliable source of labor, although the turnover is relatively high.

Part-time labor and new full-time labor may be recruited from among customers. Any frequent visitor can be chalked up as a fancier/hobbyist with a working knowledge of one or more types of livestock. Conversation will soon reveal if he is interested in work or knows some knowledgeable person who would be.

BIBLIOGRAPHY

I. Government Sources

Ross, Joe and Gores, Stan. *Starting and Managing a Pet Shop*. 1970. Small Business Administration, Washington, D. C. 20416.

Small Business Administration, Small Business Bibliography No. 76, *Pet Shops*. June 1967. Small Business Administration, Washington, D.C. 20416.

II. Nongovernment Sources

"Ben Elsinger Points Out Some Profitable Pet Trends for 1970," The Pet Dealer, January 1970.

"Betting on Real Cats and Dogs," Business Week, August 30, 1969, p. 72.

Bunn, Verne E. "Have Adequate Information When Buying and Selling," The Pet Dealer, 1970.

"Cash in on the Pet Market," American Druggist 160 (August 11, 1969) pp. 77-79.

Caswell, Charles Foster. So You Want a Pet Shop. New York: Comet Press Books, 1956.

Daykin, Leonard. "Pet Food Departments Explode," Progressive Grocer, November 1969.

"Docktor Pet Centers, Inc.," Reprint from The Franchise Guide, 1969.

Englehardt, Charles P. "Pitfalls in Franchising—But Many Probable Rewards Seen," The Pet Dealer, January 1970.

"Florida Spawns New Industry: Tropical Fish," Los Angeles Times, June 14, 1970.

Muck, Janet, "Pet Shops—The Successful Ones Don't Grow on Trees," Pet Shop Management, May 1969.

"The Pet Retail Franchise," Pet Shop Management, May 1969.

"The Pet Business is Found in Demand," New York Times, May 30, 1970.

"Rx: No Scents = K-9$'s," Chain Store Age, April 1970.

Stapp, John. "Four Rungs Up the Ladder," Pets/Supplies/Marketing, April 1967, pp. 9, 12.

"Survey Indicates Median Pet Dealer Earns $10,000 Yearly," The Pet Dealer, January 1969.

Stanford Research Institute, Long Range Planning Service—Pet Products, Report No. 252, August 1965.

Werb, Richard. "Scarcity of Help Places Big Burden on Today's Pet Shop," The Pet Dealer, August 1969.

"We're Going to the Dogs—$3 Billion a Year," Philadelphia Daily News, October 3, 1966.
"What are the Factors in Determining Dealer's Most Effective Hours of Operation?" The Pet Dealer, January 1970.
"Wholesaler Publishes Guide to Opening a Pet Shop," Pets/Supplies/Marketing, January 1967, pp. 64-65.
Your Docktor Pet Center Franchise; Docktor Pet Centers, Inc., Philadelphia, Pennsylvania 19154.

APPENDIX A

Associations

Manufacturers Only

American Pet Products Manufacturers Association, Inc., 663 Fifth Avenue, New York, New York 10022.

Pet Food Institute, 111 E. Wacker Drive, Chicago, Illinois 60601. (Dogs and cats only.)

Wholesalers/Distributors Only

Pet Industry Distributors Association, 111 E. Wacker Drive, Chicago, Illinois 60601. (Manufacturers accepted as affiliates.)

Wholesalers/Distributors/Manufacturers

Florida Tropical Fish Industries, Inc., c/o R. S. Rhinehart & Associates, Inc., P. O. Drawer 1519, Winter Haven, Florida 33880.

National Association of the Pet Industry, 431 Chauncey Street, Brooklyn, New York 11233.

Western Wholesale Pet Supply Association, Inc., 4154 MacArthur Boulevard, Oakland, California 94619.

Retailers Primarily

Illinois Retail Pet Supply Association, c/o Bernie Hoffman Animal Kingdom, 2980 N. Milwaukee Avenue, Chicago, Illinois 60618.

National Dog Groomers Association, Clark, Pennsylvania 16113.

National Retail Pet Supply Association, c/o Boyd's Pet Shop, 620 South Street, Long Beach, California 90805.

United Pet Dealers Association, Inc., 2601 E. 16th Street, Brooklyn, New York 11235.

Wisconsin Retail Pet Dealers Association, Inc., c/o Evans and Kunz Pet Shop, 4714 West Fond du Lac Avenue, Milwaukee, Wisconsin 53216.

APPENDIX B

Franchisers

Amerbrit International, Inc., 7400 N. W. 74th Avenue, Miami Springs, Florida 33166.

Docktor Pet Centers, Inc., Caroline and Charter Roads, Philadelphia, Pennsylvania 19154.

Intra Pet Distributors, Shasta Pet Centers, S. Ardmore Avenue, Valla Park, Illinois 60181.

Pet Mart, Inc., 7041 Wimsatt Road, Springfield, Virginia 22141.

Pic-A-Pup, Inc., 253-01 Union Turnpike, Floral Park, N. Y. 11426.

Pup City Systems, Inc., 2455 E. Sunrise Boulevard, Suite 503, Fort Lauderdale, Florida 33304.

Phydos, Inc., 1150 Fremont Street, Seaside, California 93955.

Scuffy Pet Centers, Inc., 53 Cottage Place, Allendale, New Jersey 07401.

Dale Pet Centers, Inc., 8951 Bay Parkway, Brooklyn, New York 11214.

Pet Hotels, Inc., 633 N. Peer Drive, Los Angeles, California 90069.

Puppy Palace Enterprises, Inc., 35 S. Letitia, Philadelphia, Pennsylvania 19106.

Ultrapet, Inc., 610 Merrick Road, Lynbrook, New York 11563.

APPENDIX C

Trade Shows

It is good for any pet shop owner or prospective pet shop owner to visit a trade show if possible. Meeting with other retailers, wholesalers, and manufacturers and seeing a wide variety of merchandise is always stimulating.

Trade Shows Permitting Attendance of Retailers

Independent Pet Industry Trade Show, usually held in April and in a different city annually. H. H. Backer Associates, Inc., 2151 N. Hudson Avenue, Chicago, Illinois 60614.

Pet Industry Distributors' Association, held in July in Chicago, Illinois, 111 E. Wacker Drive, Chicago, Illinois 60601.

The Pet Industry National Trade Show, held annually in September in New York City, 431 Chauncey Street, Brooklyn, New York 11233.

Western Wholesale Pet Supply Association, Inc., held annually in August. Rotates annually between San Francisco and Los Angeles.

APPENDIX D

Journals

The Pet Dealer, 9 East 38th Street, New York, New York 10016.

PETS/SUPPLIES/MARKETING, 1 East First Street, Duluth, Minnesota 55802.

PHOTOGRAPHIC STUDIOS

Section Contents

URBAN BUSINESS PROFILE

Photographic Studios

(SIC 7221)

I. RECOMMENDATION

A variety of opportunities exist for individuals to participate in the sizeable growth of the photographic industry. One of the most accessible opportunities for industry participation is as the owner-manager of a photographic studio that does portrait work for individuals or general photographic work for organizations and commercial enterprises. The photographer who opens such a studio has the opportunity to realize both a high degree of professional satisfaction and an attractive return on a modest investment if he serves his chosen market with insight, current techniques, and competitive prices. The photographic industry itself is, however, as turbulent as it is fast-growing. In 1969, equipment and photographic supplies stores experienced the highest failure rate of all retail businesses. The studio photographer must be able to keep abreast of the latest developments in photographic technology if he is to succeed in this easily-entered, highly competitive business. But his success is dependent primarily upon his skill in using photographic equipment to satisfy people rather than his possession of modern equipment. The photographic studio business will continue to be based on reputation and customer service, with the rewards going to those who are more than just eager amateur photographers.

II. DESCRIPTION OF THE INDUSTRY

A. Identification of Industry Activities

The photographic studio covered by Standard Industrial Classification (SIC) code 7221 is engaged in portrait photography for the general public and somewhat broader photographic services for commercial clients. It may develop film and process prints, but firms primarily engaged in processing and developing are not covered in this profile.

B. Dimensions of the Industry

The number of photographic studios has risen rapidly in recent years. From 1963 to 1967, for example, the number of studios rose from 19,544 to 26,558 while the value of their receipts climbed 50 percent to three-quarters of a billion dollars. The number of employees in studios has kept pace with the rise in the number of establishments: the 1969 figure of 42,500 photographic studio employees indicates that the industry continues to be characterized primarily by one- or two-employee operations. Individual proprietorships, in fact, make up about 80 percent of the industry by number of establishments, although they share equally with corporations in volume of industry receipts.

The growth in photographic studio operations is, of course, directly related to the rapidly increasing importance of photography in our daily lives. The 620-percent increase in the value of photographic equipment and supplies shipped to the American consumer from domestic and foreign producers between 1950 and 1969 represented nearly three times the rate of growth in Gross National Product in the corresponding period. And this growth only suggests the extent to which the American public has come to rely on accurate photographic representations of people, places, and events to communicate with each other.

The results of this increased reliance on photographic representation has had a mixed effect on the business and the professional photographer. He is more and more bypassed as the source of routine pictures, but he has been able to profit by the general public appreciation of skilled craftsmen and quality photographs created by this technology boom. The significant turnover among photographic studios indicates no lack of entrepreneurs willing to take a chance at proving their photographic skill in the marketplace.

The importance of the customer in this industry suggests a relatively attractive business opportunity for the skilled minority photographer, and minorities have already begun to penetrate the market.

A recent survey by Flourney Coles indicates that photographic studios comprise about 20 percent of the black professional service businesses in seven cities with large black populations. Spanish-speaking communities also contain a number of studios serving their ethnic market. The extent to which these photographers have tapped the larger market usually is limited, however.

C. **Characteristics of the Industry**

The photographic studio's product is more than a picture of a particular subject. The customer—whether he be an individual portrait-sitter or a business advertiser—seeks a photographic representation of his ideas about the subject being photographed. The photographer who is technically proficient in the use of camera, lighting, and development material may fail to satisfy if he cannot relate to these ideas. Particularly successful photographers not only convey the image that the customer seeks, but have the creative talent to discover new ways of expressing the concept that the customer has of himself or his product.

This understanding of the professional photographer's role suggests the range of activities in which he may engage. Commercial studios generally perform a range of photographic work in advertising, recordkeeping, and public relations for commercial clients. These studios may also take photographs of events in their locale on contract to other commercial clients. Portrait photographers specialize in portrait photography in their studios, at institutions such as schools, and on location elsewhere. Portrait photographers also cover the growing field of wedding photography. Only about 20 percent of all studios engage in both portrait and commercial photography.

The market for each of these two types of studios continues to grow strongly. Audiovisual expenditures rose to a new high of $1.37 billion in 1969, with schools and business accounting for over half a billion dollars apiece. Over 26,000 photographic studios currently compete for this commercial market with about 6,000 corporate photo departments and even more photographers employed full- or part-time by schools and companies. Business management's growing awareness of the value of photography for obtaining information, selling products, and keeping records has afforded expanding opportunities for all these industry participants.

The portrait studio, considered the more traditional part of the industry, is also riding some significant growth trends. The Professional Photographers of America estimate that one-third of all households buy at least one professional portrait in a 3-year period, and this figure is expected to rise with the growing affluence of the population and increasing acceptance of the photograph as an essential part of new life styles. The increase in the number of memorable events at which professional photographers are usually preferred—weddings, graduations, and births—is another source of strength for the portrait photographer who does onsite photo work. School photography in particular has been an excellent source of business for the studios. An industry survey taken in 1970 showed that the high school senior market alone was worth over $100 million, and at least 70 percent of all school children are photographed for class pictures every year. This business is not only profitable—the average price of a portrait package for each photographed elementary schoolchild was $4—but serves as an excellent device for introducing the studio product to a large number of homes in the area. Follow-on contracts for school yearbooks are often quite lucrative.

The volume of business available and the relative ease with which a photographer can acquire the necessary equipment and developing facilities combine to keep the competition among studios high. Customer needs for photography are usually continuing ones, however, and a photographer who breaks into a market with price discounts or artistic flair can often hold his customers with attentive service and timely reminders. Industry sources indicate that customers place the greatest volume of repeat business with studios in which they feel comfortable. This characteristic of the photography business undoubtedly accounts for the considerable number of minority-operated studios operating in larger cities and suggests that these studios have a natural advantage in serving customers from their communities. While minority portrait studios are expected to capture at least some of the extra business from increasingly prosperous minority households, there are fewer minority commercial studios that have been able to compete successfully within the commercial market. Minorities moving towards the commercial market have usually done so after establishing themselves as portrait specialists, often using "affinity group" photography (church, social, recreational, civic) to obtain work in the wider business community.

The market orientation of the industry encourages the location of the studio in an area that is easily accessible to its customers. Studios have usually been located either on the fringes of commercial areas serving the target community (portrait studios) or in downtown business districts (commercial studios). Photography is not usually purchased on impulse, so space in an office building or a walkup in the chosen commercial district is usually satisfactory, and a store front is not a requirement. Some studios find it more profitable to send out their undeveloped work for processing, reducing their space needs and rental expense at the studio. For those studios that do their own development and processing work, however, the darkroom and other necessary facilities are invariably on the premises. The commercial specialist does much of his work on location and often satisfies his minimal office needs in a location close to his clients. Both types of studio are heavily dependent on a personal vehicle for transportation to worksites.

The photographic studio is seldom a lucrative venture for a new entrepreneur. Profits for the new studio photographer are usually heavily dependent on the extent to which he includes the value of his own contribution of time and talent to the business. The small proprietorship, which typifies the industry, can usually begin operations with a minimum of investment and at a low overhead rate, and a photographer who does his own portrait and development work, marketing, and accounting and clerical work can draw over 20 percent (from which his own draw or salary will be provided) of his total sales volume. Many individual proprietors hire part-time office staff for clerical and administrative functions as their time becomes more valuable and the increased volume of work justifies such a step. A survey taken in 1967 by the Professional Photographers of America indicated an average net profit before taxes (and owner's salary) of 15 percent of gross receipts. The survey can be expected to be biased towards the more successful studios and is based on only a small portion of the industry. Of greater significance, however, is the fact that surveyed studios were not asked to estimate, and include in their profit computations, the value of services rendered by the proprietor himself. The net profit projections of 21 percent to 25½ percent of studios grossing less than $100,000 annually are, therefore, overstated by the amount of the owner's (usually the photographer's) draw. Studios grossing over $100,000 annually include most corporations in the industry; they indicate salary costs of about 25 percent and a net profit before tax of about 9 percent.

D. **Requirements for Entering the Industry**

The photographic studio business is easily entered by the ambitious photographer. The studio owner must, of course, be more heavily capitalized than the freelance photographer, but industry sources indicate that a one-man studio can be started for about $6,500. For a sales volume of up to $50,000, minimal space requirements call for an office or reception area, a shooting room of at least 15 by 20 feet, a work and storage area, a small dressing room for clients, and darkroom space if the studio does its own processing.

An important decision for the new studio operator is whether or not he will operate his own developing facilities; the inclusion of a darkroom will about double space requirements and increase initial capital requirements by an amount between $1,000 and $1,500. Most one-man studios patronize commercial processing laboratories.

Trade sources indicate an allocation of initial investment for a one-man shop as follows:

a. Photographic equipment and fixtures	$4,200
b. Supplies	500
c. Rent deposit	200
d. Initial promotion	500
e. Working capital	100
	$5,500

The photographic equipment investment can be further broken down as follows:

a. Camera, including lenses and tripod (twin lens reflex or 2¼" by 2¼" single lens reflex)	$1,000 to $1,500
b. Office equipment	600 to 700
c. Lights, meters, filters, etc.	500 to 800
d. Inventory (frames, flashbulbs, etc.)	1,500
e. Miscellaneous	200

The actual outlays for equipment depend on local prices and on how much equipment is already owned or easily secured secondhand by the entrepreneur. The quality of the equipment chosen is not as important to the new studio operator as the skill with which it is used.

The typical new entrepreneur finances a major portion of his studio setup costs out of his own pocket. A limited amount of debt financing may be available from commercial banks, especially if the applicant has contracts in hand (commercial, school, civic portraits) to support his sales projections.

Franchising has extended into the photographic studio business as it has into many others in recent years. Though not a significant force in the industry, the dozen or so franchisers provide assistance to the franchisee not only in financing startup costs but in equipment selection, advertising and promotion, and training. Several franchisers also do all the developing work, supplying the franchisee with film in the process.

III. FEASIBILITY ANALYSIS

A. Business Opportunities in the Industry

The photographic studios of both commercial and portrait types are currently handling about $1 billion worth of business per year. The average studio, however, has gross billings of only about $40,000 per year, and many marginal studios are business ventures in name only. Success for the new enterpreneur, no matter what his background, is difficult in this competitive industry and depends on two critical factors.

The primary ingredient of a successful studio photographer is his ability to combine technical proficiency and artistic ability with his "reading" of the client so as to produce a picture that assists the customer in expressing himself or his idea. Whether the subject is an individual or an ad campaign, the cameraman who can capture his insight into the customer with a perceptive portrait or picture is likely to establish grounds for continued business. The ability to empathize with the customer is demonstrated by many photographers and is generally considered to be an important factor in their success. This skill is obviously useful in insuring the comfort of the customer during what can be a trying experience. The ability of a person with similar ethnic and cultural background to more easily convey this empathic quality probably provides some advantage to a new minority entrepreneur who intends to service his community's photographic needs. Industry surveys tend to support this segmentation of the market for photographic work. As the studio develops, the work of the photographer—displayed at the studio and distributed throughout his market—conveys his style and image more effectively than most forms of advertising, permitting a certain self-selection to take place among his new customers over time. The new photographer, who correctly matches his personal and professional style to his chosen customer group, has strong possibility of success.

The second critical determinant of financial success in the studio business is the extent of the entrepreneur's profit drive. The lack of this business profit motivation is identified by industry sources as the single most important cause of studio failure or "reversion to amateur status." The photographer tends to be an artist, and the temptations to sacrifice cost control to artistic excellence and to sacrifice administrative and management performance to photographic enjoyment undoubtedly prove enticing to the new studio photographer. The new studio photographer will seldom have enough business and working capital to go first class at the beginning, unless he leaves an established firm with a block of his own customers. The new studio invariably requires the 40-plus-hour weeks required of any new small business and the avoidance of costs that can be achieved by a one-man organization. Every buying and hiring decision can be justified only if it leads to more than enough revenue to cover the additional cost. Since the new studio owner will spend a good part of his day marketing, the developing (if done in-house) and administrative work must often be done at night. Judicious use of part-time help, sales commissions, and subcontracting can help the busy photographer in his growth to a two- or three-employee shop.

The studio photographer—especially if he is alone—must, of course, possess a good knowledge of camera optics, film and paper emulsions and speeds, darkroom and lighting techniques, photographic chemistry, and projection equipment.

B. Projections of Attainable Returns in the Industry

Two of the most likely scales of operation in the new photography studio venture are the one-man portrait studio and the three-man commercial and portrait studio operation. These levels of operation are representative of the industry in general and are particularly illustrative of the minority-operated studios in urban centers. The projections are based on a 1967 industry survey.

One-Man Studio

The one-man portrait studio is assumed to be located in a shopping center or commercial district patronized by the chosen customer group. The developing and processing work is sent out daily to a processing facility located downtown. The studio itself contains 750 square feet of work, supply, and reception space, with 20 feet of sidewalk frontage. The owner works 6 days a week; a part-time bookkeeper types records and correspondence. The studio was financed by $3,500 of owner's equity and a $3,000 loan from a local Minority Enterprise Small Business Investment Company (MESBIC).

Gross receipts		$25,000	100.0%
Portrait work	$24,000		
Film developing (commissions)	1,000		
Direct expenses		$10,000	40.0%
Processing services	$ 6,250		25.0
Photographic supplies	3,750		15.0
Overhead expenses		$9,250	37.0%
Rent	$1,250		5.0
Repairs	250		1.0
Taxes, license, and insurance	1,000		4.0
Utilities	500		2.0
Office supplies and postage	500		2.0
Telephone	375		1.5
Advertising and promotion	1,125		10.0
Auto expense	375		1.5
Clerical salary	2,500		10.0
Depreciation	750		3.0
Interest on equipment debt	250		1.0
Other	375		1.5
Net profit/owner's draw		$5,750	23.0%

Three-Employee Studio

The three-employee studio is the most common single size in the industry. The owner of the proprietorship employs a darkroom man and a portrait photographer in his downtown commercial center location. The studio performs both portrait and commercial work, with the owner servicing the local business market and schools during the spring season. He also performs at numerous social events and weddings in his community. The studio does its own developing, processing, and mounting. The business was financed for the present scale of operations at $12,000, with the owner putting up $6,000 and a local bank the remainder under the stimulus of a Small Business Administration (SBA) guarantee.

Gross receipts		$50,000	100.0%
Portrait work	$20,000		
Commercial work	26,000		
Film developing	4,000		
Direct expenses		$27,500	55.0%
Salaries	$17,500		35.0
Photographic supplies	10,000		20.0
Overhead expenses		$11,000	22.0%
Rent	$1,500		3.0
Repairs	500		1.0
Taxes, license, and insurance	2,000		4.0
Utilities	750		1.5
Office supplies and postage	750		1.5
Telephone	500		1.0
Advertising and promotion	1,750		3.5
Auto expense	500		1.0
Depreciation	1,000		2.0
Interest on equipment debt	500		1.0
Other	1,250		2.5
Net profit/owner's draw		$11,500	23.0%

The return on owner's investment in each case is negligible if he takes the net proceeds out in the form of owner's draws, but retained earnings can be built up in such a business by living modestly during the startup phase. The reserves set aside to cover depreciating photographic equipment are tempting for a new business to "consume," but if the studio is even to finance its own growth it must cover future equipment needs out of operating proceeds.

IV. GUIDANCE IN ESTABLISHING A STUDIO

The first step in establishing a photo studio is to ask what unfilled or inadequately served photographic need exists in an area. If there is no such need and plenty of local competition, it is probably best to remain employed and/or an amateur photographer. It is estimated that 5,000 to 10,000 persons are required to support a photographic studio. A quick check of the volume and profitability of potential competitors may also be useful in defining opportunities.

Location of a new studio must be accessible to the chosen customer group. Of perhaps greater importance than the general area of the store is the type of neighbors surrounding the studio. The new photographer may find that a particular setting does much to enhance or detract from his chosen image. Other locational determinants are relatively unimportant.

The new photographic studio should give great care to the planning of its marketing effort. Emphasis should be on showing work samples and demonstrating technical competence. Several suggestions from trade sources may be helpful.

1. *Commercial Studios*

   a. Portfolios of varied commercial and industrial photographs that convey strong messages can be a useful device to obtain business for the new commercial studio.
   b. Advertisements in business magazines and trade journals are useful for introducing the firm's name and special talents. The Yellow Pages are also good.
   c. A cheaply printed flyer announcing the new firm's talents and hand-carried to potential clients by the photographer along with quality work samples may be another way of introducing the new firm.

2. *Portrait Studios*

   a. Portrait studios must rely more on representing their particular style of work on studio display windows and using the better pieces of early work in sample portfolios for viewing by "affinity groups" and chosen customer organizations. Contacts made in the studio, if pleasant, can lead to a large volume of outside work.
   b. Schools and other large groups are often susceptible to price discounts in their purchases of photography, and a new photographer may be able to break into a large new market with low-margin pricing on several key jobs. School contracts in particular are worth a great deal in community advertising. The contract to provide high school senior photographic work can lead to work for yearbooks, university applications, job applications, and graduation announcements; these young people may return for business the rest of their lives.
   c. Careful use of newspaper announcement sections may alert the studio to opportunities for work—solicited with congratulatory cards—in weddings, births, and graduations. Mass mailings to past customers before large family holidays is also helpful.

The new studio owner need not start out with new equipment; a more important requirement is that his equipment be well known by the operators. For those new entrepreneurs who might require new equipment, suppliers and distributors of photographic equipment in a particular local area can perhaps best be located through the telephone directory. Other sources of information are journals such as The Professional Photographer; Photographic Trade News: *Master Buying Guide and Directory Annual;* or the *Popular Photography Directory and Buying Guide*. Also of interest in determining specific equipment needs is the Printing, Graphic Arts, Photography category of publications prepared by the U.S. Government. Publications describing photographic techniques and equipment, cameras, lenses, shutters, projectors, etc., are for sale at the National Technical Information Service, 5285 Port Royal Road, Springfield, Virginia 22151.

The sources of capital most often used by the new studio are equity (family, partners, personal) and bank debt. Minority photographers may be able to take advantage of such sources of capital as MESBIC's, Community Development Corporations, banks using SBA guarantees, and coalitions of business interests supporting minority entrepreneurship. The relatively small amount of startup capital needed is perhaps best obtained from equity sources which can then be used to obtain additional funds from a bank. The SBA lease guarantee can be a useful mechanism for "buying" into a favorable location.

BIBLIOGRAPHY

Government Sources

Small Business Administration, Washington, D.C. 20416. *Photographic Dealers and Studios.* Small Business Bibliography No. 64, 1968.

U.S. Department of Commerce, Bureau of the Census, Washington, D.C. 20233. *1967 Census of Business, Selected Services;* Series BC67–SA1.

U.S. Department of Commerce, Business and Defense Services Administration, Washington, D.C. 20230. *U. S. Industrial Outlook,* 1969 and 1970.

U.S. Department of Labor, Washington, D.C. 20210. *Employment Outlook for Photographers,* 1969.

Nongovernment Sources

Apple, Ruth. "The Language of Selling Photography," The Professional Photographer, August 1970.

Chandler, Jean. "Don't Give Up Your Babies," The Professional Photographer, September 1970.

Coles, Flourney. *An Analysis of Black Entrepreneurship in Seven Urban Areas,* Washington, D.C., 1969.

Narramare, G. L. "Something New," The Professional Photographer, August 1970.

Professional Photographers of America, Inc., 1090 Executive Way, Des Plaines, Illinois 60018.

Schabacker, Joseph C. "How to Sell Product, Service, and Self," The Professional Photographer, October 1970.

Schwartz, Theodore. *The Business Side of Photography,* New York, 1969.

Wolfman, Augustus. "1970-71 Wolfman Report on the Photographic Industry in the U. S.," Modern Photography Magazine, 1970.

REAL ESTATE BROKERAGE

Section Contents

URBAN BUSINESS PROFILE

Real Estate Brokerage

(SIC 653)

I. RECOMMENDATION

Real estate brokerage is a highly cyclical business in which profit levels are largely unpredictable. It is unusually subject to the fluctuations of the national and local economies, and the broker has virtually no control over market conditions. It is, nevertheless, a business which an individual can enter with only a moderate education and with minimal training in the field. Progressing to ownership of a brokerage generally requires a few years' experience as a salesman and a moderate level of capitalization.

Minority brokers and salesmen have an inherent advantage in operating within their own community because selling real estate requires rapport with, and the trust of, prospective buyers. This kinship, however, is not a guarantee of success, and it would be unwise for the potential minority broker to rely exclusively on his race or ethnic group without making certain that he also knows the details of the business and can provide the required service.

The personal characteristics usually required to operate a successful real estate brokerage business include:

(1) A few years' experience in the business, generally as a salesman.

(2) A personality for selling in the particular market of anticipated operation.

(3) A thorough knowledge of:
  (a) The mechanics of real estate transactions,
  (b) The money market in the area of operation,
  (c) The real estate structure in the neighborhoods of anticipated operation.

II. CHARACTERISTICS OF THE INDUSTRY

A. Definition

"Real Estate" is included in Major Group 65 of the Standard Industrial Classification (SIC). This major group includes real estate operators, owners and lessors of real property, buyers, sellers, developers, agents and brokers.

SIC 653—Agents, Brokers, and Managers—includes establishments primarily engaged in renting, buying, selling, managing, and appraising real property for others. This profile will concentrate on these aspects of the industry to the exclusion of owner-operators, developers, and operative builders engaged in construction for sale on their own account.

B. Dimensions

U.S. Government figures based on social security tax filings show, for 1968, over 155,000 reporting units under the broad heading of "real estate." These establishments employed over 625,000 people for an average number of four employees per reporting unit.

Of these establishments, over 22,000 were classified as "Agents, Brokers, and Managers." These firms employed over 103,000 persons, with an average of 4.6 people per firm. In addition, many real estate salesmen work out of a broker's office but are classified as self-employed individuals for social security purposes.

The total market value of all ordinary real estate transactions (transactions up to $250,000) in the United States for a 6-month period in 1966 was placed at over $14.5 billion, yielding an annual rate of $29 billion. The number of properties involved was over 1 million, or an annual rate of over 2 million. These sales, doubled to produce annual rates, represent 2.9 percent of the properties on the assessment lists, and 3.3 percent of the total assessed value of property in the U.S.

Real estate is a broad field, and brokerage is by its very nature a widely distributed activity. While some areas of the country offer more attractive real estate opportunities than others, there are, nevertheless, opportunities for real estate transactions wherever one might choose to operate.

C. Nature of the Business

The function of the real estate broker is to bring together buyers and sellers to produce the transfer of real property under terms acceptable to both. For this service he is paid a commission based on the sale price of the property. This commission is usually paid by the seller, who normally commissions the broker as his agent in the sale.

The seller of real property is not legally bound to use a broker to sell his property. He generally does so, however, because the broker offers the time, sales talent, facilities, organization, and knowledge which permit a sale in less time and with less danger of legal or financial error than would be the case were the owner to handle the sale himself.

The broker and his sales force are generally knowledgeable about the neighborhoods and areas in which they operate. This knowledge, usually not possessed by the buyer and seller, covers such factors as price levels for real estate in the area, availability and terms of financing, building and zoning restrictions, local tax and utility rates, availability and quality of public services (schools, transportation), and shopping and other facilities, as well as such seemingly mundane matters as the best type of grass for the backyard. With his localized knowledge developed from experience in the area of operation, the broker is usually better able to present the attributes of the property for sale to the prospective buyer than is the owner himself. Also, because it is his business, the broker has the time and the facilities to seek prospects and the organization to show the property and close the deal. The owner is rarely so well equipped to handle the inquiries of the buyer, to allay his fears, and to make a sale.

D. Licensing Requirements

Every State in the United States requires that real estate brokers and salesmen be licensed. Generally, only a broker can act directly as the agent for buyer and/or seller in a real estate transaction. A real estate salesman must work under the auspices of a broker. Most States require a certain level of experience as a salesman as a prerequisite for a broker's license. All States require passage of an examination for a license. These examinations run up to 8 hours for salesmen and 12 hours for brokers. Additional requirements vary, but many States have minimum educational requirements for salesmen and require education and experience prerequisites for brokers. There are fees levied for both the license and the exam in most States. These range up to $60 and $100 for a license and are $35 and $50 for the exam for salesmen and brokers respectively. Detailed licensing requirements by State are available from the individual States or from the National Association of Real Estate License Law Officials, 1515 Grant Building, Pittsburgh, Pennsylvania, 15219.

E. Listings

Key to the success of the broker is his listings. A listing is an authorization to sell a property within a specified time, at a specified price, and under certain terms. The listings are the broker's inventory. The more extensive and varied his listings, the better is his opportunity to attract and meet the needs of prospective buyers. Listings, therefore, are the lifeblood of the brokerage business.

Listings are of various types. They vary according to the degree of commitment made to the broker by the seller.

Open listings are those in which the seller makes known that any broker who produces a willing and able buyer will receive a commission on the sale. Under such an agreement, however, the broker is not assured of any remuneration and is reluctant to use his office, sales time, and advertising budget to produce a sale.

The exclusive agency listing protects the broker's investment of time and money. Under this agreement, the broker receives his commission if he produces a sale within a certain period of time. Should the sale be produced by another broker, there is an arrangement for splitting the commission. He receives no commission if the owner arranges the sale.

An exclusive-right-to-sell listing guarantees the broker his commission if the property is sold by anyone within a specified time period under specified terms.

Multiple listing involves the pooling of listings by individual brokers in order to increase their inventory of offerings. Both the exclusive agency listing and the exclusive-right-to-sell listing can take the multiple form. Multiple listing services are generally operated by local organizations of brokers called "real estate boards." The members of boards or branches of boards agree to pool all or a selected number of their listings. The listings thus pooled are subject to an agreement among the participating brokers. This agreement spells out how the commission is to be divided between the listing broker and the selling broker (when these are different offices).

F. Marketing

Obtaining listings is the first step in the brokerage process. With an inventory on hand, the broker must then locate prospective buyers. Buyers come from various sources. Primarily, brokers make estensive use of newspaper advertising. From 10 to 15 percent of the gross income of the broker may go for such advertising. Buyers are also attracted by the property itself. They will see a sign on the property and contact the broker for further details. The broker's office may also attract potential buyers. Individuals in the market for property will "drop in" to the office for assistance. The reputation of the firm is important for attracting "drop-ins." Finally, an experienced broker will know his community well and may have a good idea that a certain individual would be interested in a certain piece of property.

Real estate salesmen and brokers generally work a limited geographic area which may be as small as a neighborhood or as large as a metropolitan area in size. They will also concentrate on one type of real estate, residential being the most common. Many further limit their markets by concentrating on rental or on sales property.

A marketing talent necessary to success as a real estate broker or salesman is the ability to match the buyer to the property. For residential property, the broker will take into consideration the income, financial position, family size, desire to buy or rent, locational needs, and age of the buyer, as well as personality and other traits which the perceptive broker or salesman can translate into neighborhood type. He will then try to match the buyer to property from his listings taking into consideration such factors as price, financing terms available, size of unit, tenure (rental or purchase), location, type of unit, and neighborhood.

The ability of the salesman to "close" a customer depends heavily on his personality and presence and his ability to relate to the buyer.

A salesman can be very good at selling professional white-collar workers and be unable to communicate and instill trust in blue-collar workers. Some sales require "hard-sell," others "soft." A salesman has a personality and a style which usually communicates best with a limited range of buyers. Some have a wider range than others, but the salesman is more likely to do well with those personality types with which he feels comfortable or, more importantly, those which feel comfortable with him.

Making a sale involves instilling the desire to buy in the potential buyer, and, equally important, arranging the loan and sale details under terms acceptable to both buyer and seller. (Whether the drapes and the carpets come with the house can become a key issue in the sale.) Closing a deal can involve a great deal of compromise between buyer and seller. The broker serves as the mediator. To close the deal and make his commission, the broker and/or salesman must successfully bring the parties involved to terms. The process may involve delicate negotiations and the role of mediator is critical to many a sale.

G. Prerequisites for Selling Real Estate

Beyond the legal, licensing, and personality requirements for real estate salesmen and brokers, an intimate knowledge of the real estate market in which one is working is crucial. For this reason, it is common for smaller brokers deliberately to limit themselves to a few neighborhoods that they know well and where they have had experience. The broker must instill trust in the buyer, and to do so he must be able to handle a very wide range of inquiries about property and its setting. "Can the garage be legally converted into a recreation room?" "Can you recommend a competent contractor to do the job?" "Do the schools have a sex education program?" "How often is trash collected?" "What does this service cost?" The salesman must be able to answer these and similar questions.

While a knowledge of the mechanics of the real estate transaction is necessary to qualify for a license, the broker must continue to maintain and enhance his competence. He must be particularly knowledgeable about various sources of financing and be capable of working out various financial arrangements, because many sales will hinge on whether satisfactory financing can be arranged. The real estate broker/salesman will want to be well informed on the various costs of mortgage money and the availability of funds for mortgages and home improvement loans from the savings and loan associations, banks, and mortgage brokers operating in his area. Real estate purchases are the largest single expenditure most people ever make. Trust in the broker is paramount when the buyer is ill at ease in the world of real estate (as most are) and about to commit himself to a purchase equal to three or four times his annual income.

Real estate sales involve long and unorthodox hours. Property must often be shown at the buyer's convenience and that, as often as not, is in the evening or on the weekend. Beyond a rudimentary knowledge of the field, most brokers would say that someone entering the business needs a sales personality and a lot of "hustle."

Both salesmen and brokers work on a commission basis. This means that their earnings are erratic. A salesman may earn $3,000 in a month and nothing for 4 months. Earnings are strictly geared to performance. Persons entering the field should be aware of the economic insecurity of their earnings and be prepared to cope with the problems inherent in such an arrangement.

H. Competition

Selling real estate is a highly competitive business. All brokers in a given area are competing with each other for exclusive listings and for sales. It is a business easily entered, especially at the salesman level. (Salesmen work on commission. Therefore, to hire an additional salesman, the broker risks only the minimum overhead required to support the salesman.)

Brokers will find it difficult to maintain a good sales force. A turnover rate of 30 percent per year is the average for salesmen in the industry. Good salesmen can usually be expected to become brokers in their own right, and, because they know the area in which they gained their experience, they will in many cases establish themselves in direct competition to the broker under whom they worked as salesmen. Upon leaving, the salesman-turned-broker takes with him all his experience and knowledge and many of his contacts. Brokers will sometimes install a bonus plan or profit-sharing arrangements in order to keep good sales personnel.

Despite the competitive nature of the business, there is considerable cooperation among brokers. Local real estate boards, affiliated nationally as the National Association of Real Estate Boards, establish and supervise codes of ethics, handle disputes among members, run multiple listing services, and establish standards and procedures for fee-splitting and other forms of cooperation. Membership in the local board is not a legal requirement, but it is considered advisable in most areas.

III. BUSINESS OPPORTUNITIES IN REAL ESTATE

A. Key External Factors Affecting Success

The local real estate market is subject to the fluctuations of the national and local economies, a factor entirely beyond the control of the broker. Residential sales depend heavily on the availability of mortgage loans and the attractiveness of the terms to the buyer. It is difficult to finance real estate purchases in a tight money market. Local conditions may also have a severe effect on business. In an area with a limited economic base, a major setback to one local industry will have economic ramifications throughout the community, including the real estate market. Unemployment will rise, population may decrease, and the broker may be left with listings galore, but no buyers. Conversely, a boom in economic activity in a community (a new plant, a large contract to an existing one) will usually translate into a boom for real estate demand and activity. The broker may, for a while, be able to sell whatever listings he can get.

Key factors in the brokerage business are the level of market activity and the level of competition. The following are suggested as variables which reflect trends in the local market:

1. Deeds recorded, 2. Mortgages recorded, 3. Foreclosures,
4. Rents, prices, and construction costs, 5. Construction volume,
6. Vacancies and density of occupancy, 7. Display, classified ads.

The level of competition can be inferred from the numbers of licensed salesmen and brokers in the area, number of firms, etc. Anyone contemplating operation in a given area should have a good feel for the competition before establishing himself in business.

B. Representative Returns to the Broker

Real estate salesmen and brokers work on a commission based on the sales price of the property they sell. The commission is usually 5 to 6 percent but may be less on higher value property. (Above $50,000, commissions will usually decrease on a sliding scale).

Because of the cyclical nature of the real estate market and the sales level of the broker within that market, it is difficult to establish norms of profitability. The following table portrays the cost structure of the industry; it represents a simple one-man operation, with the broker acting as his own salesman and with a secretary and a small office. He may employ one or two part-time salesmen. (The table reflects only the broker's commission). This oversimplified case shows what sales volumes are needed to cover overhead costs and produce various income levels for the owner-broker. In this example, the broker draws no salary.

Typical overhead for a small office for one year:

Advertising	$1,400
Automobile expense	1,200
Dues and subscriptions	300
License, bond, and insurance	600
Postage, stationery, etc.	400
Telephone	1,200
Rent	1,500
Salaries and wages	5,000
Miscellaneous expenses	400
Total	$12,000

Sales volume needed to produce various income levels for owner-broker, assuming fixed overhead:

Sales volume*	Commission (5%)	Overhead	Profit
$150,000	$7,500	$12,000	−$4,500
200,000	10,000	12,000	− 2,000
240,000	12,000	12,000	Break Even Point
250,000	12,500	12,000	500
300,000	15,000	12,000	3,000
350,000	17,500	12,000	5,500
400,000	20,000	12,000	8,000
500,000	25,000	12,000	13,000
750,000	37,500	12,000	25,000

* or double the volume for sales made by salesmen because the broker gets only half the commission in such cases.

In this case, the broker-owner must produce $240,000 in sales to cover his overhead. For an income of $10,000 a year, he must produce $440,000 in sales himself, or double that from his salesmen, or some combination thereof. Overhead is shown as a constant factor in the table. Some brokerage expenses are variable with revenues (advertising, secretarial wages, etc.), and if volume approached the upper limits of the table, overhead expenses would increase.

C. Revenue Projection

Following are two hypothetical profit-and-loss statements for two brokerage operations, one small and one medium-to-large.

These situations represent attainable revenue levels. However, operation on these scales in the real estate business by no means guarantees these profit levels. Mismanagement, a depressed real estate market, or plain bad luck could wipe out the profits shown. These hypothetical firms might perform as indicated one year and lose money the next. Real estate brokerage is a very cyclical business, with general assurance of profit levels limited to only the most established firms. Even then the degree of certainty is not great.

Case No. 1 is a small broker in his second year of operation. He has a small office, employs one secretary/receptionist and is associated with two salesmen, one full-time and one part-time. He acts as a salesman himself and sells a volume of $250,000 for the year. His two salesmen produce a total of $300,000 in sales for the year and work for half of the brokerage commission for their sales. Total revenue to the broker for the year comes to $20,000. His overhead costs are $12,000 and he retains $8,000 in earnings.

Case No. 1—Small office

Receipts			
Real estate sales			
By broker-owner	$250,000		
By salesmen: one full-time	200,000		
one part-time	100,000		
Total real estate sales		$550,000	
Sales commissions at 5%			$27,500
Commissions to salesmen: full-time		5,000	
part-time		2,500	
Net receipts to broker			$20,000
Expenses			
Advertising	$ 1,400		
Automobile expense	1,200		
Dues and subscriptions	300		
License, bonding, and insurance	600		
Postage, stationery, etc.	400		
Telephone	1,200		
Rent	1,500		
Secretary/receptionist	5,000		
Miscellaneous expenses	400		
Total expenses			$12,000
Profit before tax and broker's compensation			$ 8,000

Case No. 2 involves a larger well-established partnership which employs ten salesmen. The brokers act as administrators of the office and handle arrangements for closure. They do not sell. Their total sales volume for the office is $4.5 million for the year, some of which involves high-value property for which they receive a commission less than the standard 5 percent. Total brokerage commissions come to $200,000, half of which goes to the salesmen as their share. The two partners each draw salaries of $18,000 per year. In addition, salaried personnel include three secretaries, one receptionist, a bookkeeper, and some part-time help. Total overhead for the year is $90,000. Of the remaining $10,000, $4,000 goes to the salesmen in bonuses. This leaves $6,000 in net profit for the partners. In salary and profit, each man has an income of $21,000 for the year.

Case No. 2—Medium/large partnership

Receipts			
Real estate sales			
@ 5% Commission	$3,000,000	$150,000	
@ 4% Commission	500,000	20,000	
@ 3% Commission	1,000,000	30,000	
Total commissions		$200,000	
Commissions to 10 salesmen		100,000	
Net receipts to partnership			$100,000
Expenses			
Salary to officers		$36,000	
Advertising		7,000	
Automobile expense		2,400	
Dues and subscriptions		2,000	
License, bonding, and insurance		1,800	
Postage; stationery, etc.		800	
Telephone		3,000	
Rent		5,000	
Wages—Secretaries	$15,000		
Receptionist	4,000		
Bookkeeper	7,000		
Part-time help	2,000		
Total wages		$28,000	
Entertainment, travel		2,000	
Education		500	
Miscellaneous expenses		1,500	
Total expenses			$90,000
Profit before bonuses			$10,000
Bonuses to salesmen			4,000
Net profit to partnership			$6,000

IV. GETTING STARTED

A. Requirements

Primary requirements for starting a real estate brokerage business are experience, a broker's license, a thorough knowledge of the geographic area of anticipated operation, a personality compatible with the anticipated clientele, and capital.

A legal requirement for real estate brokerage is a license. About 35 States require sales experience for a broker's license. The required apprenticeship ranges from 6 months to 5 years, with most States requiring from 1 to 2 years.

The starting place for the novice in real estate, therefore, is at the salesman level. As a salesman, the newcomer to the field will learn the mechanics of the business, which, although complex, can be mastered by most persons. Gradually the insight and experience needed to progress to the status of a full-fledged broker will be gained. As salesman, the individual learns a particular local market well. He is afforded the opportunity to develop potential clients and to meet and get to know the principal actors in the real estate game (other professionals in the field, local businessmen, city officials, mortgage brokers, and building contractors). It is during his salesman period in the business that the individual will determine his abilities to deal with various kinds of people and will determine the market of concentration best suited for him (blue-collar inner-city, white-collar suburban, high-income executive, etc.).

Even if an individual possesses the other prerequisites for starting a brokerage operation, he still must have sufficient capital to establish and maintain an office and to meet his personal obligations until his operation becomes profitable. It is advisable that the newly-established broker plan his new business as if he were going to have to survive for a year without a sale (although if that proves to be the case, he may be in the wrong business). Assuming $12,000 for office overhead, and perhaps $10,000 to maintain one's family, startup capital of $22,000 would be required. An individual might get by with less, but in any case, $18,000 to $20,000 would seem to be the minimum startup capital requirement.

The capital necessary to establish a brokerage firm is usually derived almost exclusively from personal sources. Nevertheless, the Small Business Administration or a mortgage company may make partial loans. Technical assistance, in the form of publications and seminars, is available from organizations such as the National Institute of Real Estate Brokers.

The physical requirements for entrance into the field are not great. An office with telephone service is required and may be located either in a commercial district or in a residential area. Many new real estate offices are run out of homes (where legally permitted).

Membership in a multiple listings service can be a valuable aid to a new broker. These services are usually run by the local board of realtors and are available only to members. Initial membership in these organizations can run from $500 to $700, and continuing service is paid for as a percent of earned commissions, on a fee per listing basis, or on a monthly fee basis. Listings on a flat fee basis average about $20 per month but may run as high as $150 per month for computerized service which includes rental of terminals.

B. Opportunities for Minority Individuals in Real Estate

A key ingredient of success in selling real estate is the ability to develop a rapport with the prospective buyer. It is very important that the buyer trust the salesman. This characteristic of the real estate brokerage business suggests a special opportunity which minority salesmen can use to establish themselves in the business. The growing amount of real estate ownership in the black and Spanish-speaking communities offers commensurate opportunities for a person of those communities to service their real estate transactions. If they are treated fairly and honestly, sellers and buyers can be counted upon to convey this perception throughout their neighborhoods, rapidly increasing his business and, therefore, his real estate expertise. A poor reputation stemming from shabby or opportunistic treatment can, of course, destroy the salesman's opportunities to grow with the field.

Real estate is a business which offers women significant opportunities and in which their sex is often an asset. In residential real estate transactions, the woman in the family usually must be satisfied in order to close a sale, and women have proven particularly capable of selling to this "ultimate customer." Also, because payment is on a commission basis and the broker need only bear minimal extra overhead costs for a part-time sales person, many women have been able to combine family and career successfully by working in real estate sales part-time.

C. Growth Opportunities in Real Estate

Just as the salesman progresses to broker status on the basis of his experience and knowledge, the broker, in time, may progress further up the real estate ladder. Opportunities will present themselves for the broker to act, not as an agent for others, but as a real estate operator in his own right. Constantly in touch with the market, the broker will encounter purchase opportunities, at reasonable prices and payment terms, which have interesting potential for profit in either sale or management. To act as an operative, however, requires additional knowledge and experience and access to large capital holdings.

The operator sees value in property and capitalizes on that value. The next step in the continuum is the developer. The real estate developer creates value by substantially modifying the property in such a way as to cover the cost of modification and produce a profit after sale (or lease). Developers may concentrate on land (subdividers), residential property (operative builders), commercial property (shopping center developers), or industrial property (industrial parks and structures). Each step involves progressively greater undertakings and capitalization.

Many brokers, both to increase their income and stabilize its flow, venture into other related areas, particularly property insurance and property management. Most property is insured against loss. Handling property insurance is a logical extension of the broker's business since he is dealing regularly with new owners of property who will be seeking such insurance. Property management is also a logical outgrowth of his brokerage activities. Management, however, requires time and additional personnel; it is an unprofitable business on a small scale and requires extensive attention on a large scale.

BIBLIOGRAPHY

Survey of Current Business, U.S. Department of Commerce, Bureau of the Census (monthly publication), Washington, D.C. 20233.

Taxable Property Values, 1967 Census of Governments, Volume 2. U.S. Department of Commerce, Bureau of the Census, Washington D.C. 20233.

Aids to Real Estate Education, Department of Education, National Association of Real Estate Boards (A pamphlet describing the educational offerings of the Association), 155 East Superior Street, Chicago, Illinois 60611.

The Challenge of Real Estate, National Association of Real Estate Boards, 1959. (A pamphlet describing the field of real estate and its various specialties.)

1970 Report of the Interstate Cooperation Committee, National Association of Real Estate License Law Officials. (A complete summary of real estate licensing laws by State.) 1515 Grant Bldg., Pittsburgh, Pennsylvania 15219.

Publications of the National Association of Real Estate Boards, April 1970, National Association of Real Estate Boards.

Real Estate Reading, National Association of Real Estate Boards. Revised May 1970. (Extensive bibliography, 35 pages.)

TRADE ASSOCIATION

Apartment Association of America (Real Estate): 1022 15th Street, N.W., Washington, D.C. 20005. Founded 1964. Members, 700. Apartment and rental housing owners, managers, builders, developers, investors, financers, and others. Compiles statistics, disseminates information, and conducts research on construction, financing, management, rental, operation, and maintenance of rental housing. Publications: 1) Washington Report, monthly; 2) Rental Housing News, monthly; 3) Management Bulletins, irregular.

SAVINGS AND LOAN ASSOCIATIONS

Section Contents

URBAN BUSINESS PROFILE

Savings and Loan Associations

(SIC 6120)

I. RECOMMENDATION

Establishment of a savings and loan association offers a unique opportunity for well-qualified members of the minority community. Few businesses run for profit provide such a demonstrable service to their community, and the minority savings and loan association may be especially well placed for extending the availability of mortgage credit to lower-income and minority residents in its area of operations. Whether or not the association can provide this service at a profit to itself depends, in addition to conditions in the money market, on the size of its assets (amount of savings invested in association) and the quality of its mortgage loans. And these association characteristics depend heavily on the skill of its management and the confidence placed in the association by its community.

The successful savings and loan association is managed by individuals with skill and experience in finance, real estate, and personal salesmanship. This group need not be composed entirely of members of a locally predominant minority community; several minority associations have found that multiracial staffing of the association and its board of directors obtains critical skills and confers credibility on the association. And the perception of the association by its potential market is all-important, because the ablest staff of appraisers and financiers is powerless to place mortgage loans without a reservoir of savings upon which to draw.

Growth in association assets, assuming competitiveness with other financial intermediaries in basic savings incentives (interest rate, account insurance) resulting from government regulation of the finance industry, depends largely on effective public relations. The well-staffed minority association may be in a particularly advantageous position to attract savings dollars from both its own community and a growing portion of the larger community. In addition to the basic return on savings, it may be able to offer an "extra dividend" to its savers in the form of tangible involvement in minority community development.

II. DESCRIPTION OF THE SAVINGS AND LOAN INDUSTRY

A. Identification

There are many different types of financial intermediaries, or institutions which exist to link borrowers and savers of money. The savings and loan is one of the most specialized of all such institutions, limiting its lending activities almost entirely to borrowers of financing for home mortgages. Its primary function is to accumulate savings deposits from a wide variety of savers in interest-bearing accounts and to lend this money to home buyers and builders through the purchase of home mortgages. The savings and loan industry performs an important social function by lowering the cost of housing investment (through the provision of home mortgage financing) and by providing savers with an additional opportunity for earning a higher return or lessening the degree of risk on the savings dollar.

The activities engaged in by the typical savings and loan are those which are needed to perform this intermediation function. The association collects savings in a variety of accounts, appraises mortgage investment opportunities, makes loans to selected mortgage borrowers, collects interest and amortization payments from these borrowers, and pays a portion of these mortgage proceeds to the saver as interest for the use of his money. The savings and loan, since it is a private institution, retains the balance of the investment proceeds as a return for performing this service.

The importance of this service—savings and loans now provide over 40 percent of all the mortgage credit in the U.S.—has led to a high degree of regulation in the savings and loan industry. The Federal Home Loan Bank Board (FHLBB), as the central regulatory agency, controls the issuing of charters for new associations, the insuring of savings accounts, the structure of the mortgage portfolio, and other important determinants for those associations which are Federally chartered. A similar regulatory structure exists for State-chartered associations. The association must also act in compliance with a host of State and Federal laws meant to protect the safety of the investing and home-buying public. And yet the savings and loan association, as a private institution which serves a genuine need for housing mortgage credit and interest-bearing savings accounts in its chosen market, can provide an attractive return to its management, its board of directors and its community.

B. Dimensions

The savings and loan association is the third largest type of financial institution in the country. Only banks and insurance companies hold more assets. At the end of 1969, 5,898 savings and loans held

$162 billion in assets. The industry has earned itself a significant place among the financial intermediaries since World War II; the following table highlights its growth story:

	1945	1955	1960	1965	1969
Bank assets	$160 B	$210.7B	$257.6B	$377.3B	$527.7B
S & L assets	$ 8.7B	$ 37.7B	$ 71.5B	$129.6B	$162.2B

Another index of the dimensions of the industry—the number of associations doing business—presents an insight into this industry's growth. The first savings and loan was established in 1831 in Frankford, Pennsylvania, and the number of such associations in the still-unregulated industry had increased to 12,804 by 1927. The dominant trend since that time has been one of internal growth rather than establishment of new associations, since the total of all savings and loan associations in the United States has remained remarkably close to 6,000 since 1945. During this time the number of new association starts has just about equaled the number of mergers and failures.

The stability in the total number of associations obscures important changes in the industry, however. Many of the savings and loans which existed in the early 1900's were small organizations with part-time staffs which existed only to serve a special market. The number of such relatively inactive groups has declined due to the economic adversities of the 1930's, the increased competition for the savings dollar, and the advent in 1934 of Federal insurance coverage on deposits in qualifying associations. Federal Savings and Loan Insurance Corporation (FSLIC) coverage, provided only to active associations with full-time management, separate quarters, and a certain level of deposits, is identified by industry sources as an important factor in the development of an industry image which permits effective competition for savings deposits. Thus, continued growth of FSLIC coverage among associations—460 associations have become FSLIC-insured since 1960, increasing the percentage of FSLIC-insured associations to 76 percent and the percentage of FSLIC-insured assets to 96 percent—is a measure of industry strength.

In addition, changes are continually taking place among, and in the relative composition of, the different types of associations in the industry. The major difference among savings and loans lies in the source of their charter.

Federal Savings and Loan Associations

—chartered upon approval of application by the Federal Home Loan Bank Board under provisions of Home Owner's Loan Act of 1933;

—supervised by FHLBB's Office of Examinations and Supervision;

—automatically covered by FSLIC insurance coverage (to $20,000 on each account);

—comprise 35 percent by number, 54 percent by assets, of industry.

State Savings and Loan Associations

—chartered and supervised by State regulatory agency;

—may be covered by FSLIC insurance coverage (about 60 percent of the State savings and loans are) or by State insuring agencies (432 State associations);

—usually mutually owned, though many stock associations operate in 21 States;

—comprise 65 percent by number and 46 percent by assets, of industry.

Despite the early tendency toward industry standardization introduced by Federal regulation in the 1930's, the dual system of chartering and supervision has maintained a surprising stability. Federal savings and loans have held more than 50 percent of total industry assets since 1950, yet their portion had grown only to 54 percent at the end of 1969. This relatively constant apportionment of assets obscures an interesting trend, however. Only about half of the Federals were originally chartered as such; the remainder represent conversions from State charter. The State chartering system, therefore, has played an important role as a source of much of the "new blood" in the industry. The FHLBB has been actively assisting in the establishment of new minority-operated associations, however, and most of the new minority associations hold Federal charters.

Another distinction which exists among State-chartered savings and loans lies in the form of association ownership. All Federal and most State associations are mutually owned, an association type in which legal ownership of the association is vested in the depositors themselves. The other type of association is called a permanent stock association, in which investors contribute capital to the new association in return for stock (and therefore ownership) in the new entity. A mutual permits depositor control at the possible expense of association agility and aggressiveness; the theoretically more tightly controlled stock association sacrifices broad community policymaking for a stronger startup capital position and a potentially greater scope for aggressive placing of mortgage investments. Mutuals held $128 billion in assets at the end of 1969, while stock associations (12.5 percent of all savings and loans by number), based mostly in the dynamic California market, held $33 billion or 21 percent of all savings and loan assets.

The bulk of savings and loan business is conducted by associations of moderate size. The average savings and loan holds $27.5 million in assets. There is a growing concentration at the larger size end of the scale; the 5 percent of the associations with more than $100 million currently hold over 44 percent of all assets, and mergers, failures of small associations, and growing use of branch offices are increasing the concentration. The branching trend is an important phenomenon and is much more important in accounting for new savings and loan offices than the chartering of new associations. The growth of the branch office concept is highlighted below:

	Population	
	per association	per office (main or branch)
1950	25,240	24,624
1955	27,112	24,670
1960	28,446	22,668
1965	31,197	21,021
1969	34,074	20,378

Savings and loan associations operate in every State, the District of Columbia, and several territories. About half of all associations are located in the States of Pennsylvania, Illinois, Ohio, New Jersey, Maryland, Texas, and California. California has the largest accumulation of assets at $31 billion, and the District of Columbia has the greatest accumulation of assets per capita at about $3,000 per person.

The extent of minority participation in the savings and loan industry has traditionally been small. At the end of 1970 the FHLBB district covering the Southeast United States (Greensboro District) contained 13 Federal savings and loan associations operated by minority community individuals, and there were a total of 43 minority associations in operation (32 insured, 11 noninsured) throughout the country.

C. Characteristics

The savings and loan association supplies two important products to its community. It is the major supplier of mortgage financing in the country, purchasing 44 percent of the mortgages on new and existing homes in 1969. By providing needed financing for the sale of housing, the association bolsters the value of local real estate in its lending area. The insured association also provides an opportunity to earn a risk-free return on the savings dollar, with a variety of savings instruments at several interest rates to suit the saver. The importance of the savings and loan as a savings institution can be seen in the fact that there are now an average of over 75 savings and loan accounts for every 100 U.S. households.

The savings and loan association exists, then, to service its two forms of customers. The savings customer "buys" an interest payment with a deposit of capital, while the borrowing customer "buys" a loan of capital with an interest payment. Savings deposits constitute the bulk of the industry's liabilities (83 percent), and mortgage loans make up 86.5 percent of the average S & L's assets. The "spread" between the cost of the association's money (saver's interest rate) and the return on that money (borrower's interest rate) determines the amount of funds available to cover overhead, to provide for reserve requirements, and to bolster surplus (profits).

1. The S & L as a Savings Institution

There are several factors which can induce a person with money beyond his present needs to deposit it in a savings institution. One of the more traditional is simply the desire for safety. A more recent motivation reported by new minority S&L's is the desire on the part of several types of groups to associate with a large provider of funds to the minority community. But the overriding consideration in the mind of the saver—particularly the individual who is "investing capital" rather than "saving dollars"—is the desire to earn a return on his savings which is, for all practical purposes, risk-free.

The ability of its interest rate to attract needed working assets for the association depends on several factors.

a. Money market conditions ultimately determine much of the performance of any association. Short term market interest rates control the return on direct market instruments (e.g., Treasury notes) and may rise faster than the ability of the savings and loan industry to keep up. Long term rates affect mortgage proceeds and therefore the amount that the individual association(s) can afford to pay to compete.

b. Competition from other financial institutions—notably banks—for the savings dollar has recently bid away some of the savings that would otherwise have gone into savings and loans. Banks are also affected by money market conditions in their pursuit of savings accounts, but their full service capability enables them to escape interest sensitivity somewhat.

c. Federally imposed (FHLBB) interest rate controls have limited the interest rates payable by members of the FHLBB System since 1966.

The controls placed upon all major savings institutions are at once a government recognition of the importance of an orderly flow of capital into important segments of the economy (e.g., housing) and an effort to prevent cutthroat competition for the savings dollar. The competition has recently grown more sophisticated; the Housing and Urban Development Act of 1968, underscoring the growing interest sensitivity of the large investor, permitted S & L's for the first time to offer a variety of savings instruments at controlled rates and for different deposit durations. The use of different instruments and accounts also gives the association greater control over interest costs and withdrawals. These new instruments—basically certificates of deposit in amounts ranging up to $100,000 and for durations up to 10 years—have been the major source of new savings and loan industry assets; passbook savings actually fell from $98 billion to $90 billion in 1969 while the value of certificates rose from $29 billion to $41 billion. In fact, the amount of money in passbook accounts was about the same at the end of 1969 as it was during 1966.

About 97 percent of all savings accounts or certificates are held by individuals. Thus, the new association must reach the household market. This market is composed of two relatively distinct groups, however. The typical account holder holds a rather small balance (less than $1,000), while most of the assets come from a small number of depositors holding large accounts. In 1968, for instance, 50 percent of all FSLIC-insured accounts held only 4 percent of all assets while the 2 percent of the accounts with more than $15,000 apiece held 13 percent of all assets ($16 billion). The indication from trade sources is that the S & L serves a thrift function for the small saver (including the major portion of the minority associations' depositors) while providing liquidity and insured earnings at higher rates for the certificate purchaser. The minority association which is able to serve adequately its chosen market for mortgage credit will probably have to attract both types of saver.

The S & L industry has been characterized by a declining ratio of annual gross receipts to total savings at year's beginning in recent years, reflecting to some extent both industry maturity and the monetary situation since 1965. This means among other things that interest payments left on deposit ($6.6 billion in 1969) comprise a continually growing portion of annual net savings receipts—particularly since interest rates and frequency of payment have increased simultaneously. This growing cost of its money places particular pressure on S & L management to invest savings dollars well.

2. *The S & L as a Lending Institution*

The S & L is distinguished from all other savings institutions because it must, according to law, regulation, and custom, allocate the bulk of its savings inflows to the financing of housing. Only 1.1 percent of the S & L industry investments are not secured by some form of real estate. The total mortgage loan portfolio at the end of 1969 was $140 billion, consisting of 10.75 million loans in an average amount of $13,000 apiece.

The vast majority of these mortgage loans have traditionally been secured by single-family dwellings. Over 84 percent of all mortgage loans were so secured in 1969. The portion of an S & L portfolio which can go to other forms of real estate (multifamily dwellings, mobile homes, other investment properties) is governed by law and regulation; generally, no more than 20 percent to 25 percent of the total assets of a Federal savings and loan can be secured by such property. This portion of the average Federal association portfolio has grown, however, from 8 percent in 1960 to 16 percent in 1970.

Not only does the typical association concentrate on single-family loans, but about 94 percent of all its financing is in conventional, as distinguished from FHA- or VA-insured, loans. The use of conventional loans permits flexibility in the operations of an S & L that is difficult to attain with FHA-VA mortgage financing. Avoidance of highly standardized underwriting procedures also allows local S & L management to adapt its lending to local real estate conditions, a knowledge of which is most important. The processing delays usually associated with FHA-VA lending, the occasional locally unrealistic fixed interest rates, and the S & L industry's success with monthly loan repayment plans (hence a diminished need for government mortgage insurance) are other reasons for concentration on conventional loans. FHA- and VA-insured loans have some advantages, however, particularly in periods of tight money. And the guarantees on these loans enhance their negotiability and therefore provide additional liquidity to the home mortgage market.

The S & L has four sources of loanable funds. The annual net gain in savings has traditionally been the major source, presently accounting for about 50 percent of the pool of loanable funds. Of growing importance is the flow of funds from mortgage repayments, continually growing as the portfolio of mortgages financed 20 to 30 years ago "rolls over." The well-run association holds a growing pool of retained earnings after payment of savings interest and operating expenses. Loans and advances from the FHLBB system (from one of the 12 district banks) are the last source of loanable funds for the S & L and make up an important source of cash with which to adjust to changes in flows from the other three sources.

Over half of the average association's loans go for the purchase of existing homes. This concentration not only reflects the deficiency of new home construction but also underscores the importance of accurate real estate appraisal to an association's performance. About 22 percent of all mortgage loans in 1969 went for construction of new one- to four-family homes. The remainder of all loans go for apartments, nonresidential property, and land development.

The savings and loan association has the capability of purchasing existing loans (primarily real estate mortgages) from holders outside the savings and loan industry. In 1969, for instance, over 75 percent of the $2.3 billion worth of mortgage loans and mortgage participations with other lenders were purchases from commercial banks, insurance companies, and mortgage brokers. The need to cover interest payments and operating expenses forces the S & L to keep its savings dollars fully invested even if current housing activity is low.

III. OPPORTUNITIES IN THE SAVINGS AND LOAN INDUSTRY

A. Factors Affecting Industry Profitability

The basic operating principle of the savings and loan association is a simple one. S & L management must obtain money, the average cost of which is cheaper than the return on its investments. The extent of the "spread" between the two rates is a measure of the association's ability to cover expenses and generate a profit. For example, a typical 1969 cost of money was between 5 percent and 5.5 percent while the average terms on single-family conventional mortgage loans made by Federal S & L's in 1969 was about 8.15 percent. But several factors keep the S & L industry from being as profitable as it might appear.

The necessity of "borrowing short and lending long" which characterizes the home mortgage market locks the S & L into a position which is often out of step with current money market conditions. For instance, mortgage loans made years ago when interest rates were perhaps only 4 percent make up the bulk of those currently being paid off rather than current loans at 8 percent. Yet the S & L must pay competitive rates on savings accounts if it is to have the major portion of total loanable funds that usually comes from net additions to savings. The association's performance, then, can only be judged over a period of time which bridges cycles in the money market and in comparison to other associations facing basically the same economic conditions.

The importance to the industry of continually obtaining new net savings is therefore obvious. The S & L must compete with other investment opportunities (to the extent allowed by regulations and laws) with interest rates and with emphasis on safety and thrift; it must compete with other savings and loan associations on the basis of personal salesmanship, service, and other more intangible factors.

The importance of an association image which attracts capital from a wide variety of savers cannot be overemphasized. An association which can offer its customers an "extra return" through friendly service, customer gifts, or community relations programs may have a small but decisive advantage over other S & L's that offer the same interest rates and insurance coverage on deposits.

Another factor which critically affects profit potential in the industry is the ability of the S & L to appraise real estate and borrowers as to value and reliability respectively. The management group which knows and can appraise the people and property in its area of operations (usually limited to either 50 or 100 miles from the S & L office) has a considerable advantage over mortgage lenders who are less skilled at these critical tasks. Industry sources emphasize the importance of a strong real estate background for at least one of the key members of the S & L management team, and officers with experience in sizing up people in their market are also very important to association success.

The fact that the real growth in the S & L industry since 1955 has come through the growth of associations using branch offices underscores an industry characteristic with important implications for association profitability. As in any specialized technology (in this case, making and processing mortgage loans), there are identifiable economics of scale in the S & L business. Operating costs relative to scale of operations seem to decline continuously as association size increases. This suggests that S & L's will always be competitive with diversified intermediaries (banks) in the financing of home mortgages. But it also raises questions about the future of many smaller associations that are not able to spread the costs of the critical management function over a large volume of loans at one office or over the operation of several branches which can properly share several management functions. Industry awareness of this phenomenon has perhaps contributed to the fact that applications for new branches or mergers currently outnumber those for new associations.

A group of final profitability determinants are those exogenous features over which the individual association has no control. The one to which the others are keyed is the condition of the money markets. The ability of the association to earn an addition to surplus may be severely constrained during periods characterized by the high cost of money and the low return on old mortgage loans.

These factors all combined to squeeze industry profitability from 12.5 percent of net worth in 1962 to 4.1 percent of net worth in 1967. The primary contributing factor, according to industry sources, was the narrowing of the spread between the cost of money and the return on invested funds. Recent improvement in this spread is allowing association profitability to rise once again toward the levels that existed during most of the post World War II era.

The risks that face any new association, therefore, are considerable, but unique opportunities exist for a minority savings and loan association (one whose board is composed largely of the local minority community). The deficiency of mortgage financing available to minority neighborhood residents is well known. And yet the experience of several associations indicates that mortgage credit extended to minority home owners is well secured by carefully appraised single-family homes in predominantly minority neighborhoods. Washington, D.C., for instance, a city whose population is over 75 percent black and Spanish-speaking, currently has one of the lowest foreclosure rates in the Nation. A minority association may have special access to credit-worthy households which the predominantly white management of the typical association have not considered prime customers for mortgage loans. A minority or multiracial association which can realistically assess the general stability of these neighborhoods, can accurately appraise individual homes, can judge the credit-worthiness of loan applicants, and can attract savings dollars from a broad range of local savers may become a profitable association while at the same time serving a genuine social need.

The minority association is faced with some major challenges as it goes about this task. The savings and loan association, like the bank and other savings intermediaries, acts as a fiduciary agent for the saver, holding his savings in trust. The majority of minority associations are FSLIC-insured, but the association must do more than advertise insurance coverage to convey a sense of confidence and elicit a feeling of trust in its community. Extreme care in selecting a board of directors and expressing the operating philosophy of the institution have proved to be important factors in establishing the association image needed to build savings accounts.

Another major challenge faced by the new minority association is to overcome strong pressures to act primarily as a social institution. A recent study of the savings and loan industry prepared for the Federal Home Loan Bank Board identifies heavy "concentration of mortgage loans in failing neighborhoods" as a primary cause of association failure. Recent minority association experience shows that minority neighborhoods are not necessarily failing neighborhoods, but the successful minority association must be able to differentiate between the two in its operations. Other typical characteristics of failed associations were identified as lack of diversification among borrowers, considerable investment in mortgages on buildings not owner-occupied or whose owner held a weak equity position, and undue growth emphasis.

B. Representative Operating Statements of Federal and State Savings and Loan Associations

Financial operating statements often help to highlight the important characteristics of the industry which they portray. The following hypothetical operating statements of both Federal and State associations are based on the 1969 Combined Financial Statements published by the FHLBB and are oriented towards the average association in each of the selected asset size groups.

Representative Operating Statements for Associations of Indicated Size

A. Federal Savings and Loan Associations

	Size by assets	
	Under $2.5 million	*$7.5 to $10 million*
Assets (period average)	$1,800,000	$10,000,000
Mortgage loans (period average)	1,500,000	8,250,000
Gross operating income		
Mortgage loan interest	100,000	500,000
Investment interest	10,000	42,500
Miscellaneous income	10,000	57,500
Gross operating income	120,000	600,000
Operating expense		
Compensation	16,000	57,500
Office expense	4,000	11,250
Other operating expense	11,000	47,500
Interest charges	2,750	13,750
Total operating expense	33,750	130,000
Net operating income before income taxes	86,250	470,000
Income taxes (Federal, other)	1,000	10,000
Net income after tax	85,250	460,000
Allocation of net income		
Reserves	6,250	32,500
Surplus	2,500	31,500
Interest on savings deposits	76,500	396,000

B. State-Chartered FSLIC-Insured Savings and Loan Associations (both permanent stock associations)

	Size by assets	
	Under $2.5 million	*$7.5 to $10 million*
Assets (period average)	$1,650,000	$10,000,000
Mortgage loans (period average)	1,400,000	8,250,000
Gross operating income		
Mortgage loan interest	88,000	500,000
Investment interest	7,250	42,500
Miscellaneous income	4,750	57,500
Gross operating income	100,000	600,000
Operating expense		
Compensation	12,500	60,000
Office expense	2,500	12,500
Other operating expense	10,000	50,000
Interest charges	2,500	14,500
Total operating expense	27,500	137,000
Net operating income before income taxes	72,500	463,000
Income taxes (Federal, other)	1,500	8,500
Net income after tax	71,000	454,500
Allocation of net income		
Reserves	3,500	31,000
Surplus	3,250	31,000
Interest on savings deposit	64,000	389,500
Dividends on permanent stock	250	3,000

Several items in these representative statements bear comment.

(a) There is obviously little difference between the financial performance of the "average" Federal and the "average" State savings and loan association in each of these size groups. This basic similarity extends throughout the size ranges.

(*b*) The economies of scale mentioned earlier are apparent. Most operating expenses do not vary directly with the volume of business (mortgage loans outstanding), and there is a steady decrease in the ratio of operating expense to average annual assets. The larger of the two association sizes portrayed earns much more surplus than its larger size alone might suggest.

(c) The net income figures are presented in accordance with standard industry practice but are misleading because they have not been adjusted for the major "cost" of doing business—the cost of money expressed as interest on savings accounts. The real profit in the association's operating statement is shown by the surplus item (and dividends on preferred stock for stock associations).

(*d*) The income tax figures reflect the favorable tax situation conferred on the savings and loan industry before it became subject to corporate income tax in 1951. The associations have recently had income which is transferred to reserves (to cover losses, etc.) partially sheltered from taxation, but for 10 years beginning in 1970 a higher taxation on income in excess of $25,000 will gradually be phased in.

IV. ESTABLISHING THE ASSOCIATION

A. Organization Assistance

There is no well-defined formula for planning and establishing a successful savings and loan association. The association is a private profit-seeking entity and is, therefore, subject to the competition of all other financial intermediaries—banks, mutual savings banks, life insurance companies, and others—attempting to capture the same savings dollar and mortgage investments.

There are several opportunities, however, for the founders of the new association to obtain useful assistance in the creation of a sound and potentially profitable savings and loan business.

A particularly important source of assistance to the prospective association is the Federal Home Loan Bank Board (FHLBB) and the 12 district banks. The Board works to insure industry health and dependable mortgage credit partly by controlling entry into the industry through a chartering system and by assisting potentially viable associations to meet charter approval requirements. The FHLBB approves the association's charter only after the applicant has met certain standards reflecting on its potential for success. In particular, the association must:

(*a*) Provide tangible evidence which tends to demonstrate its ability to succeed;

(*b*) present evidence that a new savings and loan association is, in fact, needed in the chosen market area;

(c) present evidence that operations will be unlikely to cause undue injury to existing financial institutions;

(*d*) contain assurances of a broad base of support in its market community.

In addition to these requirements, the applicant must have paid-in capital (in the case of stock associations) or pledges of savings accounts (in the case of mutuals) sufficient to cover FHLBB-required reserves in order to qualify for FSLIC insurance. The FHLBB Office of Examinations and Supervision, the Office of Industry Development, and the various district banks (see list in appendix) all provide assistance to groups attempting to establish a viable savings and loan association and obtain FHLBB approval of a charter. Particular assistance has recently been extended to directors and staff of predominantly minority associations. Associations seeking State charters are also able to obtain help in developing a sound business plan from the appropriate State chartering agency.

Another expected source of assistance, especially for new minority associations, is the American Savings and Loan League. This trade group for minority associations is headquartered in Washington, D.C. The new organization is expected to focus on the training of both existing S&L management and new personnel.

All groups contemplating the establishment of a new savings and loan association will find the literature prepared by the FHLBB and the several trade groups to be of great assistance in their feasibility analysis and organizational planning. The United States Savings and Loan League, with offices in Chicago, Washington, D.C., and San Francisco, publishes an annual "Fact Book" which contains a wealth of data on the industry. The American Savings and Loan Institute, also based in Chicago, has produced a highly useful document on the workings of the industry and the individual association in its "Savings and Loan Principles." Finally, the FHLBB publishes an annual report and a monthly, The Journal of the Federal Home Loan Bank Board, which is available to interested parties for a nominal subscription price.

The relatively close regulation of the savings and loan industry may prove to be of benefit to the prospective association if it uses the resulting reports, publications, and regulatory agents to its advantage in designing and planning its new venture.

B. Approaching the Market

The new savings and loan association, to be financially successful, must have access to an adequate supply of both savings dollars and mortgage investments. The association must plan its marketing strategy, including the characteristics of its board of directors and staff, the location of its offices, the nature of its lending policies, and the style of its advertising, so as to insure this result.

Industry experience indicates that the bulk of industry savings, whether in the form of passbook accounts or certificates of deposit, are received in suburban locations. The new minority association, even though it may emphasize purchase of mortgages on single-family dwellings in predominantly minority community locations, will therefore need to attract a large part of its savings from the larger community. The association should make special efforts to sell large-denomination certificates of deposit as well, since the higher cost to the association of capital received through certificates may be more than offset by the favorable effect which such longterm money has on its liquidity needs. For these reasons a new association primarily concerned with providing mortgage credit to the minority or lower-income community may be well advised to maintain offices easily accessible to a wide variety of savers. A downtown commercial area which is close to the mortgage market but is easily accessible to business investors and suburban commuters as well as walk-in "passbook savers" would be a generally useful strategy.

A successful market strategy for a new minority savings and loan association would include a carefully planned appeal to the "conscience money" in its area of operations. Reference to the citywide benefits that are generally expected to result from the provision of mortgage credit to predominantly minority communities has proved to be an effective marketing appeal for minority association spokesmen, provided that they convey the impression that this strategy entails no additional risk to the saver. Account insurance provided by FSLIC or one of the State insuring agencies can be very useful in creating the necessary impression of stability and safety. Of at least equal importance, however, are the qualifications of the association's Board of Directors and the experience of its staff. Some predominantly minority-controlled associations have found that wide exposure of individually successful and articulate directors or staff members in citywide civic activities or meetings has been of considerable benefit to their marketing program.

The new minority association may have unique opportunities for its lending activities as well. The FHLBB has made available to member associations, through its district banks, special 10-year advances for inner-city housing so as to stimulate greater industry participation in longterm renewal and rehabilitation projects. The interest costs to associations receiving these special advances have been reduced below the normal rate to make such lending activity more attractive to the savings and loan industry. The minority association, if it is staffed by capable appraisers of property and mortgage borrowers, may be in a particularly strong position to use such low-cost advances from Federal Home Loan Banks to its advantages.

The new association may also seek to establish a correspondent relationship with a more well-established savings and loan association early in its life. The correspondent relationship, employed successfully by small rural banks for decades, and occasionally used in the S & L industry, is a means by which associations can jointly participate in mortgage loans. A minority association which develops special expertise in making sound mortgage loans on inner-city properties may have attractive new investment opportunities to offer to an established association in return for widening its own investment opportunities through participation on more conventional loans.

C. Staffing the Association

The importance to a new association of a board of directors which inspires confidence in the organization and of a staff which represents courteous efficiency should be obvious. A successful board should represent different segments of the association's target population of savers, including members of the majority community and different professional or business groupings. The most important characteristic of members of such a board will probably be successful achievement in their individual fields. The board of a successful association would undoubtedly have considerable skill and background in real estate, finance, and salesmanship, although professional occupations in these fields may not be required.

The management and staff of the savings and loan association, for its part, must have enough skill at their jobs to inspire confidence in the saving public and to make sound mortgage investments. Opportunities for minorities to acquire the necessary experience in finance, real estate appraisal, accounting, and other relevant skills have traditionally been inadequate, and any new association intending to primarily service the minority community with savings opportunities and mortgage credit will have to develop a staffing policy which mixes the hiring of experienced staff, the training of inexperienced staff, the training of inexperienced help, and the participation of board members and part-time assistance. Several programs are being developed at both national and various local levels to subsidize, with government or foundation funds, the training of new minority staff members; the Federal Home Loan Banks and the American Savings and Loan League will have information about such programs as are applicable to individual associations.

The new association will need to be as sparing as possible in its office and staffing arrangements until savings inflows and mortgage investments justify expansion. The small office can be run by one or two tellers, a loan specialist/appraiser, and an accountant, in addition to the president or manager who should be capable in all these functions. Appraisers may be retained on an as-needed basis in the smaller offices. Salaries in the industry, particularly in the smaller associations, are usually no more than competitive with business generally, and tellers' wages usually range between $2.50 and $5 per hour.

D. Startup Capital Needed

The prevailing opinion in the industry is that starting on a shoestring is no longer possible, if it ever was. The new association needs well over $1 million dollars in either paid-in stock (stock associations) or pledged deposits (mutual associations) in order to acquire and furnish an office, hire staff, buy stock in the appropriate FHLBS district bank, incur other necessary startup costs, and still have enough assets left over to assure adequate liquidity while purchasing a large number of sound mortgages from its mortgage market. Estimates of startup capital needs range from $2 million to $10 million depending upon the location and market strategy of the association.

The new association will need to pay close attention to the condition of the money markets prior to planning an opening date. The small additions to industry net savings in 1969 ($4 billion) made this a difficult time for a new association to attract working assets, for instance, while the easier credit conditions prevailing in late 1970 eased the problem of savings accumulation considerably. The situation for mortgage lending was just the opposite, of course, but if the new minority association is truly meeting an unfilled need for mortgage credit, the lending problem may be the easier of the two to overcome.

The minority savings and loan association has much to offer to its community if it is effectively serving such an unfilled market for mortgage credit. The prospective association, which honestly appraises the need for its services, thoroughly explores the sources of assistance available to it, and carefully develops a business plan based on the realities of its market area, may also yield an attractive return to its founders and management.

BIBLIOGRAPHY

Savings and Loan Fact Book 1970, United States Savings and Loan League, 111 East Wacker, Chicago, Illinois 60601. 1970.

Study of the Savings and Loan Industry, (The Friend Report), An excerpt of the Research Report prepared for the Federal Home Loan Bank Board, Washington, D.C. 20552. September 1969.

Federal Home Loan Bank Board, *37th Annual Report*, 1969.

The Journal of the Federal Home Loan Bank Board, Washington, D.C. 20552.

August	1968	Vol. 1, No. 3
July	1970	Vol. 3, No. 7
September	1970	Vol. 3, No. 9
October	1970	Vol. 3, No. 10
November	1970	Vol. 3, No. 11

The Savings and Loan Industry Financing Potentials for Small and Minority Businesses, A research report perpared by Stephen Mc-Spadden and McClinton Ford for the Federal Home Loan Bank Board, Washington, D.C. 20552. August 1970.

Combined Financial Statements 1969, Federal Home Loan Bank Board, Washington, D.C. 20552.

APPENDIX—FEDERAL HOME LOAN BANKS

FEDERAL HOME LOAN BANK OF BOSTON
One Union Street, Boston, Massachusetts 02108
District 1: Connecticut, Maine, Massachusetts, New Hampshire, Rhode Island, and Vermont

FEDERAL HOME LOAN BANK OF NEW YORK
60 Broad Street, New York, New York 10004
District 2: New Jersey, New York, Puerto Rico, and Virgin Islands

FEDERAL HOME LOAN BANK OF PITTSBURGH
11 Stanwix Street, 4th Floor, Gateway Center,
Pittsburgh, Pennsylvania 15222
District 3: Delaware, Pennsylvania, and West Virginia

FEDERAL HOME LOAN BANK OF GREENSBORO
444 Elm Street, Greensboro, North Carolina 27401
District 4: Alabama, District of Columbia, Florida, Georgia, Maryland, North Carolina, South Carolina, and Virginia

FEDERAL HOME LOAN BANK OF CINCINNATI
2500 DuBois Tower, Cincinnati, Ohio 45202
District 5: Kentucky, Ohio, and Tennessee

FEDERAL HOME LOAN BANK OF INDIANAPOLIS
111 Monument Circle, Indianapolis, Indiana 46204
District 6: Indiana and Michigan

FEDERAL HOME LOAN BANK OF CHICAGO
110 East Wacker Drive, Chicago, Illinois 60601
District 7: Illinois and Wisconsin

FEDERAL HOME LOAN BANK OF DES MOINES
Second at Center, Des Moines, Iowa 50309
District 8: Iowa, Minnesota, Missouri, North Dakota, and South Dakota

FEDERAL HOME LOAN BANK OF LITTLE ROCK
1400 Tower Building, Little Rock, Arkansas 72201
District 9: Arkansas, Louisiana, Mississippi, New Mexico, and Texas

FEDERAL HOME LOAN BANK OF TOPEKA
Seventh and Harrison Streets, Topeka, Kansas 66601
District 10: Colorado, Kansas, Nebraska, and Oklahoma

FEDERAL HOME LOAN BANK OF SAN FRANCISCO
1 Bush Street, San Francisco, California 94104
District 11: Arizona, California, and Nevada

FEDERAL HOME LOAN BANK OF SEATTLE
600 Stewart Street, Seattle, Washington 98101
District 12: Alaska, Hawaii and Guam, Idaho, Montana, Oregon, Utah, Washington, and Wyoming

SUPERMARKETS

Section Contents

URBAN BUSINESS PROFILE
Supermarkets
(SIC 5411)

I. RECOMMENDATION

While the operation of a supermarket in the inner city appears on the surface to be a natural type of business venture for a minority entrepreneur or cooperative, it is a highly risky business requiring a very complex organization with sophisticated business methods, highly experienced management, considerable capital, and large scale buying power.

Despite apparent high prices for merchandise, margins are extremely low and competition is intense, largely on the basis of price and intensive promotional schemes. The large chain supermarkets continue to increase their share of the overall business, and the independent grocer is very hard-pressed to compete unless he knows the business thoroughly and can "outmanage" the area chainstore manager.

Inner-city locations are very difficult to operate profitably. Insurance rates are exceptionally high and losses to pilferage, shoplifting, and robbery are considerable, as are the costs of guarding against such occurrences.

The fact remains that the inner city needs supermarkets and that the chainstores are not very eager to open in such locations. This creates an opportunity for the minority entrepreneur or cooperative, but adequate financing and superior management are absolutely necessary, or the venture is certain to fail. For individuals desiring entry into the food business, a more likely prospect would be the convenience store which requires a much smaller investment and less complex managerial skills.

II. Description

A. Identification

The Standard Industrial Classification (SIC) 5411 includes stores which are commonly known as supermarkets, foodstores, or grocery stores. They are primarily engaged in the retail sale of food products for consumption in the home. For purposes of this profile, the supermarket is defined as any foodstore offering primarily self-service which does a business of about $1 million annually, or in the neighborhood of $20,000 per week.

There is a classification of store known as "superette," which is a term used for stores with sales of $150,000 to $1 million annually. Much of what is said in this profile about supermarkets applies to superettes as well. Small grocery stores are those with sales of less than $150,000 annually. These last types are generally of the "mom and pop" variety which are a carryover from earlier years and which exist largely because the owner's family is willing to work long hours for very little "take-home" pay. These stores are on their way out and are not recommended for minority entrepreneur consideration.

Convenience stores are another category which may belong in either the small store or the superette class. These stores are open long hours 7 days a week, and carry a line of food items which cater to the homemaker who has run out of a necessary item.

B. Dimensions of the Industry

The retail food industry in the United States is a multibillion dollar a year business, with total U.S. grocery sales in 1967 of $74.2 billion, up from $38.2 billion in 1958. During this period, the number of all grocery stores declined from 285,000 to 226,000, with average sales per store increasing at a steady rate from $169,000 annually to $328,000. Supermarkets accounted for almost three out of every four sales dollars (72.3 percent) in the retail food industry, but they accounted for only 15.4 percent of all stores.

These basic facts about grocery stores must be kept in mind at all times:

1. There will be continuing growth along with population growth.
2. The trend has been to larger and larger stores.
3. Establishments owned by large chains have continued to grow and currently dominate the industry.

There has been a recent trend toward growth of small stores of the so-called convenience category, but these are special cases and do not pose a threat to the domination of the large chains.

Expenditures for food have grown over the years at a rate faster than the growth of population. This is generally attributed to the increase in convenience foods such as frozen foods, prepackaged meals, special mixes, and the like, which cost more than the basic foods that are prepared at home.

There has been considerable interest in minority penetration into the supermarket field in recent years, due largely to the virtual abandonment of the inner city by many chains and the need to provide a source for food to inner-city residents. In addition, there have been a number of claims that many of the chainstores charge higher prices at their remaining inner-city locations than at their suburban stores. While these charges have been denied, they are widely believed throughout minority communities.

Although a number of minority grocery stores have been established, many of these have experienced difficulties attaining sufficient volume and adequate cost controls for profitable operation. Some have failed. There are, as yet, no outstanding minority-owned successes in the supermarket field although many of those that have started in the past 5 years have shown signs of overcoming their initial difficulties and surviving.

C. Characteristics of the Industry

1. The Product

The average inventory of the modern supermarket consists of some 6,000 to 8,000 items, defined as either individual products or individual brands. Indeed, it is the large inventory which permits the supermarket to capture its volume of sales. Above all, the successful supermarket seeks to be a "one-stop" shopping center, and the larger the inventory, the more realistic is this claim.

The table below shows how many different items are carried in the various departments of one of the largest chains, and the percentage of total sales each department accounts for.

Department	**Number of items**	**Percent of total**	**Percentage of total sales**
Meat	465	7.1	28.3
Produce	241	3.7	7.6
Dairy	281	4.4	11.5
Frozen foods	286	4.5	3.3
Bakery	278	4.3	5.0
Grocery	3,837	59.0	40.5
Nonfoods	1,100	17.0	3.8
Total	6,488	100.0	100.0

The supermarket sells the convenience of one-stop shopping, and the desirability of a large number of items from which to choose. Supermarkets compete with each other on price, quality, store appearance, and location. The tendency in recent years has been to add more and more items, to establish special delicatessen departments, and to increase the number of nonfood items on which markups are higher. The average store in a large chain offered 6,488 items in 1970 as compared to 5,144 in 1957, and nonfood items increased from 654 to 1,100. Meat and produce items also increased greatly.

The quality of produce and meats is an important part of the supermarket product. While most supermarkets carry the same brands of nationally-advertised foods, there may be considerable difference in the quality of meats and produce, and many homemakers choose among supermarkets on the basis of real or fancied differences in the qualities of these items.

Many of the supermarket chains also feature their own brands of groceries. The quality of these private brands is usually high and they often offer considerable savings to the shopper willing to forego the nationally-advertised brand. Private labels are also available to independents, particularly if they deal with a large wholesaler who has established a reputation for his own brands.

Nonfood items generally consist of items such as drugs and cosmetics, small housewares, special buys in soft-goods items such as socks, dishtowels, underwear, children's wear, garden supplies, and stationery. Items such as drugs, cosmetics, and soft-goods items have become increasingly important because there is usually a larger markup on these goods than on food items. In many cases, a service jobber will supply these items and service them on the shelves or on special display fixtures. The supermarket pays only for the items which are sold.

Frozen foods have become increasingly important, and many of the newer supermarkets devote considerable refrigerated space to displays of these items.

Some supermarkets also feature their own bakery products, even to the extent of having a bakery on the premise. This, too, can be an important factor in bringing the customer to the store.

Under some circumstances, bakery, meats, and/or produce departments can be leased to specialists. If such an arrangement is possible, it may prove wise for a new entrepreneur to thus free himself to manage other departments more closely.

2. The Customer

The average urban family of four is apt to spend about $2,000 a year in the grocery store. Most of the purchases are made by women, although men are becoming increasingly important as supermarket shoppers, and many managers have recently been slanting displays of foods toward those which might promote impulse purchases from men.

Many families try to do all their shopping for food once a week, although the typical pattern is to make one trip to the supermarket for the week's shopping on Thursday, Friday, or Saturday, when most specials are featured, with an occasional trip or two during the other days to pick up forgotten items or such perishables as bread, dairy products, meats, and frozen foods.

The weekend specials are a major aspect of supermarket merchandising. However, many supermarkets are trying to change consumer habits into buying early in the week as well, and it is not uncommon to see the major chains advertising in the Monday newspapers, as well as Thursday and Friday.

While the average supermarket shopper comes to the store with a list of purchases to be made, impulse buying is a major factor in building volume. Special displays are valuable features of food merchandising, and food manufacturers often pay for the privilege of featuring their merchandise in these displays.

The new "consumerism" has brought about an increasing demand on the part of articulate consumer "spokesmen" for "unit pricing" and "open dating." Unit pricing provides the customer with a comparison of the price per standard unit for different brands and different size containers, so that she does not have to perform the mathematical computations herself. Thus the prices for a 13-ounce container, a one-pound three-ounce container, and a two-and-a-half pound container will also be shown in terms of the equivalent price per pound for each container. The customer can then see which item actually costs less.

Open dating refers to providing the customer with information on the freshness of items. Most grocery items are stamped with coded numbers which indicate when an item is to be removed from the shelf as no longer fresh. These codes were designed to be deciphered only by stores employees. However, stores have recently begun providing consumers with information with which to understand codes.

Many customers develop loyalties to particular stores based upon convenience of location, preference for the store's private brands, a belief that the store offers better bargains or has better quality meat and/or produce, a desire for the store's greater variety of items, or even friendliness with the clerks. However, such loyalties are fickle, and they change easily. Many of the chains show a considerable shift in their weekly volume, based upon the competitiveness of their weekend specials or their competitive position on special promotions. The wide use of trading stamps and special promotions tends to support the assumption that the average customer finds little to choose between the many chains on the basis of convenience, price, and quality, and therefore makes his decision on the basis of special promotions, weekend specials, and trading stamps.

This being true, it is logical to assume that a minority-owned supermarket which could compete on an equal basis with the chains when it comes to convenience, price, and quality could easily capture the loyalty of enough members of the minority community, based upon a consciousness of race and an identification with the owner of the store, to achieve profitability.

With the average urban family of four spending in the neighborhood of $2,000 a year on retail food purchases, a supermarket could attain a volume of $1 million by securing 500 such families as customers. However, since most families will split their purchases among many different outlets, a minimum-sized supermarket should seek about 2,000 to 3,000 customers.

3. Operations

While the operation of a supermarket may appear on the surface to be a relatively simple job requiring rudimentary skills, such appearances are dangerously deceptive and have led many individuals and groups into bankruptcy. In actual practice, supermarket management is a highly complex skill requiring application of diverse talents and continuous attention to many different aspects of the job.

The appearance of the store is an important feature, requiring a knowledge of point-of-sale merchandising, proper lighting, and appropriate arrangement of merchandise to facilitate shopping and assure that the customer will come back. The width of aisles, for example, is highly important. If they are too wide, they take up valuable space which could be used to stock more merchandise. If they are too narrow, the customer becomes irritated at being unable to maneuver her shopping cart easily. The store must be kept clean at all times, and yet there is a continuing tendency to become cluttered and messy. If the store has a rundown, overly-cluttered, and messy atmosphere, the shopper may conclude that the items being sold are insanitary.

Stocking the various items is another important aspect of management which requires considerable detailed supervision and knowledge. With several thousand items to keep track of, the supermarket manager must determine how much shelf space to allot to each item, and he must carry just enough of each item to turn over his stock rapidly while at the same time making sure that he does not run out of stock and disappoint his customers. Careful inventory control requires constant checking of the sales of the various stock items. Inventory control may well be the most important factor affecting profitability.

The quality of produce and meat offered for sale is yet another aspect of management full of pitfalls for the inexperienced or slipshod manager. Meat suppliers and produce houses cannot be expected to watch the quality of the product they deliver on behalf of the retailer. Just as the housewife examines every cut of meat and every piece of produce carefully, so, too, must the store management see to it that the meat it receives and the produce it buys is of the highest quality. A superior meat and produce department can make an otherwise run-of-the-mill store successful. On the other hand, meat and produce of poor quality can ruin an otherwise well-run store.

Proper purchasing of other items is also a key item for the independent supermarket manager. This means taking advantage of special buys and knowing which wholesaler can help him best. Some independents can make money by speculating on food and buying larger than usual quantities in anticipation of price rises on such high volume staples as sugar and canned goods. This requires exceptional skill and experience and can lead to disaster for the unwary store owner who stocks up on an item before the price goes down.

Careful control over stealing and pilferage is an essential aspect of supermarket management. The freedom with which customers and children roam the aisles and the small size of many items make it inevitable that many items will be slipped into pockets. Stock clerks and warehouse clerks are also prone to help themselves to merchandise freely. Sloppy checkout procedures can lead to undercharges which cheat the management and overcharges which cheat the customer and undermine the store's reputation. Cashiers who fail to ring up items for customers whom they know can also result in losses. Bad checks are another loss problem for supermarkets.

There are some established security services which provide agents and investigative services to assist the store manager in protecting against loss. It is also possible to minimize pilferage by lowering shelves, placing registers so that a better view of the store can be maintained, and using closed circuit TV.

The supermarket manager must also master the techniques of advertising, and he must play and win the game of competitive pricing of specials. This means he must know when and how to put certain items on special price and thus attract customers into the store. He will be competing with the chains, and he must study their moves and make countermoves in a constant strategic battle. Some of the larger food retailers actually make money on advertising because brand name manufacturers pay the retailer for the privilege of having their brands listed in his advertising. However, advertising in a competitive market takes an extreme amount of time, often out of proportion to other aspects of management.

An independent supermarket owner should give serious consideration to joining a retailer's cooperative or affiliating with a wholesaler who sponsors joint advertising and features independent brand merchandise. There are a number of these associations in and around the larger metropolitan areas. They offer many advantages. First of all, there is identification through advertising with a number of other stores. Second, the retailer receives the advantage of special promotions and purchases. Third, advice on store operation is generally available. Someone who is thinking of starting a new store should check with wholesalers and independents who have joined in cooperatives in order to compare the advantages offered by such groups.

Labor requirements, of course, vary with the size of the supermarket to be operated. Nevertheless, there are several critical positions which must be filled regardless of store size. The following list identifies the positions and indicates their criticality:

Clerk
Assistant department heads
  *Produce
  *Meat
  Delicatessen
  Grocery
Department heads
  (same as above)
Assistant store manager
  (usually only in larger stores and serves as grocery department head)
*Store manager

---

*Critical jobs.

Wage scales vary according to the geographic area in which the supermarket is located as they are dependent primarily on the strength of the employees' union. For example, wage scales in Washington, D.C., and Los Angeles are high, while in Jackson, Mississippi, where the union is relatively ineffective, wages are much lower.

	Washington, D. C., wages (Weekly)	Mississippi wages (Weekly)
Clerks	$130–$155	$ 45–$ 75
Assistant department heads	$175–$190	$90
Department heads	$220–$230	$100–$115
Assistant store manager	$220–$230	$100–$115
Store manager	$250+	$125–$150

Nonwage benefits differ according to area also. Typical Washington, D.C., benefits, for example cover medical, dental, hospital, and vacation expenses, while those in Mississippi include only vacation. Wages and benefits do not vary according to the size of the store, as they are controlled by the union. Therefore, wages and benefits in a certain area would be the same despite store size and capacity.

4. Competition

The independent supermarket operating in the inner city will be doing business in one of the most competitive industries in the Nation. The size of the market in any one area and the relative ease of entry virtually assure competition in any location where there is sufficient population to assure a reasonable market.

Within the industry, a 1-mile radius is usually accepted as the primary trading area for a supermarket. In 1968, the typical new supermarket had to compete with two other supermarkets with an average combined sales area of 27,000 feet and weekly sales in excess of $50,000.

The supermarket operator is subjected to many different kinds of competition. The convenience store or neighborhood delicatessen competes by being open longer hours and more days. There is also competition from special frozen food stores, bakeries, dairy stores, and in some cases butcher shops. Drugstores and discount department stores sell competitive food and nonfood items. During appropriate seasons produce vendors can be found on street corners or operating out of trucks. But the largest source of competition is the big supermarket chain which competes by heavy advertising, by lower prices, by offering a large variety of items from which to choose, and by employing a wide range of promotional "gimmicks" to get people into the stores.

However, it is possible for an ably-managed independent to compete with the chainstores. By exercising closer supervision over his store the independent can see to it that operation is cleaner and neater. He can take more trouble to know his customers and to develop a cheery and friendly atmosphere. He can be more flexible in his pricing of "specials" and from time to time make special buys which permit him to undercut chainstore prices. With a little care and attention he can offer better produce and better meats than the chains. By identifying himself with the neighborhood and the institutions of the community he can gather a large amount of goodwill which can translate into steady customers. There should be no underestimation of the difficulty of competing in the supermarket industry. But it is possible for a new entrant to do so, if he has sufficient capital, understands food merchandising, and can become an effective manager.

5. Ease of Entry

Given sufficient capital, it is very easy to enter the supermarket business. There are existing businesses which can be purchased, although this should be done with care to make certain that the business being purchased can be operated at a profit. There are also vacant buildings in the inner city, many of them formerly occupied by supermarkets, which have been closed, and these are generally available for the establishment of a business.

Superficially, it might be said that all it really takes to enter the supermarket business is to find a location, equip it with some shelves, checkout counters, and other equipment, order up the stock, and open the doors. However, the potential supermarket operator should not follow this route. Careful planning should take place to establish the right location. Arrangements should be completed for the best possible deal on equipment. Store layout is a complex problem. Stock should be carefully ordered. Personnel should be employed and trained. And considerable time and expense should be given to the opening announcement and the special inducements to get customers into the store during the first week.

With proper planning and advance arrangements, there is no reason why a supermarket cannot begin to break even within the first 3 months after opening. However, considering that mistakes will be made in determining the best inventory arrangement, it may take several more months before inventories are adjusted and regulated to enable the business to reach a break-even point.

6. Financing

Adequate capitalization and financing is one of the keys to successful operation of a supermarket. In most cases, capital is not required for land and building, because an existing building can be leased or arrangements can be made to have a building constructed by someone else and leased by the supermarket operator. Prospective operators of supermarkets in inner-city areas should be alert to leasing commercial space in new housing developments. It is almost always better to lease than to build since less capital is required and a certain flexibility is maintained. Virtually all of the chainstores follow this method.

Some capital will be required for equipment. Equipment can be expensive. For example, a supermarket with 15,000 square feet of selling area could require a minimum of 75 feet of frozen food shelving, about 100 feet of produce shelving (cooled), about 30 feet of dairy shelving and 30 feet of cooled beverage shelving, and a minimum of 50 feet for the meat section. At least six checkout stands and registers would also be required. While the total investment for such equipment is considerable, there is a strong possibility that used equipment can be picked up for some purposes and other equipment leased. However, even with leased equipment there may be considerable investment involved in installing the necessary plumbing and in meeting local building and food-handling codes.

A rough estimate of inventory investment would be about $5 to $10 per square foot of selling space or between two and four times the weekly estimated volume. However, much of this inventory can be secured on credit, depending on the relationship established with a supplier and his confidence in the store management.

Even with maximum use of lease arrangements, financing of equipment, and purchase of inventory on credit, startup costs of a new market will nevertheless be considerable, and it is recommended that $50,000 to $100,000 be available for a store with about 10,000 square feet of selling space, which anticipates a minimum volume of about $20,000 per week. Some of this may not necessarily have to be in cash, but may be in the form of a line of credit available from a bank. For a larger store of 15,000 square feet of selling space, the initial investment would be closer to the $100,000 to $200,000 range.

7. Profitability

The average gross profit among supermarkets (net sales less cost of goods sold) is about 20 percent of net sales, with net profit on sales averaging between 1 percent and 2 percent. An average net profit of 1½ percent on gross volume of $1 million would yield an annual net profit of $15,000. If this were achieved on an investment of $50,000, it would bring about 30-percent return.

The average small food retailer does not make this type of profit, while the large chains often show higher profits on those individual stores that are successful.

The key to profitability in supermarket operation is high volume and inventory control. Managers who can turn over stock rapidly while keeping costs within bounds can show a reasonable profit despite the intense competition within the industry.

Smaller stores such as superettes are characterized by lower profitability. These stores generally do not show the profit of the larger, higher volume stores and are usually justified on the basis of the opportunity afforded to the owner and his family to work in their own store. Thus, while the owner (and his family) may draw a decent living from the store, profits tend to be quite low.

The owner of a superette operating in a protected location or as a convenience store can sell at a higher gross margin and earn a somewhat better profit than a superette attempting to compete with chain-stores in the same trading area.

8. Dependence on Outside Factors

The retail food business is considered a somewhat "depression proof" business in that people always have to eat, and even in times of depression they will spend their welfare allowances, unemployment compensation, and food stamps in the grocery store. Thus, almost more than any other business, the supermarket is dependent for success on the ability of management in selecting the right location, treating the customers well, and controlling costs.

Supermarket operators planning to open in the inner city may find their location and market affected by urban renewal and highway-building programs. These can often change neighborhoods and relocate customers out of the trading area. A wise step before settling on a specific location would be to check with the city planning office to determine what plans are being considered that would change the character of the neighborhood or affect the number of people living in the trading area.

III. FEASIBILITY

A. Factors Influencing Feasibility

The major factors influencing feasibility are: location, management, volume, inventory control, store appearance, price, quality control, and merchandising.

1. Location

Ideally, the location should be within a primary trading area (radius of 1 mile) that has ample population to support the volume of sales desired and where competition is not overly intense. The cost of operating in the location (that is, rent and other charges such as utilities and maintenance) should be appropriate to the quality of the building and within reasonable limits for the volume expected.

2. Management

A supermarket operation is very complex. The average supermarket manager for a chainstore is not only carefully trained, but he receives backup services from a host of experts in merchandising, advertising, store layout, buying, personnel supervision, equipment maintenance, quality control, inventory control, and the like. The independent supermarket operator must often become his own expert in all these fields. The individual desiring to operate his own supermarket should have several years' experience as manager of another store. Without such experience, he would be well advised to seek employment first with a chainstore for several years, using the opportunity to study carefully their methods of operation.

3. Volume

The retail food business is primarily a volume business, particularly for supermarkets. The store must produce the volume required to support its overhead, or it will inevitably lose money.

4. *Inventory Control*

It is extremely important to maintain the proper balance between inventory and sales volume. On the one hand, the successful supermarket manager wants to keep enough inventory on hand so that his customers can always find what they want; but on the other, he does not want to tie up his money and his shelf space in items which do not sell rapidly. Moreover, many food items will spoil if not sold quickly. The problem is not simple. Some items do not turn over quickly, but they must be kept on hand because customers will be lost without them. The big chainstores have computers and special analysts to help in making these decisions. The independent supermarket operator must make them on his own, although affiliation with an association or a cooperative can provide some help.

Another aspect of inventory control is inventory shrinkage resulting from stealing by the staff, shoplifting by customers, or just plain carelessness. Where profit margins are so small, profits can quickly disappear unless inventory shrinkage is controlled.

5. *Store Appearance*

The big supermarket chains spend hundreds of thousands of dollars fixing up their stores so that they will be attractive places in which to shop. The independent operator may not have the capital to make this kind of investment, and he will have to be ingenious in his ability to decorate and to lay out fixtures, and diligent in seeing to it that his store is clean, neat, and appealing.

6. *Price*

Food shoppers are kept constantly aware of the comparative prices of food items by heavy advertising on the part of food retailers. Moreover, many standard items are exactly the same, and it is easy for the shopper to make price comparisons. The homemaker is more apt to be concerned about the price of food than other items since it is the largest single item in the family budget. For all these reasons, the supermarket operator must compete on the basis of price. This can be done in several ways. Sometimes a manager will deliberately cut his inventory so that he can cut prices, reduce his gross margin, and still show a profit. Sometimes price competition is more apparent than real, and the operator reduces a few weekend specials while maintaining adequate markups on the bulk of his merchandise. Again, the big chains have an advantage because they can use their huge purchasing power to secure volume discounts. The independent operator will have to be aggressive and alert to good buys in order to match their basic advantage.

7. *Quality Control*

There are many opportunities to compete on the basis of quality control in food retailing, particularly in the quality of produce and meats. Baked goods and dairy products also have quality control problems. Careful attention needs to be paid to frozen foods. When these are allowed to thaw and then are refrozen, they lose their flavor. Although there are alarm services to warn the owner when the refrigeration fails, careless handling can cause losses when frozen foods are allowed to stand outside their cases for too long a period.

8. *Merchandising*

The successful supermarket manager must be a good merchandiser. He must know how to advertise, how to set up good displays, what kinds of special promotions to feature, and how to treat his customers to give them the feeling that they enjoy shopping in his store. The use of trading stamps and special premiums is an important part of food retailing. There are many arguments for and against such merchandising techniques, and these must be understood by the successful operator so that he can use those which are most appropriate to his competitive position.

B. Special Problems and Potentials for Minority Entrepreneurs

1. *Problems*

The problems faced by a minority entrepreneur trying to establish a food supermarket will be the same as those of any independent attempting to enter a business which is dominated by big, aggressive, and amply financed chainstores, plus special factors created by racial discrimination and environmental problems.

It would be extremely difficult for an inexperienced and unaffiliated minority entrepreneur to go into the suburban shopping centers to compete with the chains on their home ground. In the first place, most shopping center operators would turn up their noses at an independent, inexperienced supermarket operator. They need one of the high volume chain operations to pull customers into their center. This limits the minority entrepreneur to the inner city or its less desirable fringes, where the chains, by and large, do not want to go. While such locations may offer less competition from the chains, they have problems of their own stemming from the character of the neighborhood, the increased cost of insurance, and excessive costs from vandalism, shoplifting, and theft.

Moreover, size is essential to success, and in the supermarket industry, size requires investment. Most minority entrepreneurs do not have access to the kinds of investment required for a supermarket of the size required for profitability, and conventional sources of financing will hardly be available when the proposal is to establish a store in a difficult area. Food retailing accounts for a major portion of minority-owned businesses. However, very few of these businesses are adequate in size, and most subsist without profit, enabling an owner to draw a minimum amount for personal income.

2. Potentials

Nevertheless, there appears to be a shortage of retail food outlets in some inner-city areas where minorities live, and thus there is an opportunity for an individual or a group with the willingness to work hard at the business, the skill to solve the many problems presented, and an access to special sources of capital for minority ventures. If plans can be carefully drawn and effective management secured, there are reasonable chances that sufficient capital can be forthcoming.

Most groups which have been established to help with the economic development of the inner city are interested in establishing retail food operations. The lack of such facilities is a hardship to the residents of the areas in question, and this factor adds a special urgency to the need for providing financing. However, a number of ventures have already been financed in many areas, and a significant proportion of these have experienced severe financial difficulties. This has made lenders somewhat more cautious than they might otherwise be.

New housing projects for the inner city offer an opportunity for the establishment of food supermarkets. These projects will bring a concentration of new families into the area, and many of them will either provide for commercial space or be located close to sites which can be developed for commercial use. In almost all cases, it will be desirable to establish a new supermarket operation in these locations. Minority entrepreneurs seeking to become supermarket operators should carefully investigate such opportunities in connection with new inner city housing projects.

C. Operating Projections

Shown below are hypothetical operating projections for two sizes of supermarkets. The first is a minimal operation, reflecting the very lowest feasible volume of $1 million annually in about 10,000 square feet of selling space (15,000 square feet overall). The second example is designed to show what might be a more typical operation for an average supermarket having 20,000 square feet of selling space and an annual volume of $2,300,000.

These figures are used as typical examples. Individual operations may vary considerably from these examples depending upon local and special circumstances.

Item		Minimal Amount	Minimal %		Average Amount	Average %
Annual sales		$1,000,000	100.0		$2,300,000	100.0
Cost of goods sold		805,000	80.5		1,851,500	80.5
Gross margin			19.5			19.5
Operating expenses:						
Labor (including fringe benefits)	$92,000		9.2	207,000		9.0
Purchased services	16,000		1.6	36,800		1.6
Promotion and advertising	11,000		1.1	23,000		1.0
Rental of premises and equipment	21,000		2.1	43,700		1.9
Supplies	10,000		1.0	20,700		0.9
Taxes, licenses, and insurance	14,000		1.4	32,200		1.4
Utilities	9,000		0.9	18,400		0.8
Maintenance and Repairs	7,000		0.7	13,800		0.6
Depreciation and amortization	10,000		1.0	20,700		0.9
Total		190,000	19.0		416,300	18.1
Operating profit		$ 5,000	0.5		$ 32,200	1.4
Other income (discounts earned, advertising allowances, etc.)		4,000	0.4		13,800	0.6
Total income		$ 9,000	0.9		$ 46,000	2.0
Capital investment		$ 75,000			$ 150,000	
Return on investment			12.0			30.7

Typical operating ratios for supermarkets in 1969 are shown below:

Gross profit with warehouse	21.1%
Gross profit without warehouse	19.3%
Net operating profit ratio before taxes	1.5%
Sales by department:	
Grocery	67.5%
Meat	25.2%
Produce	7.4%
Average hourly labor cost	$ 2.77
Grocery inventory turnover rate	19.4 times per year
Typical sales per man-hour	$34.69
Typical sales per customer	$ 6.02
Typical sales per square foot of selling area (weekly)	$ 4.15

IV. STARTING THE NEW STORE

A. The Location

The first step in starting a new supermarket is to select the right location. Assuming that the potential new entrepreneur or cooperative already knows the general area in which the supermarket is to be located, a search must be made for an appropriate location. A thorough investigation must be made of all potential locations. These could be: (1) a store presently being operated which is available for purchase; (2) a store which was formerly occupied by a supermarket, but which is now vacant; (3) other vacant commercial space which could be adapted for supermarket operation; (4) newly-constructed commercial space in a proposed shopping center or in the commercial portion of a new housing project; (5) vacant land on which a foodstore could be constructed.

A careful study should be made of all potential locations on the following basis:

1. The Total Market

An estimate should be made of the total market for retail food purchases within the primary trading area of the store. While a rough rule of thumb is a 1-mile radius for the primary trading area of a suburban-type supermarket with ample parking space, a smaller radius should be used to identify the primary trading area in the inner city where many of the customers will have to walk in order to shop. The number of people in the trading area should be determined and their average income estimated. From these data, it is a relatively simple matter to determine their annual food purchases. The advertising departments of local newspapers or radio stations can provide this information. Each prospective location should be analyzed on this basis to see which offers access to the largest market.

2. Competition

The largest market may not necessarily be the best due to competitive factors. Thus, an analysis should be made of the competition serving the same markets and the amount of business each of the competitors does. (This latter estimate can be judged roughly on the basis of the square footage of selling space—which can be paced off by the individual making the study.) After judging the portion of the market potential competitors are taking, an estimate can be made of the potential share of the market that the proposed new supermarket might expect in each location. When this potential is applied to each prospective location, a judgment can be made on which location offers the best opportunity to build volume.

3. Amount and Quality of Space

A comparison should be made of the amount of space available in each of the locations and whether or not the space is sufficient to provide a selling area large enough to support the volume desired. In determining the desirability of space, consideration should be given to its cost and its condition. Thus, one location may have less space available than another, but it may cost less per square foot and be in better condition. It is also important to look at the shape of the space and any posts or other structural characteristics which would handicap use as a foodstore. Moreover, in determining cost, consideration should be given not only to the monthly rent, but also to the cost of renovation, maintenance, and other payments which the tenant is expected to pay.

Sufficient parking space will have to be available along with the store space, if significant business is to be expected from customers who will shop by automobile. A small supermarket depending almost wholly on customers who come by automobile would probably want about 3 square feet of parking space for every square foot of selling space. Thus, a store with 10,000 square feet of selling space would require 30,000 square feet of parking. However, if it expects to do a high volume in that selling space, it may require more parking space. If a significant proportion of customers will come to the store on foot, smaller parking spaces will be sufficient. Obviously, in a city where land costs are high, the supermarket operator generally tries to make do on less space for parking than in the suburbs where land costs are less and all customers come by automobile.

4. Special Factors

There are special factors influencing location to be considered. The quality of the neighborhood is one factor. The potential operator should determine whether the proposed location is becoming a better neighborhood in which to do business or worse. Are there large projects being planned which will relocate customers out of the area? Are new housing projects being planned on vacant land? What kind of neighboring commercial establishments are in the area? Obviously, it is better to be located in a progressive shopping area tenanted by good merchants than to be in an area where seedy bars and grills predominate.

The potential entrepreneur should array all these factors carefully and study them to determine which location is the most advantageous for his purposes. The importance of this kind of locational study cannot be overestimated. It is essential to the establishment of a new supermarket. The average chain spends close to $5,000 on research before selecting a new location. The new entrepreneur may not be able to afford that kind of investment, but he can spend his own time gathering the facts and looking over potential sites carefully. If funds are available, it may be wise to hire an expert economic research firm to help choose the best location.

B. Operational Planning

After the location has been secured, careful plans must be drawn which can be shown to financial backers and others. A determination must be made of what is needed to get the store started, including: renovation of the proposed location; purchase or leasing of equipment; amount of startup inventory; and startup expenses for promotion and training of personnel. A statement should be prepared indicating the cost of all these items and how they are to be financed. A pro forma operating statement should be prepared showing anticipated annual volume and costs.

C. Arranging for Equipment

Visits should be made to local grocery store equipment suppliers for information and prices on refrigerated equipment, special produce counters, shelves, cash registers and the like. A determination should be made of what can be purchased secondhand and what can be leased. Care should be taken to make sure the refrigeration equipment will work. Faulty operation of refrigerating devices can result in considerable loss.

D. Preliminary Lease Negotiations

Preliminary discussions should be held with the owner of the land or building to determine the nature of the lease and the cost. It is generally desirable to have an experienced lease negotiator assist with these discussions. The new operator should try to get a relatively short lease with options to renew at an agreeable rate. The owner of the property will try to get a long lease and some type of guarantee, so that if the operator is unable to continue operations, the lease commitments will be met. Finding an acceptable middle ground between these two points of view is the purpose of negotiations and should be determined by how badly the owner needs to find a tenant and how desirable the proposed building is compared to other possibilities.

A common lease arrangement calls for a fixed minimum payment with additional payments as volume increases, thus enabling the owner to share in the store's success. The supermarket operator should be careful to avoid giving away all his potential profits to the owner of the building, but if he can get a lower minimum by agreeing to a larger share of increased volume, it may lessen the risk of potential failure.

E. Arranging for Inventory

Preliminary discussions should be held with a grocery wholesaler to determine the basis on which an opening inventory can be secured. Generally, the grocery business requires payment in 7 days; while the product business requires payment on receipt of goods. Consideration should be given to the reputability of the wholesaler, his prices, and his willingness to supply credit. It is also advantageous to affiliate with a wholesaler who provides group advertising and brand names, thus giving the new supermarket an established identification in the minds of the consumer. There are many such arrangements in metropolitan areas throughout the country. In the Baltimore area, there is a cooperative arrangement for black-owned grocery stores called Jet Stores; in the Miami area, there is an organization for minority foodstore operators called Farm Stores International, Inc.

F. Arranging for Capital

After the location has been determined, operational planning finished, and preliminary negotiations held with the landlord, equipment suppliers, and grocery suppliers, the new entrepreneur will need to arrange additional financing. Presumably, he will have some idea of where he can secure financial backing for a feasible plan prior to starting the whole process. Such financing can come from a number of sources: (1) the potential new owner or group of owners may have financial resources of their own which can be used or pledged as collateral for a bank loan; (2) if a cooperative, shares may be sold throughout the community to members; (3) there may be special sources of financing from local organizations established to help minority entrepreneurs, such as agencies funded under Title I-D of the Economic Opportunity Act, the Urban Coalition, or a local Minority Enterprise Small Business Investment Corporation (MESBIC); (4) a local bank under a loan guaranteed by the Small Business Administration. The potential new operator should take his plans to the appropriate source of financing and complete the arrangements.

G. Securing a Work Force

A competent work force should be trained and ready for the opening day. While potential employees may be secured from the public employment office or a local employment training program, every effort should be made to secure a nucleus of experienced personnel. If necessary, it would be wiser to pay a premium to lure experienced employees away from some of the supermarkets. Under no circumstances should the new operation start with a completely inexperienced work force.

It is particularly important to try to get experienced personnel for the produce department and the meat department. These are specialized functions which require considerable background.

The work force will need considerable training on such items as checkout counters, customer courtesy, stocking merchandise, display, preparation, and handling of meat and produce, and similar items. If the new management does not have the ability and time to undertake such training, arrangements should be made to employ someone to do so. A check should be made with the local manpower development and training office or concentrated employment program to determine whether such training can be arranged and paid for out of public manpower training funds.

H. Opening Day

The opening day of a new supermarket operation should be carefully planned. Prizes and premiums should be secured to induce customers to come in and see the store. The store, itself, must be spotless and in attractive condition. Opening week special prices should be prominently featured in advertising and store displays. A good impression on opening day can mean early attainment of break-even volume, and this achievement can result in lower startup costs.

Many of the above procedures can be abbreviated where an existing business is being purchased. But the prospective purchaser should be certain of what he is purchasing in all these areas and make sure that he is not simply buying another person's problems.

V. SUMMARY

A food supermarket is one of the most competitive businesses in our economy. Operating margins are very small and leave virtually no room for inefficiency or mistakes. Large, highly organized chainstores provide intense competition for the newcomer to the field. Capital requirements are larger than they are for most retail operations. Management is extremely complex.

Supermarkets do not offer an attractive opportunity for inexperienced, undercapitalized entrepreneurs. However, because there is a need for more quality food outlets to serve consumers in the inner city, it may be desirable actively to encourage new supermarkets for the inner city and to provide considerable extra assistance to entrepreneurial ventures of this type, or to the formation of cooperatives. If so, extreme care should be taken in planning the new operation and every effort should be exerted to make certain that it will be capably managed and adequately financed.

BIBLIOGRAPHY

Government Sources

U.S. Department of Commerce, Bureau of the Census, Washington, D.C., 20233. *1967 Census of Business, Retail Trade.*

U.S. Department of Commerce, Business and Defense Services Administration, Washington, D.C. 20230. *U.S. Industrial Outlook, 1970.*

Nongovernmental Sources

"Annual Survey of Food Retailing," Progressive Grocer, April 1970.

Appelbaum, William, *Guide to Store Location Research*. Addison-Wesly, 1968.

"Behind the New Wave Discount Super Revolution," Chain Store Age, November 1967.

Bucklin, Louis P., *Shopping Patterns in an Urban Area,* Berkeley, 1967.

"Can Black-Run Supers Free the Inner-City World?" Progressive Grocer, April 1969.

Kane, Bernard, *A Systematic Guide to Supermarket Locational Analysis,* New York.

"16th Annual Study of Shopping Center Trends," Chain Store Age, May 1968.

"The Chain Supermarket—a 10-Year Progress Report," Chain Store Age, July 1967.

"The Cost of a Supermarket," Chain Store Age (Exec.).

"The Inner City," Food Topics, October 1967.

The Supermarket Industry Speaks, 1970, Supermarket Institute, Inc., 1970.

"The True Look of the Discount Industry," Discount Merchandiser, June 1968.

"Why Boom in Negro-owned Supers," Chain Store Age, September 1968.

TRADE ASSOCIATIONS

National Association of Food Chains, 1725 Eye Street, N.W., Washington, D.C. 20006.

National Association of Retail Grocers of the U.S., 360 North Michigan, Chicago, Illinois 60601.

Supermarket Institute, 200 East Ontario Street, Chicago, Illinois 60611.

Preparing a Business Profile

Section Contents

INTRODUCTION

The purpose of the business profiles on the preceding pages is to provide potential small businessmen with information and insight into some of the problems and potentials of these businesses. The businesses reviewed in this series were selected for inclusion on the basis of their recent growth within urban areas.

However, any limited selection of industries may not contain the particular type of business in which a potential investor has interest. Therefore, to help a new businessman develop a profile on the business of his choice, this supplement to the Urban Business Profile Series has been prepared.

This supplement consists of two parts. Part I contains a description of the methodology used in the preparation of a business profile. Part II presents a detailed outline of such a profile.

A business profile, as described herein, does not substitute for a thorough feasibility study. Indeed, the two types of studies are complementary, and not substitutes for each other. The profile gives the businessman insight into the problems and potentials of a business, whereas a feasibility study is needed to determine whether a particular business, in a specific, identified site, has reasonable chances of success, considering all pertinent factors.

Information on the preparation of a feasibility study may be obtained from a local Small Business Administration office, an investment bank, or an affiliate of the Office of Minority Business Enterprise. The address of the local Small Business Administration office can be obtained from the telephone directory. Lists of the OMBE affiliates and of the Minority Enterprise Small Business Investment Companies are appended to this publication.

PART I: METHODOLOGY

The methodology used in preparation of the profiles involves the following steps:

1. Basic data should be accumulated from published government and private sources. Statistics relating to number of firms by employment size for the time period 1962 through 1970 are available in the County Business Patterns for State and metropolitan areas. More detailed data are contained in the 5-year Census of Business and Census of Manufactures. These three series are published by the Bureau of the Census, U.S. Department of Commerce. National projections are published for major industries by the Bureau of Domestic Commerce, U.S. Department of Commerce, U.S. Industrial Outlook. These publications are available in most public and university libraries.

   Additional material may be available from profiles published by the Small Business Administration, the Agency for International Development, and the Bank of America Small Business Reporter series.

2. Communication should be made with appropriate trade associations in order to identify and obtain the types of information available to the public from these sources.

The names and addresses of trade associations can be found in the "Directory of National Trade and Professional Associations in the United States," published by Potomac Books, Inc., Washington, D.C., or the "Encyclopedia of Associations," published by Gale Research Co., Detroit, Michigan. Important publications for each industry can be identified by these trade associations.

3. Where franchise operations are important to a particular type of business, major franchisers or their representatives should be contacted and their literature reviewed.

4. Interviews should be conducted with operators of existing businesses within the locality of the proposed business. In view of the special interest which minority group members have in the development of urban businesses, a particular attempt should be made to identify existing minority businessmen and interview them concerning special problems and potentials which may be encountered.

5. Drafts of the profiles should be discussed with and shown to persons familiar with the business (e.g., trade association executives, owners, or persons who have worked in the various businesses) to make sure that all essential aspects are covered and the information is substantially complete and correct.

PART II: PROFILE OUTLINE GUIDE

I. SUITABILITY OF BUSINESS

Specifications of conditions relating to markets, experience, location, financing, and labor availability, under which a new business might reasonably be expected to succeed.

II. DESCRIPTION OF BUSINESS

A. Identification, including the Standard Industrial Classification (SIC), of types of business activities covered by the profile.

B. Statistics pertaining to the dimensions of the industry including number and size of establishments, volume of sales, etc. and changes in these dimensions over time. Note significant national, regional, and local variations and extent of minority participation as appropriate.

C. Characteristics of Business

1. Nature of product

What human need is it designed to satisfy?

Is it a staple or an impulse item?

Is it a repeatedly purchased item or service?

Is it a "big-ticket item" or an inexpensive one?

How is the product or service sold?

2. Nature of customer

Where is the customer in the production or consumption chain (manufacturer, distributor, wholesaler, retailer, consumer)?

Is the customer likely to develop loyalty to a particular seller? On what basis?

Does the business have commonly understood guidelines for "minimum market size needed" or other such standards for market analysis?

What are the locational determinants of the business?

3. Technology

What skill levels are required to produce this product or service?

What wage rates prevail?

How capital intensive is the business?

Are there significant economies of scale in the production and/or selling of the product or service which clearly affect the size of firms in the business?

Is a Research and Development (R & D) capability important to success in the business?

4. Competition

How clearly defined is this business (what other types of businesses satisfy the same need)?

How concentrated is the business (how much of total sales is controlled by major firms)?

What organizational forms characterize it (franchise, proprietorships, partnerships, corporations, conglomerates)?

Is the business a new and/or rapidly changing one, or a mature and stable one?

What are the areas (price, service, quality, image, etc.) in which producers or sellers compete in this business?

5. **Ease of new firm entry**

   Is the business easy to enter in terms of licensing, capital, locational requirements, penetration of markets, and availability of qualified staff or work force?

   What is the usual lead time required to establish a new firm in the business and to achieve break-even operations?

6. **Capital requirements and forms of financing**

   What sort of capital requirements exist for each of the most common forms of firms within the business (e.g. franchise, chainstore, proprietorship, etc.)?

   How are these capital requirements usually financed—equity (owners or "parent" group), debt, lease credit, trade credit, etc.?

   What special programs or sources of capital exist for establishing new ventures in this business?

   What is the average gross margin, return on sales, return on investments, etc., within the business?

   Do profit measures vary by size, scale, and organizational form of the firm?

   What have been the profit trends in the business?

7. **Dependence on outside factors**

   How the firm's success is affected by such factors as:

   a. business cycles,
   b. rapidly changing tastes and markets,
   c. labor supply,
   d. sources of material supply,
   e. regulatory and legal authorities,
   f. money markets,
   g. other noncontrollable factors.

III. ANALYSIS OF BUSINESS FEASIBILITY

A. Identification of factors which clearly influence or determine performance in the business, i.e., location, adequate capital, service, customer loyalty, volume, R & D, production efficiency, etc.; (based on analysis of information in Part II).

B. If appropriate, identification of particular problems and possibilities for new minority ventures (special markets, financing sources, personnel requirements, etc.).

C. Projection of attainable returns on investment for the several sizes of firms most common in this business (different scales of operations, forms of control, levels of investment, etc.).

IV. GUIDANCE IN ESTABLISHING A BUSINESS

A. Approaching the market

1. Discussion of business practices in market segmentation—pricing, discounts, service, advertising, etc.
2. If appropriate, identification of special markets open to minority entrepreneur.
3. Discussion of standard or common marketing strategies for different situations, e.g., high advertising-high volume, low margin-low labor skill. For instance, a suburban shopping center furniture store will probably carry a higher priced line and adopt a more liberal credit policy for its higher and steadier income market segment than would an inner-city or low-income market store. Further consequences of choosing a particular market would be requirements in space, service, staffing, advertising, discount sales, and other items of marketing policy.

B. Establishing plant requirements

1. Land
2. Building and plant
3. Equipment

   Identify space, plant, and expected equipment needs. Industry and business sources are the most likely places to obtain the information and cost data.

C. Employing a work force

1. Discussion of business practices with respect to wages, productivity, unions, etc.
2. Discussion of possible relationships between labor and capital requirements.
3. Projection of probable staff levels and staffing costs.

D. Obtaining financing

1. Discussion of traditional forms of financing used.
2. Discussion of opportunities for minimizing cash needs through lease, finance, subcontract options.
3. Identification of special programs which may be available to minority entrepreneurs.
4. Presentation of financing plans considered most suitable.

   (Assistance in preparing financial plans should be sought from Community Development Corporations, the Small Business Administration, Minority Enterprise Small Business Investment Companies (MESBIC's), or a local investment bank).

APPENDIX

LICENSED MINORITY ENTERPRISE SMALL BUSINESS INVESTMENT COMPANIES (MESBIC's)

AS OF DECEMBER 13, 1971

Date Licensed		
8/13/68	1.	Arcata Investment Co. 2750 Sand Hill Road Menlo Park, California 94025
9/2/69	2.	Pioneer Capital Corp. 1440 Broadway Room 1967 New York, N. Y. 10018 212/594-4860
12/16/69	3.	Palo Alto Capital Co. Post Office Box 11066 Palo Alto, Calif. 94306 415/321-2762
2/26/70	4.	UCC Venture Corp. UCC Tower–Suite 1008 Post Office Box 6228 Dallas, Texas 75222 214/637-0445
3/19/70	5.	City of Commerce Investment Company 1117B South Goodrich Boulevard Los Angeles, Calif. 90022 213/724-6141
3/10/70	6.	Prudential Minority Enterprises, Inc. 22 Plaza Building Newark, N. J. 07101 201/336-5425
4/13/70	7.	Motor Enterprises, Inc. General Motors Building 3044 Grand Blvd. West Detroit, Michigan 48202 313/556-4273
4/20/70	8.	Hartford Capital Corp. 77 Main Street Hartford, Conn. 06103 203/547-2000
5/26/70	9.	Baltimore Community Investment Company 1102 Mondawmin Concourse Baltimore, Md. 21215 301/669-2863
6/12/70	10.	Phillips Industrial Finance Corporation Phillips Building Bartlesville, Okla. 74003 918/336-6600
6/29/70	11.	Pioneer Enterprises, Inc. 11255 Olympic Blvd. Los Angeles, Calif. 90064 213/479-4374
6/18/70	12.	Provident Enterprises Corporation 81 Encina Avenue Palo Alto, Calif. 94301 415/329-9200
7/2/70	13.	Minority Assistance Corporation 40 West 40th Street New York, N. Y. 10018 212/484-5157
7/14/70	14.	Forsyth County Investment Corporation Suite 305, Pepper Bldg. Winston-Salem, N. C. 27101 919/724-3676

Date Licensed		
7/16/70	15.	Broad Arrow Investment Corporation Route 5S, Ft. Hunter Rd. P.O. Box 151 Amsterdam, N. Y. 12010 518/843-3900
7/28/70	16.	Rutgers Minority Investment Company 18 Washington Place Newark, N. J. 07102 201/648-5287
9/24/70	17.	Equal Opportunity Finance, Inc. 1202 South Third Street Louisville, Ky. 40203 502/635-6321
10/16/70	18.	Vanguard Capital Corp. 222 West Chester Ave. White Plains, N. Y. 10604 914/694-4251
10/23/70	19.	REC Business Opportunities Corporation 316 Fifth Street Racine, Wisc. 53402 414/637-8893
11/13/70	20.	Business Ventures, Inc. 152 Temple Street New Haven, Conn. 06506 203/787-6735
11/13/70	21.	MESBIC of Washington 3300 Rainier Avenue, S. Seattle, Wash. 98144 206/PA 3-0555
12/22/70	22.	Amoco Venture Capital Company 910 S. Michigan Avenue Room 1766-A Chicago, Illinois 60605 312/856-6523
1/13/71	23.	Combined Opportunities, Inc. 5050 North Broadway Chicago, Illinois 60650 312/275-3871
3/4/71	24.	North American MESBIC, Inc. 114 State Street Boston, Mass. 02109 617/523-8024
2/19/71	25.	Progress Venture Capital Corporation 1501 North Broad Street Phila., Penna. 19122 215/849-2200
8/10/71	26.	Greater Springfield Investment Corporation 134 Chestnut Street Springfield, Mass. 01109 413/734-5671
3/10/71	27.	The Urban Fund, Inc. 1525 East 53rd Street Chicago, Illinois 60615 312/955-0080
3/22/71	28.	Pooled Resources Investing in Minority Enterprises, Inc. (PRIME, Inc.) 2990 West Grand Blvd., Room M-15 Detroit, Michigan 48202 313/872-2212
4/18/71	29.	The Circle K Investment Corporation 900 Magoffin Avenue El Paso, Texas 79901 915/532-4971
4/30/71	30.	BanCap Corporation 420 Lexington Avenue New York, N. Y. 10017 212/684-6460
5/7/71	31.	The Equitable Life Community Enterprise, Inc. 1285 Avenue of the Americas New York, N. Y. 10019 212/554-4978
5/17/71	32.	Minority Equity Capital Company, Inc. 470 Park Avenue New York, N. Y. 10016 212/889-0880

Date Licensed		
6/4/71	33.	Minority Investments, Inc. 1200 U Street, S.E. Washington, D.C. 20020 202/833-8380
6/18/71	34.	Alyeska Investment Co. 2805 Denali Street Anchorage, Alaska 99503 907/279-9584
8/18/71	35.	Model Capital Corporation 1106 East Spring Street Seattle, Wash. 98122 206/626-5440
9/15/71	36.	Indianapolis Business Investment Corp. 1241 N. Penna. Street Indianapolis, Ind. 46020 317/639-9413
9/23/71	37.	Opportunity Capital Corporation, Calif. 101 Howard Street San Francisco, Calif. 94105 415/781-5560
9/23/71	38.	Capital Formation MESBIC, Inc. 5 Beekman Street New York, N. Y. 10038 212/222-9650
10/8/71	39.	Southern California Minority Capital Corp. 2651 South Western Ave. Los Angeles, Calif. 90018 213/731-8211
10/15/71	40.	ECCO MESBIC, Inc. 32 Broad Street Sparta, Georgia 31087 404/444-5269
10/20/71	41.	Alliance Enterprise Corporation 1616 Walnut Street, Suite 802 Philadelphia, Pa. 19103 215/985-1636
11/15/71	42.	Coalition Small Business Investment Corp. 131 East 23d Street New York, N. Y. 10010 212/533-1900
12/9/71	43.	LaRaza Investment Corp. 132 South Central Ave. Suite C Phoenix, Arizona 85004 602/252-7401

OFFICE OF MINORITY BUSINESS ENTERPRISE (OMBE) AFFILIATE ORGANIZATIONS

Albuquerque

National Economic Development Association (NEDA)
1801 Lomas, N. W.
Albuquerque, N. M. 87104
508/843-2386
Victor M. Casaus, Regional Vice President

Atlanta

Atlanta Business League (NBL)
329 Walker Street, S. W.
Atlanta, Georgia 30314
404/524-5449
Franklin F. O'Neal, Executive Director
Wendell White (OMBE Representative)
404/526-6304

Baltimore

Morgan State College Minority Business Enterprise Project
2108 North Charles Street
Baltimore, Maryland 21218
301/685-0610
Ralph J. Ross, Executive Director

Boston

The Roxbury Small Business Development Center
126 Warren Street
Roxbury, Massachusetts 02119
Bernard Wiley—Acting Executive Director
617/427-6333
Frank Bispham (OMBE Representative)
617/223-2381

Chicago

Chicago Economic Development Corporation (CEDC)
162 North State Street, Suite 600
Chicago, Illinois 60601
231/368-0011
Garland Guice, Executive Director
Bennett Johnson, Jr. (OMBE Representative)
312/353-4460

NEDA
537 Dearborn South
Chicago, Illinois 60605
312/939-2607
Gilbert M. Vega, Regional Vice President

Cincinnati

Determined Young Men
3880 Reading Road
Cincinnati, Ohio 45229
513/221-0180
Merven Stenson, Executive Director

Cleveland

Greater Cleveland Growth Corporation
690 Union Commerce Building
Cleveland, Ohio 44115
216/241-4313
Melvin Roebuck, Executive Director

Minority Economic Developers Council (MEDCO)
10518 Superior Avenue
Cleveland, Ohio 44106
Armond L. Robinson, Administrator

Dallas

Dallas Alliance for Minority Enterprise (DAME)
7200 North Stemmons Freeway
Suite 1006, UCC Tower
Dallas, Texas 75222
214/637-5170
Walter Durham, Executive Director

Denver

Colorado Economic Development Association (CEDA)
1721 Lawrence Street
Denver, Colorado 80202
303/255-0421
Edward Lucero, Executive Director

Detroit

Inner City Business Improvement Forum (ICBIF)
6072 - 14th Street
Detroit, Michigan 48208
313/361-5150
Walter McMurtry, President

El Paso

NEDA
First National Building
Suite 10B
109 North Oregon Street
El Paso, Texas 79901
915/533-7423
Jose Manuel Villalobos, Regional Vice President

Indianapolis

Indianapolis Urban League
445 North Pennsylvania Street
Indianapolis, Indiana 46204
317/639-5391 or 253-5418
Sam Jones, Executive Director

Kansas City

Black Economic Union (BEU)
2502 Prospect
Kansas City, Missouri 64127
816/924-6181
Curtis McClinton, President

NEDA
703 North 8th Street
Kansas City, Kansas 66100
913/342-6663
Richardo Villalobos, Regional Vice President

Los Angeles

South Central Improvement Action Committee (IMPAC)
8557 South Broadway
Los Angeles, California 90003
213/751-1155
Louis Wilson, Director

The East Los Angeles Community Union (TELACU)
1330 South Atlantic Boulevard
Los Angeles, California 90022
213/268-6745
Claude Martinez, Director of Development

NEDA
5218 East Beverly Boulevard
Los Angeles, California 90022
213/724-6484
Silvestre Gonzales, Regional Vice President
Jack Wilburn, Coordinator
213/824-7691
Powell McDaniel (OMBE Representative)
213/824-7715
Joseph Luna (OMBE Representative)
213/824-7715

Memphis

Memphis Business League (NBL)
384 E. H. Crump Boulevard
Memphis, Tennessee 39126
901/574-3213
Leonard J. Small, Sr., Project Director
Harold Jones (OMBE Representative)
901/534-3216

Miami

NEDA
8551 Coral Way
Suite 307
Miami, Florida 33155
305/221-5531
Dr. Antonio Machado, Regional Vice President

Newark

MEDIC Enterprises, Inc.
287 Washington Street
Newark, New Jersey 07102
201/642-8054

New Haven

Greater New Haven Business and Professional Men's Association
226 Dixwell Avenue
New Haven, Connecticut 06511
Gerald S. Clark, Executive Director
203/562-3819

New York

Puerto Rican Forum, Inc.
156 Fifth Avenue
New York, New York 10010
212/691-4150
Hector I. Vasquez, Executive Director

New York (continued)

Capital Formation, Inc.
215 W. 125th Street, Room 313
New York, New York 10027
Hirom C. Cintron, Director, Harlem Office
212/222-9650

Brooklyn Local Economic Development Corporation (BLEDCO)
1519 Fulton Street
Brooklyn, New York 11216
212/493-1663
Preston Lambert, Executive Director

NEDA
19 West 44th Street
Room 407
New York, New York 10036
212/687-1128
David J. Burgos,
Regional Vice President

Philadelphia

Entrepreneurial Development Training Center
1501 North Broad Street
Philadelphia, Pennsylvania
215/763-3300
Alphonso Jackson, Director

Phoenix

NEDA
Amerco Towers
2721 North Central
Suite 727 South
Phoenix, Arizona 85004
602/263-8070
Joseph Sotelo,
Regional Vice President

Pittsburgh

Business & Job Development Corporation (BJDC)
7800 Susquehanna Street
Pittsburgh, Pennsylvania 15208
412/243-5600
Forrest L. Parr, President
Marian Diggs (OMBE Representative)
412/644-5529

Richmond

National Business League
700 North Second Street
Richmond, Virginia 23219
703/649-7473
Allen Roots, Acting Project Director

San Antonio

NEDA
1222 North Main Street
Kallison Tower, Room 422
San Antonio, Texas 78233
512/224-1618
Cipriano F. Guerra, Jr.
Regional Vice President
Jesse Rios (OMBE Representative)
512/225-5511

San Francisco

Plan of Action for Challenging Times (PACT)
635 Divisadero Street
San Francisco, California 94117
415/922-7150
Everett Brandon, President

Seattle

United Inner City Development Foundation
1106 East Spring St. - Xavier Hall
Seattle, Washington 98122
206/626-5440
Wilson Gulley, Executive Director

Washington, D. C.

Mayor's Economic Development Committee (MEDCO)
1717 Massachusetts Ave., N. W., Room 704
Washington, D. C. 20036
202/667-6480
Michael D. Wallach, Director,
Business Assistance Center
Curley King (OMBE Representative)
202/967-5051

Howard University's Small Business Guidance & Development Center
Post Office Box 553
Washington, D. C. 20001
202/636-7447
Dr. Wilford White, Director